Uncle John's
BATHROOM
READER®
PLUNGES INTO

Uncle John's
BATHROOM READER®
PLUNGES INTO
NEW JERSEY

Bathroom Readers' Hysterical Society
San Diego, California

Uncle John's Bathroom Reader
Plunges into New Jersey

Copyright © 2005 by Portable Press

For information, write
The Bathroom Readers' Hysterical Society
Portable Press, 5880 Oberlin Drive, San Diego, CA 92121
e-mail: unclejohn@advmkt.com

Library of Congress Cataloging-in-Publication Data

Uncle John's bathroom reader plunges into New Jersey /
Bathroom Readers' Hysterical Society.

p.cm.

ISBN 10: 1–59223–381–3
ISBN 13: 978–1–59223–381–6

1. New Jersey--Miscellanea. 2. New Jersey--Humor. I. Title:
Plunges into New Jersey. II. Bathroom Readers' Hysterical
Society (San Diego, Calif.)

F134.6.U53 2005
974.9--dc22

2005047549

Printed in the United States of America
First printing: July 2005

05 06 07 08 09   10 9 8 7 6 5 4 3 2 1

Project Team

Allen Orso, Publisher

JoAnn Padgett, Director, Editorial and Production

Amy Briggs, Developmental Editor

Jennifer Browning, Production Editor

Olivia Tabert, Editorial Assistant

Robin Kilrain, Copy Editor

Tamar Schwartz, Proofreader

Vincent Archuletta, Cover Design

Lois Stanfield, Interior Design

Thank You!

The Bathroom Readers' Hysterical Society sincerely
thanks the following additional people whose advice
and assistance made this book possible.

Cynthia Francisco

Mary Lou GoForth

Catherine Gustavsen

Kristine Hemp

Gordon Javna

Julia Papps

Stephanie Spadaccini

Sydney Stanley

Deborah Taylor

Jennifer Thornton

Connie Vazquez

Acknowledgments

Thank you Hysterical Scholars!

The Bathroom Readers' Hysterical Society
sincerely thanks the following people
who contributed selections to this work.

Myles Callum
Jeff Cheek
Jenness Crawford
Debbie Hardin
Kerry Kern
Robin Kilrain
Lea Markson
Kathleen McCabe
Debbie Pawlak
William Dylan Powell
John Scalzi
Susan Steiner
Olivia Tabert

Contents

Lights! Camera! Action!

Native Sons & Daughters

Puzzles

Preface

We here at the Bathroom Reader were scratching our heads trying to figure out just which state to choose for the next volume in our series devoted to the 50 states. We didn't scratch for long. After taking one look at New Jersey—the little state with the great big attitude—we knew it was a perfect place for a plunge.

The birthplace of baseball, the Boss, and Bubble Wrap—New Jersey's got it all. And *Uncle John's Bathroom Reader Plunges into New Jersey* covers it all, Bathroom Reader style. Uncle John put together a team of Jersey experts to do justice to a state so crammed full of interesting people, places, and things, from the shores of the Delaware River to the rounded peaks of the Kittatinny Mountains. It wasn't easy to fit everything in between these two covers, but we think everyone did a bang-up job. Here are just a few of our favorites:

- **Jerseyana:** In case you've ever asked, "Is there a difference between North and South Jersey?" and "Just what is a 'benny' anyway?" Don't worry. Here are the answers.
- **Hometowns:** Get the scoop on places called home by some in New Jersey—from Hopatcong down to Cape May.
- **Washington's Winter Whereabouts:** Learn not only where

George Washington slept in Morristown, but also the true story behind the painting *Washington Crossing the Delaware*.

- **Famous Mysteries:** Read all about mysteries in Jersey's history: the Lindbergh Baby, the *Hindenburg,* and the *U-Who.*
- **Puzzles and Quizzes:** See how much you know about Thomas Edison, Atlantic City, and the famous folk who came from the Garden State.

So whether you're down the Shore, stuck in traffic, or "thinking deeply" at a rest stop on the Turnpike, *Uncle John's Bathroom Reader Plunges into New Jersey* will be a valuable companion on a trip through the Garden State.

As always, go with the flow . . .

Cousin Amy
Editor

The Jersey Devil

In New Jersey you won't see Sasquatch or a chupacabra and there's no Loch Ness. But you might catch a glimpse of the Jersey Devil.

Sometimes called the Flying Death, Jabberwok, Kingowing, Woozlebug, or Phantom of the Pines—the Jersey Devil occupies a mysterious but central place in Jersey culture. If you journey to the Pine Barrens, a vast, dense wilderness of pine trees and oak forests, be careful. You just might encounter this most enduring and scary of all Jersey legends.

Once Upon a Time

Tracking down the Jersey Devil may be a challenge, but tracking down its exact origins is almost impossible. The most popular version of the story begins on a dark and stormy night in 1735. Mother Leeds, in her cabin somewhere in the Pine Barrens, lay in labor. A mother of 12 already, when Mother Leeds found she was pregnant yet again, she cried, "Let this one be a devil!" When her "lucky" 13th child was born, he appeared to be healthy—at first. But then, before the eyes of the terrified midwives, he soon transformed into a hideous beast, sprouted wings, and flew up the chimney.

There are dozens of origin stories for the Phantom of the Pines. Some say the Devil devoured its mother, some that

Mother Leeds abandoned the healthy boy in the forest, where he transformed into a hideous monster. Still others place the origin of the Devil in 1778, when a young girl from Leeds Point fell in love with a British soldier: the Jersey Devil was the offspring of this treasonous union.

Sources are just as unclear as to where the monster was born. If you had passed through the Pine Barrens before the 1950s, the locals might have shown you the Shourds house in Leeds Point. This shack, no longer standing, was the reputed birthplace. Or fellow devil hunters might have pointed you to South Main Street in Pleasantville, or Estellville, or Mullica River. All of these places claim to have spawned the Jersey Devil.

Taxidermist's Nightmare

If you want to find the Jersey Devil, it might help to know what it looks like. Unfortunately, no two witnesses of the Flying Death have ever agreed on its appearance. The general consensus is that the Jersey Devil has the body of a kangaroo, the head of a horse, antlers, a forked reptilian tail, a man's torso, a goat's legs and hooves, and giant leathery wings—if you can picture that.

The Devil's Territory

Throughout the 18th and 19th centuries the Jersey Devil was blamed for all manner of misfortunes in the Pine Barrens. Wherever livestock died or crops refused to grow was the Devil's territory. Parents also used the legend to discipline their children, and criminals used the legend to keep intruders out of the Pine

Barrens as well. The legend served a valuable purpose, but it would become much more than a piece of folklore after one eventful week in 1909.

From January 16 to January 23, the Jersey Devil was spotted all over the Delaware River Valley. From South Jersey, the Devil zigzagged up through Camden and Philadelphia, Pennsylvania, leaving its hoof prints in places no man could reach. Never mind that the Devil would have needed its own jetliner to be sighted in such varied places in such a short span of time. People were scared.

The Devil attacked a trolley car and was, in turn, fired upon by police. But it escaped. Later, one William Wasso of Clayton claimed to have seen the unfortunate creature's demise. As Wasso watched, the Jersey Devil trailed its tail over the third rail of an electric railway and exploded in a ball of fire. Oddly enough, the sightings continued unabated. Citizens were so terrified of the Flying Death, many refused to leave their homes—even in daylight. Mills in the Pine Barrens closed. In the town of Mount Ephraim, school was canceled—the state's first (and last) closing for supernatural causes.

At the end of the week, without explanation, the sightings and footprints stopped. The spate of sightings in such a short time frame has never repeated itself, to the disappointment of devil hunters everywhere. Of course, such a panic provided ample opportunity for hucksters and hoaxers to cash in. G. W. Green of Salem admitted decades later to having made many of the prints, but he could not have been the only one.

Devil Impersonators

Smelling profit, others began to jump on the Jersey Devil band-
wagon. The Philadelphia Zoo announced an award of $10,000—a
hefty sum in 1909—to anyone who could deliver a live specimen
to the zoo. It would doubtless be a popular exhibit, the zoo's
superintendent reasoned.

Jacob F. Hope, an animal trainer, and Norman Jefferies, a pub-
licist, managed to answer the zoo's call. Hope and Jefferies, working to publicize the Ninth and Arch Street Museum in
Philadelphia, announced that they had a creature in their posses-
sion that matched the Devil's description. This beast had unfortunately escaped right before the many sightings and doubtlessly
caused all the furor. They offered a reward of $500 for its capture.

Jefferies then obtained a kangaroo and brought it to
Philadelphia. Once there he painted it green; the poor kangaroo
almost died after it licked off the poisonous paint. Jefferies
repainted it (this time with less toxic paint). Then he attached
large false wings, which the kangaroo soon demolished. Jefferies
attached a second, sturdier set, made of a bronze frame covered
with rabbit fur. Finally, having created an acceptable-looking
devil, Jefferies gathered up a team of farmers, set the "Devil"
loose in Huntington Park, and made a big show of capturing it
again. Afterward the creature was displayed in a cage with
gnawed bones on the floor; viewers were allowed to see the creature for only one second. (Eat your heart out, P. T. Barnum.)

Speak of the Devil

Sightings of the Devil have died down since the early 20th century, but if you're wondering where to see a Jersey Devil now,

there are plenty on the ice at the Meadowlands Sports Arena in East Rutherford. The New Jersey Devils, the state's National Hockey League team, has its home base there.

In recent years the Jersey Devil has been honored in an episode of *The X-Files*, a B horror movie, and a video game (in which it hunts down radioactive carrots). There is a sculpture of the Jersey Devil in Penn Station, New York, and the beast lends its name to a drink in South Jersey bars. You may not spot the beast mauling cattle anymore, but the Phantom of the Pines is alive and well—at least in the minds of Jerseyans.

DID YOU KNOW?

New Jersey predicts the weather with Dom Jr., a coatimundi, at the Cohanzick Zoo. Every Groundhog Day, Dom Jr. looks for his shadow to predict when spring will come. The zoo director swears these Central American relatives of raccoons are more accurate than plain old groundhogs.

Jersey Basics

Think you know the Garden State? Then grab a pencil and find out what your J.Q. (that stands for "Jersey Quotient") is.

1. What's the state capital of New Jersey?
   A. Newark
   B. Trenton
   C. Atlantic City
   D. Jersey City
   E. New Brunswick

2. Okay then, so what city has the largest population in New Jersey?
   A. Newark
   B. Trenton
   C. Atlantic City
   D. Jersey City
   E. New Brunswick

3. According to the last U.S. census, how many people call New Jersey their home?
   A. 1 million
   B. 20.5 million
   C. 6.2 million

D. 8.4 million

E. 10 million

4. How many species of poisonous snakes live in New Jersey?
   A. Zero
   B. One
   C. Ten
   D. Two
   E. Fifteen

5. You may not know it, but there are also big wild animals in New Jersey. Can you tell which of these hunters currently lives in the state?
   A. Black bear
   B. Coyote
   C. Bald eagle
   D. All of the above
   E. None of the above

6. Which one of these bridges doesn't have one foot in the Garden State?
   A. Commodore Barry Bridge
   B. George Washington Bridge
   C. Ben Franklin Bridge
   D. Verrazano Narrows Bridge
   E. Delaware Memorial Bridge

7. Traffic often stops on the Garden State Parkway, but luckily there are plenty of rest stops along the way except for:
   A. Cheesequake
   B. Forked River

C. Vaux Hall

D. Great Egg

E. Ocean View

8. Where is the state's highest elevation, 1,803 feet above sea level, located?

   A. Hightstown

   B. High Point

   C. Highland Park

   D. Hi-Nella

   E. Lower Township

9. Calling all cars! What's the fastest posted speed limit on New Jersey highways?

   A. 65 mph

   B. 70 mph

   C. 55 mph

   D. 60 mph

   E. 80 mph

10. And last, what is the official state song of New Jersey?

   A. "Born to Run"

   B. "I'm from New Jersey"

   C. "Jersey Bounce"

   D. "No Left Turns in Jersey"

   E. None of the above.

Turn to page 315 for answers.

Inside, Outside, Upside Down

You want thrills? You want twists and turns? You want speed? Well, New Jersey's got some of the fastest, tallest, and scariest roller coasters in the country. Whether you like wood or if steel is your thing, there's something for everyone in New Jersey.

Wood You Like a Ride?

There are only three wooden roller coasters in the entire state, which makes them all pretty special. So if you're a classic-coaster fan, these are the ones to ride.

Rolling Thunder

Location: Six Flags Great Adventure, Jackson

A good old-fashioned wooden coaster, this dual-track, sit-down ride made its debut at Great Adventure in 1979. Made of 850,000 feet of Douglas fir lumber, Rolling Thunder reaches a top speed of 56 mph as riders hurtle over hill after hill after hill. The first drop is the steepest at 85 feet.

Great White

Location: Morey's Piers, Wildwood

Located on the Spencer Avenue Pier, the Great White first

plunges riders 25 feet down into a dark tunnel under the board-walk. Before they know it, they are plummeting down a second, larger hill (125 feet!) and reaching speeds in excess of 50 mph. According to Morey's, the Great White is one of the biggest wooden roller coasters in North America—it has over 3,300 feet of track! Even though it's not as flashy as some of its steelier cousins, the Great White is Morey's most popular ride.

Tsunami
Location: Clementon Amusement Park, Clementon
Built in 2004, Tsunami replaced Clementon's famous wooden roller coaster, the Jack Rabbit. Even though patrons were sad to see the old model go, they were thrilled by the brand-new coaster's first drop—105 feet high with the steepest vertical angle (62 degrees) on a wooden coaster in North America. The ride reaches a top speed of 56 mph and features two more big drops—82 feet and 65 feet—before it's through.

Feeling Steely
Using steel in roller coasters has made for some great new advances. Now we can go faster, flip over more often, and scream louder than ever before.

Great American Scream Machine
Location: Six Flags Great Adventure, Jackson
When it opened in 1989, the Great American Scream Machine claimed to be one of the longest, tallest, fastest looping steel roller coasters in the world. Well, it has certainly lived up to its billing. The coaster is 17 stories tall, plummets 155 feet down the first hill at a 55-degree incline, and reaches a top speed of 68

mph. If that's not enough, riders go upside down seven times in three loops, a corkscrew turn, and two boomerang loops. In keeping with the patriotic theme, the three trains are each painted red, white, and blue.

Superman Ultimate Flight
Location: Six Flags Great Adventure, Jackson
It's a bird. It's a plane. It's a . . . person on a roller coaster? Riders don't sit on this roller coaster—they fly headfirst, just like Superman. Passengers are strapped in and lie horizontally in hanging cars. This 115-foot-tall, pretzel-shaped thrill ride reaches speeds of 60 mph as it takes riders through spirals, highly banked curves, and a 360-degree in-line roll. Be warned: the red cape is not included.

Great Nor'Easter
Location: Morey's Piers, Wildwood
Located on the 25th Avenue Pier, the Great Nor'Easter, named for the vicious storms that tear up the Atlantic seaboard, does live up to its namesake. It's an inverted coaster, meaning that the cars hang from the track and the riders dangle beneath them. Made of over 2,100 feet of steel, this ride is 150 feet tall and speeds along at over 50 mph. Riders go upside down four times. Best of all, the ride hovers high over the Raging Waters water park, bringing passengers so close they feel like they're going to crash into the pools below.

Bizarre Buildings

Some offbeat architects have definitely put their stamp on New Jersey.

Cookie Jar House, Glendora
This oval-shaped house was built in 1947 as a prototype for a model community of jar-shaped houses, but the idea didn't take off. Luckily, the cookie jar house remains. Privately owned and occupied, the steel-framed building often makes visitors feel disoriented because there are no corners on the inside.

Chair House, Eagleswood
Located about 30 miles from Atlantic City, the Chair House looks normal enough from the outside, until you look up. The three-story Victorian house has a very tall steeple—with an empty wooden chair on top. Exactly how and why the chair got there is a mystery. Legend has it that the owner of the house in the 1930s put it there, but no one is quite sure why.

The Flagship, Union
On Route 22, there's a big white building that looks a lot like a boat with a pointed bow, portholes, and a deck. The Flagship was built in 1938 and was originally an ocean-themed nightclub. But over the years, the building has been a men's clothing store, a furniture store, and a U-Haul agency. Today, it's an electronics store. Oddly enough, boats and boating accessories have never been sold there.

Camp Morristown

Morristown had an important part to play in the American Revolution: it served as the winter headquarters for the soldiers twice. Here's a little background on how the troops lived and how the Father of Our Country lived during those harsh winters.

History Central

Morristown is one of New Jersey's most history-rich places. The first English settlers arrived in 1715, and the area became the county seat in 1740, receiving its name from then governor Lewis Morris. The city's historic past is still evident in its brick sidewalks, stone churches, and Victorian mansions.

What attracted the first colonists to the area in the 1700s— the lush countryside, abundant natural resources, and easy access to New York City—still attracts people today. Situated in the north central part of the state, Morristown is home to approximately 19,000 people and a wide variety of businesses and corporations. Among its many claims to fame, Morristown's greatest may be that it served as George Washington's winter headquarters not once, but twice during the War for Independence.

Washington Slept Here . . .

The swamps and mountains surrounding historic Morristown made life tough for the early settlers, but George Washington thought this the perfect spot for wintering the Continental army during the Revolutionary War. The Watchung Mountains provided natural protection from attack by invading enemies, and the city had established roads and communication routes to New York, Pennsylvania, and New England.

Believing that the commanding officer should always maintain dignified quarters, Washington took up residence during the winter of 1776–1777 at the Arnold Tavern, a large house on the corner of the Green (on what is now North Park Place). From the tavern on January 1, 1777, he issued his famous edict that allowed citizens who had been coerced into pledging loyalty to the British Crown to clear the slate by formally swearing allegiance to the United States. A historical marker is all that remains today of the tavern.

Washington returned to Morristown in December 1779. During this visit he took up residence at the home of Theodosia Ford, a wealthy widow. Her Georgian-style home, one of the finest in the state, had been completed in 1774. In addition to Mrs. Ford's own service staff, the mansion had to accommodate 15 officers (including Alexander Hamilton), 10 aides, and more than 20 servants that Washington had brought with him. Eleven rooms in the manor house, plus the stable, were transformed into Washington's winter command center. It was so crowded that the kitchen had to be used as the sleeping room for the servants. Out of necessity, a log building was constructed on the side of the house as the working kitchen. Mrs. Ford and her four children lived in the remaining two rooms.

Since winter precluded most military battles and was a time of preparation, it was the only time of the year that Martha Washington could visit her husband. She joined her husband during his stay at the Ford Mansion, which is known locally as

Washington's Headquarters and is owned now by the Washington Association of New Jersey.

And the Soldiers Slept There

The enlisted men of the New Jersey Brigade didn't fare as well as their commander. In the first Morristown encampment in 1777, approximately 3,000 soldiers were cut off from supplies and had little to eat and only meager housing. A smallpox epidemic broke out, killing hundreds of soldiers and nearly one fourth of the 400 townspeople. (The following winter was spent in Valley Forge, Pennsylvania, where 2,500 men died of disease and exposure.)

A much larger contingent of soldiers—thought to number more than 13,000—arrived back in Morristown for the 1779–1780 encampment. The soldiers were based several miles southwest of town in Jockey Hollow, where Washington instructed them to erect a "log-house city." The encampment surrounded Fort Nonsense, which provided a view as far as New York City on a clear day.

Clearing acres and acres of trees during the coldest December in 80 years was no easy feat. The soldiers slept on beds of loose straw in tents—if lucky—until the 1,200 log huts were ready in February. The encampment swelled to the point where it became one of the largest (albeit temporary) cities in the colonies. Seven blizzards dumped more than five feet of snow, cutting off all food and supply deliveries. The soldiers were forced to search the nearby farms for food and were able to survive the winter with only about 100 deaths.

More History in the Making

On March 2, 1933, President Herbert Hoover declared that four Revolutionary War sites in the Morristown area would become the first national historical park. Washington's Headquarters at the Ford Mansion was restored to its 1779 condition, and an adjacent museum was erected to display artifacts of the time. The encampments at Fort Nonsense and Jockey Hollow have been whittled down to just five reconstructed huts, but there are more than 25 miles of trails available for those who want to walk these historic hills where brave (and very cold) men endured hardship for the sake of a new nation.

DID YOU KNOW?

All roads into Morristown meet at the Green, a block-square parcel of land in the center of town. Today, the Green is the site of several festivals during the year and is transformed each December into a winter wonderland of holiday lights and decorations, including a train and miniature fire trucks for the kids to ride. Santa arrives with great fanfare on the rooftop of a nearby department store and then takes up residence in his house on the Green for December.

New Jersey Firsts

From tripping the light fantastic in outer space to making turkey condiments, New Jerseyans did a lot of things first.

Getting Lit

We all know about Thomas Edison's pioneering work on the light bulb, but did you know that Roselle was the first town in the nation to be lit by electricity in 1883?

Berry Good

Cranberry grower Elizabeth Lee of New Egypt boiled some damaged berries instead of throwing them away. The result? The first cranberry sauce. She liked the tasty jelly so much that she started the Ocean Spray company. Thanksgiving has never been the same since.

Tastes Grape!

The first bottled grape juice (not counting wine!) came out of New Jersey. Thomas Bramwell Welch figured out how to make grape juice without the kick, which was the start of the Welch's Grape Juice Company.

"Board"-dom

The world's first boardwalk was built in Atlantic City in 1870, forever keeping sand out of our shoes and giving us a good place to eat funnel cake and salt water taffy.

Dates and Drive-Ins

New Jersey's teenaged couples were the first to get their kicks at the drive-in movie. The very first one opened in Camden in 1933.

Walking in Space

Montclair native son Buzz Aldrin was the first man to "walk" in space, during the Gemini 12 space flight in 1966. (He was the second man to walk on the moon. Hey, you can't always be first!)

The First to Deep Six

From deep space to deep ocean: the first submarine was built in 1878 by John Holland of Passaic County.

Commuters, Rejoice!

New Jerseyans know a lot about commuting and have for a long time. The first ferry service in the United States began in 1811, shuttling workers between Hoboken and Manhattan.

The Guitar Plugs In

No one needs to tell you that New Jersey rocks. But even before the Boss and Bon Jovi, Les Paul invented the first solid body electric guitar in Mahwah in 1940.

And the Hops Just Keep on Comin'

Almost no one argued with the wisdom of opening the first beer brewery in America in Hoboken in 1642. Could the first beer bellies be far behind?

Fishing Holes

Yeah, it may be called the Garden State, but it could just as easily be the Fishing State too!

If you fish, you know that New Jersey has wonderful waters (both freshwater and saltwater) in which to wet a hook. Check out a few of the state's most savory swimmers.

American Shad

Also known as Poor Man's Salmon, these giant herrings abound in the Delaware River, spawning for their annual run from the end of March through June. Some of the juiciest spots include Byram, Lambertville, Bulls Island Recreation Area, and anywhere in the Delaware Water Gap Recreational Area. Here's the trick: Watch the Delaware's depth. If it's above normal, fish from the shore, casting a shad dart upstream and letting it bounce around the bottom. If the water level is normal or low, fishing from a boat is your best bet.

Bass

Largemouth, smallmouth, and striped bass make up most of the state's bass action. New Jersey stripers became so popular in the 1970s and 1980s that the population was in danger (swift wildlife management restored them). Fish for largemouth in early spring and summer; stripers only come into freshwater tidal flats to spawn in the summer; while smallmouths can be caught all year long. Look for stripers in the Delaware River and Delaware Bay.

Blue Crabs

Maryland may boast about their blue crabs, but New Jersey has plenty of them all along its tidal waters, especially in shallow bays. Lure them on baited string lines and net them as they get close (not-so-fresh chicken or fish heads make good blue crab bait), or use a cage trap, for sale at local sporting goods stores. If you see one with red claws and a brightly colored sponge on the bottom, throw it back. That's an expectant mother blue crab and catching those is not just ungentlemanly: it's illegal. The crabs are ripe for the picking May through December.

Bluefish

A saltwater fish, New Jersey bluefish can grow more than three feet long! You can catch adults by chumming (dumping oily, ground-up fish into the water) from a boat or surf casting. Young ones, known as snappers, can be caught with small lures in bay areas. Bluefish are aggressive eaters and tend to strike at anything put in front of them. You'll find them from May to December; you'll also find them good eating. They're divine grilled whole with olive oil and garlic and provide a big meal—a single fish can net around five pounds of succulent meat.

Catfish

And you thought catfish only swam in the South—it turns out that there are plenty of Yankee catfish, too, and some live in New Jersey. From the small brown bullhead variety to the larger white catfish and revered channel catfish, summer is the best time to reel in these tasty kitties. The most prized New Jersey catfish is the channel catfish, which grows to trophy size and likes to come out at night. The best places to fish for them are on the bottom of the Delaware River and its many tidal tributaries. Catfishing doesn't require any fancy equipment. A plain old worm on a hook will do.

Crappie

One of Uncle John's favorite fishes, both black and white crappie can be found in Jersey. Black crappie are preferable to white and are best caught in the colder months. Lake Musconetcong, along with Delaware, Union, Assunpink, and Smartswood lakes, all have great crappie fishing. Live bait works best. This is a good fish to beer batter, bake, stir-fry, or sauté.

Fluke

Also known as summer flounder, this is the must-have fish on the Jersey coast. Experts say it's the most sought-after sport fish in the region from May through October. It's a saltwater fish, so you need to be coastal to catch one; but it can be caught either from a boat or from the shore. Using strips of squid and smaller baitfish, keep your bait in constant motion and drag it along the bottom. Fluke are delicious broiled, and yes, the fish did give rise to the word *fluke*, meaning a "lucky chance."

Marlin

At an average weight of about 100 pounds, this beautiful finned fish will give you both a healthy fight and enough meat for a large dinner party. Marlin live only in the Atlantic; both the white and blue varieties can be found off the Jersey coast in deep waters during the summer and early fall. Trolling and casting both work on these guys, using trolling baits or lures during the day and squid at night. Just be careful because these fish can get pretty big: The record blue marlin catch in New Jersey waters weighed 1,046 pounds!

Perch

These tasty catches are another New Jersey favorite, good for fishing all year round (even when ice fishing!). These little fighters prefer the open water and travel in thick schools. You can find both yellow and white perch in New Jersey, and both species are easy to catch with a fish finder if you can come across a school. White perch are found in a number of Jersey lakes, including Greenwood, Hopatcong, Swartswood, Lenape, and Malaga. Look for white perch in the Delaware River and its lower tributaries.

DID YOU KNOW?

The world's largest striped bass used to swim off the coast of Atlantic City until she was caught in 1982. Al McReynolds hooked a big "cow bass" (most of the big ones are ladies) while fishing on the Vermont Avenue jetty after a nor'easter had blown through town. It took him over 90 minutes to land the massive fish, which measured over 4 feet long and weighed 78 pounds, 8 ounces.

Count Basie
Red Bank's Royalty

William "Count" Basie is often associated with Kansas City jazz, but this music giant, born in 1904, comes from Red Bank.

Armed with a deceptively simple piano style (as one band member commented, "Count don't do nothin'. But it sure sounds good."), there was no hotter jazz musician that Count Basie in the 1930s. His super-swingin' sounds of a full orchestra evolved into more intimate piano duets and small-group albums in the 1970s. No matter what he did, he made it all sound easy. Here are facts about the man and his music you might not know.

He Really Wanted to Play Drums

As a child, Basie's first instrument wasn't the piano, but the skins. He played drums with his school band. But when it turned out another kid in school played the drums better, Basie got discouraged and quit the instrument. Fortunately for him, his mother was an enthusiastic amateur pianist and encouraged him to take up the keys (his father played the E-flat horn, in which Basie apparently never showed an interest). The piano suited Basie well, and by 1924 he'd headed to Harlem to learn at the knee of legendary jazz pianist Fats Waller. Waller recommended Basie to a traveling vaudeville show, where he got his start ticklin' the ivories. In 1927 one of these vaudeville tours folded, and Basie found himself in Kansas City, where he stuck around playing piano until 1936. Then he and his orchestra headed for New York and national fame.

Incidentally, the kid who played drums better than Basie? A guy called Sonny Greer, who would eventually play drums for Duke Ellington for three decades.

He Wasn't Really a Count

Well, you probably figured *that* one out. He was the son of a coachman and a laundress, humble beginnings for jazz royalty. But the reason he's known as "Count" Basie dates back to the 1930s, when Basie formed a band from the remnants of two earlier bands (formed by musicians Walter Page and Bennie Moten) and performed with the group on a Kansas City shortwave radio station. The radio announcer, riffing off the royalty names of jazz greats Duke Ellington and Earl Hines, dubbed Basie a count. The nickname quite naturally stuck. Basie was also known as the Jump King in Kansas City, because of his band's relentless rhythm. That's a lot of titles for one guy.

He Got Ripped Off for His Earliest Recordings

Musicians in modern times like to complain about the rapacious nature of the music industry. But today's music companies have nothing on the sheer effrontery of the music industry in the 1930s. Basie's first recording contract is a fine example of how musicians got manhandled: In exchange for 24 "sides" (this was in the days of 78-rpm records) over three years, Basie got a mere

$750. Royalties? Forget about it. This is why Basie never made additional money from early hits like "One O'clock Jump," or "Jumpin' at the Woodside."

His Musical Career Is Divided up into "Testaments"

Basie's career has an old testament (prior to 1950) and a new testament (everything after 1952). The dividing line falls during this two-year gap when the bottom seemed to drop out for swing and jazz orchestras. For economic reasons, in 1950 Basie had to drop his full orchestra and continue with just an eight-piece band. In 1952 things picked up again, and Basie was able to hire a full orchestra once more.

On either side of this gap, Basie's orchestras were substantially different. Basie's old testament musicians relied on memorizing arrangements (these were known as head arrangements because the changes and parts were stored in the musicians' noggins) rather than reading music. The new testament orchestras, on the other hand, were filled with sight readers (players who not only read music but read it well enough to play it right away), which gave Basie more flexibility with his arrangements.

Which testament is better? That's a personal choice, of course. Both testaments, however, were known for their excellent musicians. Old testament musicians included Lester Young (often regarded as the best tenor saxophonist in jazz history), trombonist Dicky Wells, and even singer Billie Holiday, who joined Basie for a stint in 1937. New testament standouts included saxophonist Eddie "Lockjaw" Davis, trumpeter Clark Terry, and vocalist Joe Williams.

The Count Remembered His Roots

Despite the fact that Count Basie is almost always associated with Kansas City, he never forgot his hometown; one of the best known numbers from his *Atomic Mr. Basie* album (1957) is "The Kid from Red Bank."

Red Bank has repaid Basie's compliment and honored its son's memory: In 1984, the year Basie passed away, the city renamed its Monmouth Arts Center the Count Basie Theater. In 2004 the city's annual Red Bank Jazz & Blues Festival, which draws more than 200,000 music lovers annually, celebrated the centennial of Basie's birth. In jazz, apparently, you *can* go home again.

DID YOU KNOW?

For almost 50 years, every new baseball used in the Major Leagues has its sheen rubbed off with mud from New Jersey. This magic mud, harvested every year from a secret spot (a favorite fishing hole of the company's founder) in South Jersey, is produced by Lena Blackburne Baseball Rubbing Mud.

Classic Crank Calls

*Making crank phone calls has always been something of an adolescent rite
of passage. But two New Jerseyans elevated the practice into an art form.*

Reportedly the first words spoken into a telephone by its inventor, Alexander Graham Bell, were, "Come here, Watson, I want you." It probably wasn't long thereafter before some mischievous kid uttered the immortal question, "Is your refrigerator running?" (With the punch line "Well, you'd better hurry up and catch it!") The crank call has been around for almost as long as there have been telephones (some things just never get old). But the art form really didn't hit its stride until the 1970s, when two bored guys from Jersey City discovered how much fun they could have with a phone and a tape recorder.

The Grandaddy of All Prank Calls
It was the early 1970s, and John Elmo and Jim Davidson spent their free time making crank telephone calls and having fun at someone else's expense. These guys were true innovators: Instead of the tried and true "running refrigerator" and "Prince Albert in a can" gags, they would call business establishments—usually bars and taverns—and ask to have someone paged. Of course, when the false first and last names were spoken together, they formed a humorous phrase. Hearing their victim call out for Sal

Lami or Cole Cutz provided endless hours of amusement.

One day, quite serendipitously, Davidson remembered a bar that he passed each day on his way to school; he decided it would be the next victim. When he called the Tube Bar in Jersey City and owner Louis "Red" Deutsch answered, Deutsch's raspy voice struck him as so funny that he never got around to making the joke. He just cracked up and hung up the phone. That call led him and Elmo on a year-long practice of calling the bar just to hear Deutsch's voice and get a rise out of him.

Elmo and Davidson couldn't believe their luck when they called Red and heard him page "Phil Mypockets," "Pepe Roni," or "Al Coholic." Once Red Deutsch figured out that the callers were having some fun at his expense, he would become enraged and let loose a torrential outpouring of obscenities that would make the saltiest of sailors blush. He would threaten the callers with extreme bodily harm if he ever got his hands on them. And odds are that he probably would have.

Seeing Red

Red himself was a larger-than-life character. At 6 feet 2 inches tall and weighing over 200 pounds, he had become a regular fixture of Journal Square, the hub of downtown Jersey City. Beginning in the 1930s, Red had run a fruit and vegetable stand there. The square stood at the crossroads of several rail lines, so there was always a lot of pedestrian traffic. Everyone seemed to know him.

When Prohibition was repealed in 1933, Red opened a tavern in Journal Square, catering to the thirst of commuters and travelers. He named his establishment the Tube Bar, in recognition of the underground tubes (better known now as tunnels). The bar quickly became a popular success, and the colorful proprietor became something of a celebrity. Despite his popularity Red ran his bar with an iron fist. In his tavern the customer was seldom right, and patrons had better heed the "boss" and abide by his rules. Or else.

Paging Rufus Leakin

Red Deutsch didn't take guff from anyone, especially not a couple of punk kids on the telephone. When the prank calls began, he quickly learned to recognize his tormentors' voices. He would immediately go on the offensive, spewing out exquisite details of what he would do to various portions of their anatomies when he got his hands on them (slicing open their bellies was a favorite). He also cast aspersions on their lives and habits—reserving his most colorful descriptions for their mothers' sexual practices. The more enraged Red got, the funnier he became to the two callers.

Sadly, the character of Journal Square changed during the 1970s: A new underground transit depot opened and pedestrian traffic dropped off. Red sold the bar in 1980 and moved to Palm Springs, Florida (where he would die a few years later). But the tapes were about to take on a life of their own.

And the Tape Rolls On

Luckily for us, Elmo and Davidson had the foresight to record their prank calls to the Tube Bar and their heated conversations with Red Deutsch on big reel-to-reel tapes (remember, this was the 1970s). When they entertained friends with the tapes, everyone asked for copies. Soon those friends made copies for *their* friends, who made copies for *their* friends, who made copies for . . . (you get the idea). Soon the tapes were all over the country.

A manager for the New York Mets heard the tapes and played them for the team. The players enjoyed them so much that they played them for their friends on other teams, and soon all the major leagues had heard them. The L.A. Dodgers even had Tube Bar T-shirts printed. The Miami Dolphins football team was rumored to play the tapes at practices. Still, no one knew who the tapes' authors were.

D'oh, But No Dough

Because the tapes' originators remained anonymous, they received no compensation. At first the tapes were passed from person to person. But soon some people along the way saw an opportunity to make money. Bootlegged versions of the tapes surfaced for sale, but Elmo and Davidson received no royalties.

Eventually the pair got tired of seeing others profit from their work. In 1993 they copyrighted their recordings. Calling themselves the Bar Bum Bastards (a term coined by another bartender they loved to annoy), they released *The Tube Bar* tapes under the Detonator label. As of this writing, they have their own Web site where you can purchase the recordings and Tube Bar–themed merchandise, including a Red Deutsch wall clock.

If this story sounds familiar, it may be because TV's *The Simpsons* has a running gag that honors the Tube Bar tapes. Bart Simpson calls Moe, the bartender at Moe's Tavern, with requests to page a false customer. When Moe, whose gravelly voice sounds an awful lot like Red, realizes that he's the victim of a prank, he lets loose a string of invective and threats, to Bart's delight. There seems little doubt that the bit is an homage to the iconic New Jersey bar, its legendary owner, and the two crank callers.

Hometowns
Named for a Queen?

Here's the first in our series of snapshots of New Jersey hometowns. One of the oldest settlements in the state, Elizabeth has been a hub of industry and trade since its founding.

The Town: Elizabeth
Location: Union County
Founding: 1665
Current Population: 121,000 (est.)
Size: 11.69 square miles (Originally the township encompassed all of Union County. It shrank to its current size as 12 towns broke away over the years.)
What's in a Name? You may think it was named for Queen Elizabeth I, but it's not. Elizabethtown ("town" was dropped from the name in 1740 when King George II granted the town's charter) was named for another Englishwoman who never set foot in North America—Elizabeth Carteret, wife of the coproprietor of East Jersey, Sir George Carteret. (Her husband never set foot in New Jersey either.)

Claims to Fame
- In 1664 the Native Americans of Staten Island sold the land

where Elizabeth now stands for "20 fathoms of trading cloth, two coats, two guns, ten bars of lead, two kettles, two handfuls of gun powder, and 400 fathoms of white wampum."

- Site of the largest seaport in the United States.

- The Elizabeth Marine Terminal was the world's first port designed specifically to handle standardized containers. Exit 13A on the Turnpike was built to give trucks direct access to the containerport.

- Home to Jersey Gardens, the largest outlet mall in the state.

DID YOU KNOW?

Josh Saviano, who played Paul Pfeiffer on the TV show *The Wonder Years,* grew up in North Caldwell. Contrary to urban legend, he did not become the lead singer of the band Marilyn Manson. He became something much scarier: a lawyer.

The Blue and the Buff

There's a lot of information on New Jersey's state flag. Let Uncle John be your guide to the true colors of the Garden State.

The Buff

Why a yellow background and blue shield? Because none other than General George Washington picked them out in 1779. The colors—Jersey blue and buff (as the yellow is called)—honor the Dutch, New Jersey's original European settlers. The colors first appeared on the insignia of the Netherlands. Washington selected this color scheme for the uniforms of New Jersey's regiments in the War for Independence; in 1780 soldiers had to carry a state flag that matched their uniforms, and New Jersey's colors have been the same ever since. The traditional flag was made official in 1896.

The Blue

The blue-hued part of the flag features the state's seal: two ladies flanking a shield crowned by a knight's helmet with a horse's head on top. Underneath this arrangement is a banner that reads "Liberty and Prosperity, 1776."

- The banner features the state motto along with the year of independence from Britain.

- The two women represent the state motto's words: Liberty and Prosperity. "Liberty" holds a staff topped with a funny-looking hat; it's called a Phrygian helmet, or a liberty cap. "Prosperity" has a proper name, Ceres, the Roman goddess of the harvest and agriculture. Her overflowing cornucopia stands for all the good Jersey fresh produce.

- The three plows on the shield reemphasize the importance of agriculture to the state.

- The knight's helmet is a traditional European sign of state sovereignty and independence; the horse's head stands for strength and speed.

- No one agrees on who designed the state seal. Some argue that Pierre Eugene du Simitiere, designer of the United States seal, is the artist. Others claim that Francis Hopkinson, a signer of the Declaration of Independence and designer of the first American flag, put it together.

The Lindbergh Baby
Part I: The Crime of the Century

In 1932 famed aviator Charles Lindbergh's young son, Charles Jr., was kidnapped from his bedroom in Hopewell. The mystery and criminal investigation riveted attention on New Jersey as millions hoped the boy would be found and the kidnapper brought to justice.

The Price of Fame

When Charles Lindbergh moved to Hopewell Township, New Jersey, he was a reclusive man—who just happened to be America's favorite hero. On May 20, 1927, Lucky Lindy successfully completed a solo, nonstop flight of 33½ hours from New York to Paris in his single-engine plane, the *Spirit of St. Louis*. Lindbergh was the first person to fly nonstop over the Atlantic and, overnight, became a world-renowned hero. In 1929 he married an equally shy New Jersey heiress and poet, Anne Morrow. The following year their son, Charles A. Lindbergh Junior (publicly nicknamed the Eaglet), was born. The media couldn't get enough of the proud parents and their little boy.

The couple lived quietly on the Morrow estate in Englewood, New Jersey, but found it difficult to maintain their privacy there. So they built a large stone house on an estate in Hopewell—accessible only by a private airfield or a winding dirt road. By

January 1932 the Lindberghs spent their weekends in the mountains and returned to Englewood on Mondays. But on March 1, 1932, a Tuesday, they strayed from their routine and stayed an extra few days in Hopewell because little Charlie had a cold.

The rainy night began quietly enough. The nurse tucked Little Lindy into bed in his second-floor nursery at 8:00. In the living room at around 9:00, Lindbergh Sr. heard a cracking noise "like an orange box falling off a chair." And at 10:00, when the nurse checked on the baby, he wasn't in his crib. After a panicked search of the estate, Lindbergh called the New Jersey State Police in Trenton to report that his son had been kidnapped.

Clues and the Clueless

When the police arrived they found outside the house a chisel and a broken, handmade extension ladder. Footprints in the muddy ground led away from the house. But the biggest clue of all was in the nursery, where Lindbergh discovered an envelope with a note inside.

The misspelled note, in part, read: "Have 50,000$ redy. . . After 2–4 days we will inform you were to deliver the Mony. We warn you for making anyding public or for notify the polise the child is in gute care." The note's signature—two interlocking, partially shaded red circles with three holes punched in the design—would be an indication for all correspondence from the kidnapper. Unfortunately police found no fingerprints on the note.

By the next morning, news of the crime was public. Twisting roads or not, reporters and gawkers were immediately trampling the Lindbergh estate and destroying evidence from the crime scene. Police had not taken casts of the footprints, and the throngs ruined the chance to cast them and to look for more evidence outside the house.

Media Madness

A happy Lindbergh family had been news, but their tragedy was, as journalist H. L. Mencken put it, "the biggest story since the Resurrection." The crime made headlines around the world, with top billing on radio and in newsreels. Posters of little Charlie's blond dimpled image were everywhere.

Police and FBI agents joined in the hunt as tips and Charlie sightings poured in from Michigan to Mexico. Thousands volunteered to help Lindbergh find his son. Al Capone himself declared that if he were freed from his Chicago jail cell, his underworld contacts could return the child immediately. Psychics contributed their visions. Not to be outdone in the supernatural department, the local paper, the *Hunterdon County Democrat* decided to get a "nature reading" from James Lakamont, the county's only Native American. He told reporters, "He whom you seek is not in the mountains. Only if he is dead will the child be found in the woods." The remarkable prophecy was printed, then forgotten as leads, hoaxes, and frustrations built up in the Lindbergh case—until March 8, when a letter to the kidnapper ran in the *Bronx Home News*.

In the Bronx

One of the many citizens offering help to the Lindberghs was Dr. John "Jafsie" Condon, a retired principal living in the Bronx. Jafsie often wrote letters to the *Home News* when he was indignant. And the kidnapping upset him so much that, like thousands of others, he declared himself willing to negotiate with the kidnapper. Amazingly Jafsie received a letter accepting his mediation offer—a letter marked with the distinctive punched-circle design.

As head of the New Jersey State Police, Colonel H. Norman Schwarzkopf (whose son General H. Norman Schwarzkopf Jr. became famous in the 1991 Gulf War) was officially in charge of the kidnapping investigation. In reality Schwarzkopf was in awe of the heroic aviator, and it was Lindbergh who ran things. And it was Lindbergh who agreed to do whatever the kidnapper wanted.

Regardless of police objections, Lindbergh authorized the inexperienced, self-promoting (and some said suspicious) Jafsie Condon to negotiate on his behalf. Condon received more letters from the kidnapper—who, to prove he had the baby, also sent along the Eaglet's pajamas. Following the kidnapper's orders, Jafsie went to a Bronx cemetery on April 2, 1932, and with Lindbergh nearby, he delivered $50,000 in gold certificates to a man with a foreign accent—a man he nicknamed Cemetery John.

The Eaglet Falls

For all that cash, Jafsie received only another letter that claimed little Charlie was alive on a boat called the *Nellie*. A search ensued, and Lindbergh flew for days over the coast, but the *Nellie* was never spotted. Sadly, about a month later, all hope of finding Charles Jr. alive ended.

On May 12 a Trenton truck driver stopped about four miles from the Lindbergh home, went into the woods to relieve himself, and stumbled over the remains of a toddler. The body was later identified as the Eaglet. The coroner deduced from the condition of the body that the baby had been lying in the woods since the time of the kidnapping. He died from a blow to the head. Cemetery John had lied and disappeared with Lindbergh's money.

The Investigation Continues

As the Lindbergh family mourned, the public clamored for quick justice. But the investigation dragged on for two years as investigators pursued suspects and clues that didn't solve the mystery. A few if them were:

- **Suspect:** Jafsie Condon. Although Lindbergh continued to support Jafsie, the police didn't trust him. They questioned him, searched his property, and tapped his phone in an attempt to discover if the old man was actually in league with Cemetery John. Finally they decided Jafsie was an eccentric but likely innocent.

- **Suspects:** Lindbergh's staff. How did the kidnapper know the Lindberghs were in Hopewell? Or where the baby slept? Cops questioned insiders, particularly Violet Sharpe, a maid who refused to verify her alibi. Sharpe committed suicide, but it turned out her alibi was solid: the night of the kidnapping, she had gone to a speakeasy with a man who wasn't her fiancé.

- **Clue:** the money. The serial numbers on the gold notes paid to Cemetery John were all recorded and the numbers given to banks. In May 1933 ransom gold notes were turned in to the Federal Reserve Bank in New York City. The deposit slip for the exchange of the currency was signed by J. J. Faulkner—who was never found.

An Arresting Development

But on September 15, 1934, the cops finally got their break, thanks to a suspicious attendant at a Bronx gas station. After a customer paid with a gold certificate that the attendant thought might be counterfeit, he wrote down the customer's license plate number and called police. The cops checked the serial number on the certificate and recognized it as part of the Lindbergh ransom. The customer's license plate ultimately led authorities to Bruno Richard Hauptmann, a 35-year-old carpenter from Germany.

Hauptmann was an illegal immigrant whose description was said to match that of Cemetery John. When police arrested him they found a Lindbergh ransom bill in Hauptmann's wallet and more than $11,000 in ransom money stashed in a tin can hidden in the garage. Authorities were sure they had their man, but Hauptmann and his wife insisted they'd been together at home on March 1. The stage was set for what would become known as the Trial of the Century.

Turn to page 209 to continue to
"The Lindbergh Baby, Part II: The Trial of the Century."

DID YOU KNOW?

1,500 types of insects make their homes in the average backyard in northern New Jersey.

Jersey Sing-Along

The songs that all Jerseyans know, that some Jerseyans love, and others just tolerate.

When you live in a place like New Jersey, there are certain songs that are inescapable. Overplayed by radio stations, jukeboxes, and barroom DJs alike, these songs have soaked into the very earth of the state and seeped into the subconscious of almost every resident—until there's nothing left to do but give in to them.

"Jersey Girl" by Tom Waits
Listeners may be more familiar with Springsteen's rendition, but Tom Waits wrote and sang this masterpiece about how nothing matters in this whole wide world when you're in love with a Jersey Girl. Sha, la la la, la la, la la . . .

"My Way" as sung by Frank Sinatra
Ol' Blue Eyes's affirmation of doing things his way is a late night jukebox staple at diners all over the state. Probably best known and loved for the classic and somewhat contradictory line: "Regrets, I've had a few. But then again, too few to mention."

"America" by Simon and Garfunkel
Hands up! Who's counted the cars on the New Jersey Turnpike?

"Bitchin' Camaro" by the Dead Milkmen

This little ditty about heading down the Shore in the car that does donuts on the lawn is a true classic of suburban adolescence.

"Born to Run" by Bruce Springsteen & the E Street Band

Like it or not, it's impossible to be from Jersey and not know this one. Some may remember when a grassroots campaign sprang up to adopt this tune as the state's official song, but it was unsuccessful. Somehow an anthem about how this place "rips the bones from your back" and how "we gotta get out while we're young" didn't really work as a celebration of the state.

"Having a Party" by Southside Johnny and the Asbury Jukes

This is such a swinging song that they're probably still having such a good time, dancing with their baby. Perfect for parties everywhere—from wedding receptions to keggers.

"Bad Medicine" by Bon Jovi

What's a list of New Jersey songs without Bon Jovi? Incomplete, that's what. We chose this favorite from their *New Jersey* album. If you lived in Jersey in the late 1980s, there was no escape.

"Rock and Roll, Part 2" by Gary Glitter

Some say the three-time Stanley Cup–winning New Jersey Devils first used this song to rev up their fans. (Others say it was the New York Rangers, who have only won the cup twice, who skated to it first.) Either way, it's a great way to cheer on your favorite ice hockey squad.

Hometown
For Spacious Skies, for Jersey's Land of Maize

Along the banks of the Hudson River sits the town of Weehawken, a former dueling ground turned Jersey town.

The Town: Weehawken

Location: Hudson County

Founding: Originally part of Hoboken, Weehawken broke off to become its own town in 1859.

Current Population: 13,500 (est.)

Size: 0.85 square miles

What's in a Name? Despite its sound, Weehawken does not refer to some small predatory bird. The widely accepted derivation of the town name is that it comes from the Algonquian term for "land of maize."

Claim to Fame

- Weehawken is home to one end of the Lincoln Tunnel, the world's only "three-tube underwater vehicular tunnel facility," first opened in 1937. Today it's the busiest traffic tunnel in the world—an average of 120,000 cars per day pass through it.

Down the Shore

*As any Jersey native knows, you never just go to the beach in that state—
you go down the Shore. Here are 30 Shore destinations, all wonderful
on a hot day. Surf's up!*

ABSECON	LONG BEACH
ALLENHURST	LONG BRANCH
ASBURY PARK	LOVELADIES
ATLANTIC CITY	MANASQUAN
AVALON	MARGATE
AVON BY THE SEA	NEPTUNE
BAY HEAD	OCEAN CITY
BELMAR	ORTLEY
BOARDWALK	SEA GIRT
BRIELLE	SEA ISLE CITY
BRIGANTINE	SOMERS POINT
CAPE MAY	SPRING LAKE
DEAL	STONE HARBOR
HOLGATE	SURF CITY
LAVALLETTE	WILDWOOD

```
S S B R T S U R F C I T Y B T R S T
S D K B R I E L L E A O B S N A S H
L O C E A N C I T Y Y B W S E R O O
C O E S O S K T D E R D N S U V N L
A W N N I A B E I A E C E H E E O G
P D A G O A A U K A L H N L A N O A
E L O Y B L V E R A T E O A G U E T
M I E T E R A I R Y L L V B D T H E
A W A I N L A V B L P G E O A P A O
Y T I C C I T N A L T A N G L E M R
E E N E T R O R C L C O R I T N A E
A T M L B V T P O H L A N K R O N A
E E U S A N Y Y S T M E I R I P A G
N E N I T N A G I R B A T G G O S S
A K L A W D R A O B E Y A T A O Q T
S D A E H Y A B B E L M A R E G U B
T C O S T O N E H A R B O R S A A A
E P A N A A C A Y N O C E S B A N A
```

Turn to page 316 for the solution.

The Boss Sings About Jersey

Bruce Springsteen paid tribute to the Garden State in some of his best songs.

It goes without saying that Bruce Springsteen is as close to a Songwriter Laureate as New Jersey has ever had; any man whose very first album is *Greetings from Asbury Park, NJ* is a man who has rooted himself hard and fast in the Garden State soil. And while many of his songs could happen anywhere, some of his most memorable songs take place in Jersey itself. Here is a small sample of the Boss's geographically pertinent tunes.

Atlantic City

Album: *Nebraska* (1982)

Sample Lyrics: "Well now everything dies baby that's a fact/But maybe everything that dies someday comes back/Put your makeup on fix your hair up pretty/And meet me tonight in Atlantic City"

Geographic Facts: Atlantic City, of course, is New Jersey's famous gambling mecca, where the casinos exist somewhat uneasily with the city. The song is filled with references to gambling and also the mob (the Chicken Man who blows up in the first line of the song is a reference to a Philly-based mobster named Phil Testa, who was killed in mob warfare to control Atlantic City).

The E Street Shuffle

Album: *The Wild, the Innocent & the E Street Shuffle* (1973)

Sample Lyrics: "Sparks fly on E Street when the boy prophets walk it handsome and hot/All the little girls' souls grow weak when the man-child gives them a double shot"

Geographic Facts: E Street—referenced in the song title, the album title, and the name of Springsteen's backing band—is the street in Belmar where the mother of Springsteen's then-piano player, David Sancious, lived. Springsteen named the band for the street because he thought it was a catchy name. Ironically, Sancious left the band after this album.

4th of July, Asbury Park (Sandy)

Album: *The Wild, the Innocent & the E Street Shuffle* (1973)

Sample Lyrics: "Well the cops finally busted Madame Marie/For tellin' fortunes better than they do/This boardwalk life for me is through/You know you ought to quit this scene too"

Geographic Facts: Asbury Park is a seaside resort town that has seen better days. Its fall from greatness inspired Springsteen and gave birth to some great lyrics, including this bittersweet tribute to the Asbury Park boardwalk. The woman referred to is Madame Marie Castello, a fortune teller who plied her trade there in the Temple of Knowledge. She took a brief hiatus, but has recently returned to her career in foresight. The town itself is trying to make a comeback, as well, with a new wooden boardwalk and plans to revitalize its oceanfront neighborhoods.

In Freehold

Album: Unreleased: The song made its first appearance at a 1996 concert in Freehold

Sample Lyrics: "Well, the girls at Freehold Regional they looked pretty fine/Had my heart broke at least a half dozen times/I wonder if they miss me, if they still get the itch/If they'd dump me if they knew I'd strike it rich"

Geographic Facts: Springsteen's shout-out to his hometown, which bills itself as Western Monmouth's Family Town on its Web site. The site also notes that "residents in our community enjoy an award-winning Parks and Recreation Department, an excellent school system, one of the lowest municipal tax and water and sewer rates in the region." Maybe Bruce should move back. It sounds like a nice place.

Tenth Avenue Freeze-out

Album: *Born to Run* (1975)

Sample Lyrics: "From a tenement window a transistor blasts/Turn around the corner things got real quiet real fast/She hit me with a Tenth Avenue freeze-out/Tenth Avenue freeze-out"

Geographic Facts: Tenth Avenue, like E Street, runs through Belmar. The song itself refers to the band, with saxophonist Clarence Clemons making an appearance as the Big Man and Springsteen as Scooter. ("The Boss" suits him better in our opinion.)

Rotten Tomatoes

Uncle John presents a collection of the worst Jersey jokes around.

Ah, the ubiquitous Jersey joke. Often unfunny and often repeated, these little suckers have been around since Ben Franklin. In honor of the tradition, Uncle John has assembled some of the worst. We like to call them "Rotten Tomatoes."

The Classic Questions
You're from New Jersey? What exit?
You're from the Garden State? Whadd'ya grow there? Smokestacks?
You're from the Garden State? It oughta be called the "Interstate."

Jokes from Across the Hudson
Why does New Jersey have all the toxic waste dumps and New York all the lawyers? *New Jersey got to pick first.*
Why are New Yorkers so depressed? *Because the light at the end of the tunnel is New Jersey.*

Politics Is a Dirty Business
What's the difference between New Jersey and a banana republic? *New Jersey doesn't grow any bananas.*

Jersey's Own Jaws

In a world of innocence, in a time of war, man faces the ancient struggle against the elements. Just when you thought it was safe to go in the water ... shark attack!

The summer of 2001 was dubbed Summer of the Shark by the media. With a total of three shark fatalities in the United States, the press clamored about the rise of shark attacks. Vacationers all along the Eastern seaboard were afraid to go in the water. But 2001 had nothing on the summer of 1916 in New Jersey.

At the dawn of the 20th century, Americans didn't have the Discovery Channel or Jacques Cousteau; they didn't have Peter Benchley or Steven Spielberg. So they learned about sharks the hard way—up close and personal. Before July 1916, most educated Americans didn't even believe in man-eating sharks. They thought old sailors' tales about them were no more real than the kraken or sea serpents. One fortnight on the Jersey Shore proved all the scientists wrong. Five attacks, four deaths, and one mean shark.

Beach Haven or Hell?

That fateful summer Charles Vansant, a recent college grad from Philadelphia's upper class, was escaping the sweltering city heat with his family at Beach Haven, a resort on the Jersey Shore. In the late afternoon of July 1, 1916, Vansant partook in the new fashion of long-distance swimming and dove into the ocean waves.

As Vansant swam, admirers on the shore spotted a lone fin heading straight for him. They started to yell, "Watch out! Watch out!" but he could not hear them. When Vansant was less than fifty feet from shore, in water only 3½ feet deep, something slammed into him and closed its powerful jaws around his left leg.

With no thought of his own safety, future Olympic swimmer Alexander Ott rushed into the bloody water to Vansant's aid, starting a tug-of-war with the predator. With the help of others from the crowd, Ott managed to drag Vansant to shore. Only a bloody stump remained where Vansant's left leg should have been. In modern times these injuries would not have been necessarily fatal, but in 1916 Charles's father, a doctor, had no idea how to treat him. Charles Vansant died of blood loss shortly after the attack.

Despite the fact that Vansant's was the first death certificate in the United States to list "shark" as the cause of death, the hotel at Beach Haven didn't warn any other resorts of the potential threat. Most people didn't believe it could have been a shark; after all, sharks didn't eat people. When reported, the story of Vansant's death was buried on the last page of the *New York Times* three days later under the innocuous headline "Dies After Attack by Fish." So all along the Jersey Shore, vacationers continued their carefree aquatic recreation.

For Whom the Bellboy Tolls

Five days after Vansant's death, Charles Bruder, the head bellboy at a hotel in Spring Lake (another resort, about 50 miles north of Beach Haven), took a break from his duties, and, like Vansant before him, went for a swim in the ocean. He was a quarter mile from shore when observers saw a spray of water erupt around him. As rescuers hauled him into the bottom of a boat, they saw with horror that a shark had taken off both his legs and gouged his abdomen and chest. Bruder remained conscious until they reached shore, where he died before a doctor could reach him.

Mass Hysteria

The hotel manager at Spring Lake immediately put out the first coastwide shark alarm in the United States. After July 6 thousands of swimmers rushed back to dry land as a full-scale shark panic set in. Dozens of men launched out to sea aiming rifles into the waves to kill the murderous shark. Many beaches set up nets around the shore, assuring swimmers that it was quite safe to swim within their confines.

There were still naysayers who believed the attacks were committed by a killer whale or a giant sea turtle—some even said it must have been a swordfish. Most notably, Dr. Frederick Lucas, director of the American Museum of Natural History, called the idea of a shark attack ridiculous, saying that a shark could not "nip off a man's leg like biting a carrot."

Up the Creek Without a Paddle

In the early morning of July 12 old sea captain Thomas Cottrell saw a shark while on his morning constitutional. There was only one problem: He was in Matawan, *10 miles* from the ocean. The shark he saw must have swum through Raritan Bay and up Matawan Creek, a freshwater creek only 17 feet at its deepest point. Cottrell rushed to town to sound the alarm—and was soundly laughed at. A shark in the creek? Pshaw! But the townsfolk would soon regret their quick judgment.

Meanwhile six adolescent boys were enjoying a cooling dip in the creek. Lester Stilwell, a scrawny boy prone to fits, floated on his back and called out, "Watch me float, fellas!" When the fellas, mere yards away in the creek, turned to watch, they saw Lester floating . . . as the jaws of a shark surrounded him. The tail of the shark slammed one of the other boys into the pier as it claimed its prey.

The five survivors ran down the main street of Matawan screaming, "Shark! Shark!" In a matter of moments a rescue team appeared, but they scoffed at the boys' tale. They simply thought Lester had had one of his fits in the water and drowned.

Who Rescues the Rescuers?

They trawled the creek for the body but had little success. Two men, Stanley Fisher and George Burlew, dove into the deepest part of the murky creek and tried to locate the boy's body in the muddy water. After a while, Fisher surfaced and cried, "I've got it!" He had found Lester's body—lodged in the jaws of a feeding shark.

In a moment of startling stupidity, Fisher pried the body from the man-eater and made for the surface, but the shark struck him as he reached it. Fisher had to drop Lester's body in order to struggle to shore. Only as he was climbing out of the creek did he notice his left leg—and how little of it there was left. The shark had taken one giant bite and stripped the leg from hip to knee.

Dr. Reynolds, the local general practitioner, thought the bite was poisonous and wouldn't touch it. The nearest hospital was 10 miles away, and Fisher died just as he reached it, more than three hours later.

Hysteria kept spreading. Fishermen raced up and down the creek in boats, yelling at swimmers to get out of the water. But it was too late for a group of boys swimming just a quarter mile downstream from the site of the two previous attacks. As Joseph Dunn made for the ladder, he felt something hit him. He watched in horror as a shark turned around and grabbed his leg, trying to pull him into deeper water. Fortunately for Joseph, the water was so shallow there the shark could not maneuver. It let the boy go and swam away. Joseph's leg was mangled, but he survived his encounter.

Never Mind the Germans

For the rest of that day, the citizens of Matawan hunted the killer shark. They dynamited the creek; then, seeing the movement of bubbles caused by the dynamite, fired their rifles shouting, "Shark! Shark!" Dr. Lucas pointed out that the blood from all the fish killed by the dynamite might actually attract more sharks, but the shark hunters were undeterred.

A shark panic unrivaled in history swept the coast as fishermen killed dozens of sharks during the next weeks. Angry citizens wrote letters to President Wilson demanding that he make Jersey's waters safe again. Some saw the shark as a dark companion of the U-boat *Deutschland* that had appeared on the coast at the same time. Wilson met with his cabinet on the subject but decided that an all-out war on sharks was out of the budget.

Shark: 4, Man: 1

John Murphy and Michael Schleisser launched their small motorboat into Raritan Bay on July 14 for some recreational fishing, trailing a net behind them. Their boat suddenly slammed to a halt: They had something big in their net, and it was pulling their boat backward and under the water. The catch turned out to be a big shark that turned and started chomping at the two men over the gunwales of the boat. Schleisser grabbed a broken oar handle, the only weapon available, and managed to beat the shark to death.

Schleisser, also a renowned taxidermist, brought his prize home to stuff. When he opened the stomach he found what the Museum of Natural History confirmed were human bones. There was no way to match the bones with the victims for certain, but most believed the man killer was gone for good.

Expert Opinion

So what was the cause of these shark attacks on Jersey's shore? The most common theory is that all attacks that summer were due to a single rogue shark. It is a known fact that individual lions or tigers can develop a taste for humans and become man-eaters. However, modern shark experts dismiss the rogue shark theory. They posit that cluster attacks, such as those in 1916, can be the result of coastal water temperature changes that draw sharks to the beaches.

It's more likely that the tragedies of the summer of 1916 were the result of the new sport of ocean swimming. Humans pushed into the deep *en masse* for the first time—and ran afoul of a creature that had always been there. The high number of fatalities had more to do with the quality of medical attention than the fierceness of the predator. Medical knowledge is more advanced now than it was in 1916, and as a result more victims of shark attacks survive their encounters. But even so, sharks still make people afraid to go in the water, even in New Jersey.

New Jersey Notables
A Quiz

New Jerseyans are excellent in a wide variety of areas. Not content to specialize, the state has produced some of the finest artists, scholars, and heroes the world has ever known. Care to see how diverse your knowledge is?

1. Charles Addams
2. Donna Weinbrecht
3. William J. Brennan Jr.
4. Grover Cleveland
5. Lauryn Hill
6. Dorothea Lange
7. Patricia McBride
8. Joe Theismann
9. Molly Pitcher
10. Queen Latifah
11. Antonin Scalia
12. H. Norman Schwarzkopf Jr.
13. Ruth St. Denis
14. Alfred Stieglitz
15. Dionne Warwick
16. Franco Harris

The Artists

A. Born in 1864 in Hoboken, this pioneering photographer fought to put photography on the same artistic level as painting. His photographs were the first accepted as art by major museums in Boston, New York City, and Washington, DC. He married Georgia O'Keeffe in 1924; some of his most famous photographs are of her.

B. Another photographer from Hoboken, this artist was born in 1895 and is best known for documenting the destitute conditions of migrant workers who traveled to California during the Great Depression. She was the first woman awarded a Guggenheim Fellowship for photography.

C. Born in Westfield in 1912, this famous cartoonist created a pop culture phenomenon and beloved TV show inspired by his fascination with humor, macabre, and the ironic. He was given a Mystery Writers of America award and the Yale Humor Award.

The Singers

D. This successful actress and singer was born in East Orange in 1940. Her hits spanned the 1960s and included memorable songs such as "Do You Know the Way to San Jose?," "Walk on By," and "I Say a Little Prayer."

E. Born in South Orange in 1975, this rapper became well known first as a member of The Fugees, whose album *The Score* became one of the highest-selling rap albums of all time. Blending lots of musical styles, her first solo effort in 1998 won five Grammys, including Album of the Year, Best New Artist, Best Female R&B Vocal Performance, Best R&B Song, and Best R&B Album.

F. Her name means "delicate" and "sensitive" in Arabic. Born in 1970 in Newark, she was the first female rapper to have an album go gold (it was her third release, *Black Reign*). Her biggest single "U.N.I.T.Y." would win a Grammy that year for Best Solo Rap Performance. Not limiting herself to music, she has also excelled in acting and was nominated for an Academy Award in 2003.

The Dancers

G. Modern and spiritual dancer extraordinaire, this Newark native born in 1879 left a major impact on ballet and modern dance. As a dancer and choreographer, she was greatly influenced by Asian and Anglo-European culture and was fascinated by exotic dance steps and costumes.

H. Best known for her performances with the New York City Ballet, this famous ballerina was born in Teaneck in 1942. She joined the NYCB in 1959, and by 1961 had become its youngest principal dancer. She has worked with some of ballet's greats: George Balanchine, Jerome Robbins, Rudolf Nureyev, and Mikhail Baryshnikov.

The Heroes

I. General George Washington commemorated this New Jersey revolutionary for her heroic role at the Battle of Monmouth. The battle was fought on a hot June day, and this woman hauled water to the battlefront for the men. When one soldier fell, she took his place at the cannon and kept it firing. This hero was born in Trenton in the 1750s.

J. This army general was born in Trenton in 1934 and is a graduate of America's most elite military school, West Point. He is best known for his success as Commander of Operations of Desert Shield and Desert Storm during the first Gulf War.

The Politicians

K. A bastion of liberalism, this man was born in Newark in 1906. The son of Irish immigrants, he believed the Constitution to be "a sparkling vision of the supreme dignity of every individual." President Eisenhower nominated him to become a Supreme Court justice.

L. Born in Trenton in 1936 this Supreme Court justice, nominated by President Reagan, is considered one of the most consistently conservative justices. He is known for his acerbic wit and once said, "A law can be both economic folly and constitutional."

M. This famous politician was born in Caldwell in 1837, became governor of New York, and eventually landed in the White House. While taking many unpopular stands, he performed his office honorably and became the first, and as yet only, president to be married in the White House.

The Athletes

N. Born in 1949, this All-American quarterback grew up in South River, graduated from Notre Dame University in 1970, and went on to earn 25,206 yards passing with the Washington Redskins. He led his team to victory in Super Bowl XVII and was eventually voted into the New Jersey Sports Hall of Fame.

O. Moguls freestyle skiing was a pretty new event when this athlete became the first American to medal in it in the 1992 Olympic Games. A West Milford native, this sports pioneer would become a skiing phenomenon and one of the most victorious American skiers ever.

P. Born in 1950 and another inductee into the New Jersey Sports Hall of Fame, this Fort Dix–born football star is probably best known for his famous catch—the Immaculate Reception—while playing for the Pittsburgh Steelers. A triple-sport athlete at Rancocas Valley High School, he played basketball and baseball in addition to football. This superstar running back rushed for 1,000 yards per season eight times, won four Super Bowls, and was selected the Most Valuable Player of Super Bowl IX.

Turn to page 316 for answers.

DID YOU KNOW?

A 19-year-old New Jersey college student was the first person to down the six-pound "96er" hamburger at Denny's Beer Barrel Pub in Pennsylvania. Nobody had finished the behemoth burger in under three hours until Kate Stelnick did in 2005. Her secret? She didn't eat for two days before taking on the big, bad burger.

New Jersey's Best Diners

New Jersey is the undisputed Diner Capital of the World. There are more diners here than in any other state. Here's Uncle John's guide to these American icons.

What Is a Diner, Anyway?

Depends on whom you ask. But according to the American Diner Museum, it's a prefabricated restaurant made in one place and shipped to another place for business. Typically they're fitted with stools and counters and offer reasonably priced food, including breakfast served anytime. From there, the definition gets a little fuzzy. Some are the shiny-hulled prefabricated railcars; others are retrofitted trolleys. Many have a 1950s retro theme. Most have a jukebox. Some are even in strip malls today. But two things are for certain: they're all American and all over New Jersey.

Why New Jersey?

Historians trace the earliest precursor to the diner back to horse-drawn "night lunch wagons" in Rhode Island, Massachusetts, and New England. Providence, Rhode Island, restauranteur Walter Scott was the first man credited with selling lunch out of his wagon to night workers. While New Jersey wasn't the first to think of the idea, it was the first to run with it. The earliest attempts at what we recognize today as a diner came from companies such as Kullman, Paramount Diners, and the Jerry Mahoney Company of Bayonne.

Mahoney was the patriarch of the 24-hour pancake house and became the New Jersey diner king of his day. From a horse-drawn carriage, he began selling such salt-of-the-earth menu items as pork and beans and corned beef. And by the time the Great Depression rolled around he'd built quite a business premanufacturing railcarlike restaurants (dining by rail back then was a classy affair, so the train theme made the experience a little more special). But despite the railcar aesthetics, New Jersey diners were a dependable way to get a cheap meal—and that's what originally made them a hit during those tight times. Mahoney started shipping his diners all over the country, with financing offered, and eventually he took his company public. So it's partly because of him that when people think of diners, they think of New Jersey.

But Mahoney didn't do it alone. There were many manufacturers cranking out prefab food cafés up and down the East Coast. And among them, New Jersey entrepreneurs were doing what they do best—trying to make more of them than anyone else. Plus, the abundance of highways makes New Jersey a very mobile state, perfect for the proliferation of travel-friendly fare. During the 1950s, the diner's heyday, the combination of an economic boom and a population boom in the Northeast made an inexpensive cup of coffee and a quick slice of meatloaf or apple pie a hot prospect in the Garden State.

Diners to Visit

There are over 500 diners in New Jersey—from die-hard prefab originals that look like they've been in a time warp for the last 60 years to fancier, engineered diner franchises. Listing them all (in one sitting) is impossible. But here are some that are well worth their saltines.

Bendix Diner (Hasbrouck Heights)

It's hard to imagine a more dinery-looking diner than this one. This original art deco–style diner was built in 1947. It has become a Jersey legend for its quality and simplicity, with no apparent plans to go upscale and start serving tapas. From the Formica counter to the big neon lettering, this place looks so much like your typical diner that Hollywood types love to film there (it was the backdrop for the movie *Diner*). Go there at night and you might catch Johnny, the diner's star waiter. The level of fast, friendly service he gives customers, despite being blind, brings shame upon every bad waiter who's ever mixed up an order.

Tick-Tock Diner (Clifton)

Mmm . . . time for an angioplasty. If cholesterol is the base of your food pyramid, there's no better place to visit than the Tick-Tock Diner. Its original 1940s facade (the building is an authentic 1949 production) comes complete with a neon clock and the mantra EAT HEAVY. It's possible to eat light there, but why would you want to? All the standard diner fare is accounted for, and it's all good. From Greek salad to Belgian waffles, there's decadence for everyone—plus portions are so huge they get mentioned in every first-year macroeconomics course at Rutgers.

Miss America Diner (Jersey City)

Americana expert Peter Genovese called this "the best diner in New Jersey," adding that there wasn't even a runner up. The Miss America got its name when a German immigrant bought this 1950s model and wanted to use the name to declare his patriotism. With its stainless steel and bold neon, the Miss America has become a Jersey City landmark to the usual patrons and nearby students at New Jersey City University. People come from all around to stake their claims along the Formica for the good food and good coffee.

Americana (East Windsor)

Diehards may scoff at the Americana's size and newness (it was built in the 1970s). But Uncle John's guess is that if you got them there, you wouldn't hear much complaining. True, original diners didn't come with a 110-inch TV screen, martinis, or a full-service bakery complete with tea cookies. Yet it's safe to say that any of Jerry Mahoney's patrons would have been happy to eat in this classy joint.

Its menu boasts such diverse goodies as Szechwan chicken, matzoh ball soup, and salmon. There's still great coffee, killer omelets, and big neon to create a real authentic diner atmosphere. While there are many diners named Americana, this one really feels like Americana—probably why the *New York Post* voted it one of the top 15 reasons to visit New Jersey.

Summit Diner (Summit)

Right when you sit down, you know this is the real deal. The Summit Diner is a down-to-earth eatery with classic diner aesthetics: a small, silver Mahoney with a counter, stools, and eight prefabricated booths (which, on some mornings, you have to stake out early because they fill up fast). The food is cheap enough for college students, but good enough for students of classic American cuisine. And breakfast is the Summit's high point: big, fluffy pancakes, classic omelets made fast to order, and coffee that's still actually coffee-flavored. It's been in business since it rolled into town in 1938 and is an official government-designated historical landmark.

WHAT TO EAT AT A DINER

- Breakfast. Anytime.
- Cheese Fries Swimming in Brown Gravy. Great for late-night snacking, not so great for your waistline.
- Coffee. Lots of it.
- Lemon Meringue Pie. Heavy on the meringue.
- Strawberry Milkshakes and Root Beer Floats.

New Versus Old

In 1664 Sir George Carteret, the British coproprietor of the lands between the Hudson and Delaware rivers, had the honor of naming the English colony. He called it New Jersey, in honor of the Isle of Jersey where he had served as governor. Ever wonder how New Jersey compares to its namesake?

	Old Jersey	New Jersey
GEOGRAPHY	A British island in the English Channel, with a population of less than 100,000.	An American state and peninsula, with a population of almost 8.5 million.
HISTORY	Won from the French in 1204; has independent government.	Won from the British in 1776; has independent women.
PROXIMITY	Very close to France, but no longer wanting to actually be part of France.	Very close to New York, but no longer wanting NY trash on NJ beaches.

	Old Jersey	**New Jersey**
LANGUAGE	Official languages are English and French, but has its own language, lé Jèrriais, which resembles French, with phrases like *côtil* (meaning a steep hillside field) and *temps pâssé* (meaning times past).	Official language is English, but also retains its own dialect with phrases like *jug handle turn* (meaning left-hand turns from the right lane) and *Fuggedaboutit,* (meaning "Don't worry. All is well.").
TOURING	Within 10 miles, you could travel from one side of the island to the other, as the crow flies.	Within one 25-mile radius, you could visit seven huge shopping malls, as your credit allows.
EDUCATION	Kids go to school until they're 16 and typically go away for college, maybe taking a few transferable college courses before they go.	Kids can choose between almost 50 colleges including Princeton, Seton Hall, and Rutgers, typically making all their parents' money go away.
HUSBANDRY	Known for the Jersey milk cow, the only breed of cattle allowed on the island since the 1700s.	Known for growing world-famous tomatoes, cranberries, and blueberries.

	Old Jersey	New Jersey
SNAILS	Its Durrell Wildlife Conservation Trust has a snailarium where you can adopt endangered snails for just a small price.	With more than 700 Zagat-rated restaurants, New Jersey residents in any city can ingest a snail without driving more than a few blocks.
ECOLOGY	For centuries seaweed, known locally as *vraic*, has been harvested from the beaches to help fertilize the land.	Centuries ago Hoboken gave America its first brewery, in 1664, harvesting hops to help fertilize the locals.
PEOPLE	A little more than half of the people living on the Jersey island were born there.	A little more than half of the people living in New Jersey were in front of you on the Parkway this morning.
FASHION	Famous for the Jersey pullover, a luxurious sweater that flaunts 400 years of knitting heritage.	Famous wearers of jerseys. (When an NFL player wears a jersey for the Jets, Giants, or Eagles, he's paying homage to Old Jersey's pullover for which the word was originally created.)

Hometowns
Named After a Mall?

Cherry Hill (the town) shares a name with Cherry Hill (the mall), but there's more to this town than just shopping.

The Town: Cherry Hill
Location: Camden County
Founding: 1695
Current Population: 70,000 (est.)
Size: 24 square miles
What's in a Name? Cherry Hill has had three names. When founded, it was called Waterford but then changed its name to Delaware Township in 1844. It didn't officially become Cherry Hill until 1961, the same year that the Cherry Hill Mall opened. Some say the town named itself after the shopping center, but the official explanation is that it was in honor of the old Cherry Hill Farm.

Claims to Fame

- The town's Arts Center, Croft Farm, was a major station in the Underground Railroad.

- Home of the Cherry Hill Mall, the first enclosed mall in the East and "South Jersey's Fashion Destination."

- Site of the Scarborough Covered Bridge, one of two still standing in New Jersey. Built in 1959 and dedicated on Valentine's Day when 101 couples smooched to make it an official kissing bridge.

- Corporate headquarters of Pinnacle Foods International, makers of Duncan Hines, Vlasic Pickles, and Swanson's TV Dinners.

- Site of the biggest theater in the Loews Cineplex chain. It has 24 screens!

- Springdale Farms is situated on 100 acres in Cherry Hill and has been a working farm for over 53 years. Throughout the year, you can find more than 30 kinds of produce and flowers there. Customers get a hands-on experience by actually picking their own fruits and vegetables right off the vine!

DID YOU KNOW?

Jersey Lightning isn't just a meteorological phenomenon. It was an apple brandy distilled by the colonists in northeastern New Jersey.

Palisades
Amusement Park

Towering atop cliffs lining the Hudson River, this park provided sizzling summer entertainment for three generations.

On Palisades Avenue in Cliffside Park, New Jersey, in front of high-rise condominium Winston Towers 300, is the Little Park of Memories. Behind the bus stop, this park is—literally—paved with memories: Underfoot are bricks bearing happy remembrances of fans of the late, great Palisades Amusement Park—one of the first, and best, amusement parks ever built. Plaques and flags at this site celebrate the 74 years that the fun park occupied the surrounding 38 acres and offered rides, games, shows, food, and fun to millions.

A Park by Any Other Name . . .

The internationally known amusement park, then called the Park on the Palisades, began simply as a trolley park in the late 1800s. Trolley parks were areas created at "the end of the line" by trolley companies eager to entice riders to spend their spare time—and money—going to the countryside with their families. For almost 10 years, the park successfully fulfilled this role while offering visitors (besides a breathtaking view of New York City) wooded groves, picnic grounds, and flower gardens. Late in 1907, though, the trolley company received an offer it couldn't refuse, and the park was sold to a man with a background in designing, managing, and remodeling theatrical and cultural institutions. This former bucolic setting would soon transform into a world-class amusement park.

On opening night as many as 3,000 people showed up to see the new park. Food, rides, entertainment acts, games of skill, and 15,000 electric lights were introduced into the reopened and renamed Palisades Amusement Park. A miniature train ride, a carousel, a man billed as the World's Most Daring High Diver, a Wild West show, and balloon flights across the Hudson River were just a few of the new attractions. It was bigger, brasher, and brighter than the trolley park had ever been. In the following year, a zoo, puppet show, and Toboggan Slide roller coaster would be added to the roster.

Two for the Price of One

The park was resold and renamed a few years later to brothers Joseph and Nicholas Schenck. They renamed the park after themselves in 1910 and brought in even more attractions. That first season (seasons ran from May to September) Schenck Brothers' Palisades Park's biggest draws were automobile races (since few people had their own car at that time), the Sleigh Ride Coaster, and the Big Scenic Coaster. But the Schencks' masterpiece would come three years later.

Bathing in Brine

Before June 1913 getting cool at the park meant just basking in the breezes off the Hudson River. Faced with growing competition from New York's Coney Island attractions (including a natural beach), the brothers came up with something big: They installed a "beach" of their own. Saltwater (1 million gallons of it!) was pumped up from the Hudson River every day to fill the massive wave pool. (The same engineer who designed the carousel mechanism that makes the horses go up and down designed the machinery to churn out the waves.) As wide as a city block, the vast body of water was billed as the world's largest outdoor saltwater pool, allowed Palisades to advertise "surf bathing," and brought more people to the park.

Say "Uncle!"

In 1935 the park, under new owners Irving and Jack Rosenthal, once again became Palisades Amusement Park. "Uncle" Irving (kids who called him that to his face were rewarded with a dollar bill—Uncle John makes no such promise) was an extremely imaginative promoter. The park thrived with his creative advertising gimmicks.

A new billboard (said to be the world's largest moving sign) built on the cliffs featured 32,000 light bulbs. Matchbooks featured ads for the park—and provided free admission. To grab the interest of kids, coupons for the park were printed in comic books. Superman even became the park's official spokesperson. Discount tickets and special free admittance offers abounded: Uncle Irving knew that the trick was to get people inside the gates. Once they were there, they'd end up spending even more money. Legend has it that for years kids would sneak into the park through a hole in the fence; Rosenthal knew about the hole and ordered his men not to fix it.

Rosenthal's methods of measuring a day's success were also a bit unorthodox: He relied on the trash at the end of the day. Park supervisor John Rinaldi remembered, "He'd walk the grounds, check the garbage, and say, 'We had a pretty good day.'"

A complete list of all the rides offered by the park over the years would be too long to print here. New rides were always being rotated into the mix: The Lake Placid Bobsled coaster arrived in 1937. In 1944 the Skyrocket coaster (after having been damaged by fire) was rebuilt as the Cyclone, which became one of the most famous coasters in the world. Palisades Park was a mecca for roller coaster lovers.

A Win-Win Situation

Contests and pageants also drew more people to the park. The Diaper Derby, New Jersey Donut Dunking Championship, Most Photographic Triplets, Eyeglass-wearing Beauty Contest, and Little Miss America Pageant were just a sampling of the many competitions that were held under Irving's reign.

All sorts of free shows lured the public back again and again. The 1950s and 1960s meant rock and roll at the park. Even major-name singers performed for merely the phenomenal publicity: Chubby Checker, Fabian, the Jackson Five, the Four Seasons, and Diana Ross and the Supremes, to name just a few. Television, radio, and live shows were hosted by well-known DJs, like Bruce "Cousin Brucie" Morrow.

All Things Must Come to an End

Ironically the park's success eventually proved its downfall. While screams of excitement came from inside the park gates, cries of *foul!* came from outside them. Grumblings from nearby residents over the years hadn't amounted to many adjustments, and the good people who lived in the vicinity of the park had finally had enough. Noise had always been an issue, and the traffic and parking situations had indisputably reached saturation levels. The natives were definitely restless.

The famous midway was on its way out—and high-rise development on its way in—when, in 1967, rezoning propositions passed in the towns of Cliffside Park and Fort Lee (the other town in which the park's property lay). Irving Rosenthal, aging and in dubious health, didn't fight the new zoning at this point. He bowed out gracefully and sold the property.

Gone but Not Forgotten

To the disappointment of untold numbers of kids and parents alike (including a group of school children who waged a write-in campaign to then president Richard Nixon to keep the park open), the beloved summer stomping grounds closed its gates for the final time on September 12, 1971. Some attractions went to other amusement parks; some rides, such as the famous Cyclone roller coaster, ended up being demolished. Condominium towers went up on the cleared acreage.

Twenty-seven years later, almost to the day, the Little Park of Memories was created, to the delight of an estimated 1,000 spectators at its dedication ceremony. One of this site's plaques states what may be the sentiment of many of those among the three generations of folks who savored summer seasons at the park: "Here we were happy, here we grew!"

Against the Law

Think you're a law-abiding citizen of New Jersey? Think again! You may be breaking the law without even knowing it!

Behind the Wheel

- Need some shut eye? Then don't even think about getting behind the wheel: Jersey's made it a crime to drive while tired.

- If you need another reason not to drive after having a few drinks, a driving-while-intoxicated conviction in New Jersey means you may never again apply for personalized license plates.

Fashion Police

- Don't wear anything on your head or in your hair in the streets of Secaucus that can accidentally (or purposely!) inflict a cut on another person.

- For that matter, avoid wearing hat pins (with or without hats) throughout the state: It is illegal to wear them in public. (It is presumably okay to poke your friends with hat paraphernalia in private.)

- Don't cross-dress in Haddon Township: Men may not wear

skirts in public. (This law applies even if you *do* have the legs to pull it off.)

Animal Behavior

- In Cresskill, birds need to be able to see and hear those puddy-tats. Cats have to announce their presence properly by wearing three bells to warn our bird friends of their imminent arrival.

- Felines and humans alike should steer clear of homing pigeons. It is illegal to delay or detain one anywhere in the state.

- And while we're talking about birdbrains, consider the following: In Essex Fells it is illegal for ducks to quack after 10:00 p.m. We're not sure who would pay the price for violations, however. Would the fowl be sentenced, say, to a steaming hot bath in a nice orange sauce?

Keep It Clean

- In Blairstown, keep your oaks to yourself. No street-side trees are allowed, lest they "obscure the air."

- Garden at will in Cranford, but keep your boat off the lawn. No aquatic vehicle parking is allowed.

- Better not toss a pickle on the street or you may be arrested: Cucumber littering is illegal throughout New Jersey.

- In Raritan they'll do more than wash your mouth out with soap if you swear. Public profanity was banned in 1994.

- Smoke 'em if you've got 'em—but better not drop ashes from a cigar on the sidewalks of Blairstown. It is illegal to dirty the walkways with tobacco byproducts.

Greed, Gluttony, and Needlework

- You may not dig for uranium in Jefferson Township, no matter how rich it might make you; you can't carry it around in your back pocket either.

- Soda jerks take notice—in Newark it is illegal to sell ice cream after 6:00 p.m., unless your customer has a note from his or her doctor.

- It is against the law for a man to knit during fishing season.

Mind Your Manners

- Throughout the state, you better not slurp your soup. Audible eating could result in a citation. No official word on elbows on the table or eating peas with a knife.

- Be nice to law enforcement because it is against the law across the state to frown at police officers—even when they're writing you a ticket.

Washington's Rubicon

Cloak furling in the wind, standing majestically on one foot, George Washington led his troops across the Delaware River to win the Battle of Trenton, right? Well, it was something like that.

By Christmas Day 1776 General George Washington's Continental army had shrunk from 30,000 men to 3,000. The American Revolution seemed lost. That night Washington gathered his remaining troops and crossed the Delaware River from Pennsylvania to New Jersey in flat-bottom Durham boats. The grueling crossing through the ice-choked river lasted from 6:00 p.m. to 4:00 a.m.: Just one of the four launches made it. Only 2,400 soldiers, some without shoes on their feet, crossed the river that night to march to Trenton and surprise the Hessian troops stationed there. The short, two-hour battle was a rout: 30 Hessians were killed, 84 wounded, and nearly 900 captured—without a single loss to Washington's side. The victory marked a turning point in the war, giving the Continental forces the courage to fight five more years before the British conceded defeat. Dozens of eyewitness accounts of the crossing exist, in soldiers' diaries and letters. But in the minds of most Americans the crossing looks like one painting by Emanuel Leutze, created in 1851.

Art for Art's Sake

Emanuel Leutze's mammoth painting—12 feet by 21 feet—hangs in the Metropolitan Museum of Art in New York City. In the foreground of the famous image stands Washington holding a spyglass, one foot propped up in the lead boat. Behind him future president James Monroe clutches the Stars and Stripes. The boat's 11 other occupants beat against the chunks of ice in the river, struggling to row toward the farther shore. Leutze dressed the soldiers in garments from all over the colonies. An art student can pick out an African-American, a New England seaman, a Scottish immigrant, western riflemen, farmers from New Jersey and Pennsylvania, and soldiers from Delaware, Maryland, and Virginia.

Where's a Photographer When You Need One?

The striking image represents struggle in the face of insurmountable odds and the patriotism of the American. Unfortunately it does not represent what actually happened. For one, the crossing happened at night, not during the day, and it was sleeting, not partly cloudy. The boat is the wrong type, and the ice would have been submerged under the sluicing current. The flag Monroe so desperately holds is all wrong since the Stars and Stripes design was not adopted until six months later in 1777. And if Washington had stood on one leg in his boat like that he would have gone headfirst into the river, and America might still be part of the British Commonwealth.

European History 101

Leutze did not have historical accuracy in mind when he started his masterpiece. A German-American immigrant born in 1816, he moved to the United States as a child. When the Revolutions of 1848 broke out in Europe, he returned to Germany to support the democratic cause. And how does an artist aid the Revolution? With art, of course. Leutze took inspiration from the struggles of his adopted country and used the image of Washington to capture the spirit of freedom. He began work in 1848.

As Leutze worked, the Revolutions failed, and it was with a sense of desperation that he finished in 1850. *Washington Crossing the Delaware* stood as a symbol of the eleventh hour miracle that had saved the American Revolution and, he believed, might still save Germany's. The original painting found its way to the Bremen Art Museum, where it was destroyed in 1942 in a bombing raid by the British Royal Air Force.

Fortunately Leutze painted a full-size copy in 1851 that he had sent to America, where it was an instant success. The painting was displayed in the Rotunda of the National Capitol and eventually donated to the Metropolitan Museum's permanent collection.

A Secular Icon

Leutze's image is now iconic, reproduced in thousands of drawings, carvings, and cross-stitches. In 1998 New Jersey chose the image for the back of their state quarter, creating the first currency with Washington on both sides.

Life Imitates Art

On a blustery Christmas Day in 1953 seven men in an open boat crossed the Delaware in full Revolutionary dress. Led by Saint John Terrell, who would continue to play George Washington every Christmas for decades, these men started a modern tradition of reenactments of the historic crossing.

Of course, not every year goes off without a hitch. In 2000 police grounded the trip for safety reasons; it was just too darn cold. The history buffs instead pushed their boat along the Pennsylvania shore in conditions that actually resembled the original 1776 crossing. In past years the reenactors have marched over the nearby bridge instead of rowing and once forded the Delaware on foot after a drought left the water level so low the boats couldn't be put in the river. Washington should have been so lucky.

The tradition, inspired in no small part by the painting, continues today. If you trudge out to Washington Crossing State Park next Christmas, you'll see reenactors struggling to maintain the poses of Leutze's painting as they push across the river, anachronous flag and all.

DID YOU KNOW?

Pilesgrove hosts the longest running Saturday night rodeo in the United States. Started in 1929 and held regularly on Saturdays since 1944, the Cowtown Rodeo is Jersey's own slice of the West.

Sinatra Sampler

Everyone knows Hoboken's favorite son—Francis Albert Sinatra.
Call him Frank, Ol' Blue Eyes, or the Chairman of the Board,
Sinatra and his singing have made him a Jersey legend for life. For
those who aren't as familiar with his work, here are ten songs from
three eras, all created by one voice.

Frank Sinatra was a man for all musical seasons. From his early years as a teenybopper favorite to his mature years as a smooth, jazzy crooner, a Frank fan would never have a problem finding a song to fit any mood or any situation. But where does that leave a Sinatra neophyte, who doesn't know his or her way around the catalog? Rather than leave you to fend for yourselves, we've created this "tasting menu." These are not necessarily the songs you already know, but they do give you an idea of the range of Frank's voice and talent. And in case you want to take a listen for yourself, we've also listed the albums that you can find them on today.

The Early Years

Sinatra's earlier years are the least known to current audiences—many of us know of this musical era of Sinatra's only from the old Looney Tunes cartoons that portray him as being thinner than a blade of grass. But it's during those years that Sinatra developed the phrasing that would make him special—and the popularity that would carry him through the decades.

The Song: "Night and Day"
Where You Can Hear It: *Frank Sinatra/Tommy Dorsey Platinum & Gold Collection*
This lush, languid take on the Cole Porter classic is from the 1940s, when Sinatra sang in front of the Tommy Dorsey orchestra. Sinatra's on record as saying that Dorsey's fluid trombone playing inspired him to "play" his vocals like an instrument, and you can hear some of those early attempts in this version.

The Song: "Nancy (With the Laughing Face)"
Where You Can Hear It: *Super Hits*
Another lush ballad. Sinatra's voice is light and effortless, with phrasing that sounds just a lilt or two from speaking—a sort of offhand delivery that's as approachable as it is irresistible. No wonder the girls all screamed for him.

The Song: "I've Got a Crush on You"
Where You Can Hear It: *Sinatra Sings His Greatest Hits*
Frank Sinatra and Cole Porter go together like peas and carrots; Sinatra's easy, pleasing cadences wrap around Porter's arch and sassy lyrics. It takes work to make it sound this effortless.

Sinatra Swings!
The Sinatra everyone remembers is the jazzy, snappy Sinatra with the hat at a jaunty angle and the suit jacket hooked over his shoulder. This is exactly the Sinatra you're getting with these next songs.

The Song: "Come Fly with Me"
Where You Can Hear It: *Come Fly with Me*
The quintessential jet-set song, from the quintessential jet-set album. This song gets a kick from the breezy Billy May arrangements and Sinatra's whiskey-tinged vocals. At this point, his voice was well seasoned and deeper than in the 1940s.

The Song: "Witchcraft"
Where You Can Hear It: *The Complete Capitol Singles*
Frank sings, "It's witchcraft, wicked witchcraft," but doesn't really sound like he's complaining about being put under a spell, as his arch delivery over lighthearted horns makes abundantly clear. The perfect song by which to show one's "etchings."

The Song: "Come Dance with Me"
Where You Can Hear It: *Come Dance with Me*
Did you bring your dancing shoes and your "Basie boots"? You had better, because this one from Sinatra's best-selling album of the 1950s brings back Billy May's big, brassy arrangements to match Sinatra's swinging vocals—and sets everybody's toes tapping. It's a quick one (2:30), but that's all the time it needs to get your feet moving.

The Song: "I've Got You Under My Skin"
Where You Can Hear It: *Songs for Swingin' Lovers!*
It's Sinatra and Porter again, and it can't be beat. Sinatra's pacing and bite are masterful, and the song plays out at just the right tempo for dancing close, but not necessarily dancing slow. No one's done this song better, ever—an utterly perfect performance.

Sinatra Saloon Songs

But not every Sinatra song was about the upside of love. He made entire albums of so-called saloon songs (or, as they were also called in darker moments, "suicide songs"). In these Frank took on the role of a jilted lover, spilling his guts to the bartender while drowning his sorrows.

The Song: "In the Wee Small Hours of the Morning"
Where You Can Hear It: *In the Wee Small Hours*
The first track of Sinatra's first full album of saloon songs, and it sets the tone marvelously. It paints the picture of heartbreak and insomnia—a soul-squashing combination if there ever was one. Try not to listen to this if you've just broken up with someone; you might never get out of bed again.

The Song: "One for My Baby"
Where You Can Hear It: *Sinatra Sings Only for the Lonely*
The album title alone hints this won't be a cheerful swinging time at the turntable. And boy, isn't that true. Johnny Mercer wrote this song, the perfect distillation of the saloon song, where Sinatra actually sings it to the bartender. Apologizing for keeping the poor guy in the saloon to hear his tale, Frank tells it anyway, and you can't help but listen.

The Song: "That Old Feeling"
Where You Can Here It: *Nice 'n' Easy*
It would be terribly unfair to shuffle you off with "One for My Baby" still ringing in your ears. So to finish up, here's this lovely yet poignant tune, in which Sinatra spies an old flame and experiences a delightfully sad flare-up. Frank knew how to sing heartache. But he sings it so well, you almost don't mind having it.

Big Booming Business

Even though it's not the biggest state on the block, New Jersey is home to some pretty big businesses.

Let's Go to the Videotape

Somewhere in New Jersey, there's a huge vault of more than 100 million feet of film—all of it footage of professional football. An obsessed fan's basement? Perhaps, but we're talking about the official home of NFL Films, which has been in Mount Laurel for more than 40 years.

I Am Stuck on Jersey, Cause Jersey's Stuck on Me

Just about everything in your bathroom can come from Johnson & Johnson, a leading manufacturer of health-care products. Making everything from Band-Aids to baby shampoo, Johnson & Johnson has made its home in New Brunswick since its founding in 1886. The company has grown to include 190 operating companies in 51 countries, with $27.5 billion in sales. That's a lot of boo-boos.

You're a Grand Old Flag

No matter what country you hail from, showing your patriotism is a lot easier with flags—something the Annin Flag Company is very happy about. Annin, the world's largest and oldest flag manufacturer, makes its home in Roseland and offers more than 10,000 different flags and flag-related products: from the Stars and Stripes and the Jolly Roger to windsocks and flagpoles. The official flag maker for the United Nations, Annin has made the American flags that flew on the Moon and at every presidential inauguration since 1849.

The Rock of Ages

The financial behemoth Prudential Financial got its start in 1875 as the Prudential Friendly Society in downtown Newark, where its headquarters are still located today. The Pru has expanded from a business that provided life insurance for the working class to one of the largest financial service providers in the world.

Oh Where, Oh Where Has My Devil Dog Gone?

Mmm . . . Devil Dogs, Ring Dings, and Yodels. (Oh my!) If you like chocolate snack cakes, then Wayne—home of the Drake's Bakery—is the place to be. It's the only place where these treats are made in the United States. So if you're interested in the Drake's trifecta, you know where to go.

Gotta Getta Stuffed Animal

Need a teddy bear? How about a floppy stuffed dog? Look no further than Edison, where Gund's headquarters are. This stuffed toy manufacturer trademarked their "understuffing" methodology, which created the softest, most squishable toys suitable for repeated bouts of hugging.

A Blind Man's Best Friend

It's hard to remember a time when Seeing Eye dogs weren't around. We have the Seeing Eye in Morristown to thank for that. It is North America's oldest guide dog–training institute. Located in New Jersey since 1931, the Seeing Eye was founded with the goal of helping blind people to live independently with the help of these specially trained dogs. Nearly 13,000 dogs have been placed with the blind since the school's founding.

Tiny Bubbles

Every time a heavy package comes in the mail, what's inside is often protected with Bubble Wrap, another New Jersey innovation. Marc A. Chavannes and Alfred W. Fielding were trying to develop textured wallpaper by capturing air between two thin layers of plastic. The wallpaper idea didn't take off, but the two realized that their invention was a perfect protective packing material. Bubble Wrap was born (and would become a favorite plaything for kids who couldn't get enough of popping those little plastic bubbles). In 1960 the two men founded the Sealed Air Corporation, headquartered in Saddle Brook, that still makes Bubble Wrap and other protective packaging gear today.

Books, Bounty Hunters, and the Burg

Janet Evanovich, Jersey-born author, has created a series of best-selling novels set in Trenton that feature a bounty-hunter babe named Stephanie Plum. So what's the story behind the stories?

You Can't Take the Jersey out of the Girl

Star of her own literary mystery series (now up to 10 titles in print!), the fictional Stephanie Plum is a hilarious bounty hunter from Trenton. An unemployed discount-lingerie buyer, Stephanie was forced by hard economic times (and the end of her disastrous marriage) to work as a bounty hunter for her sleazy cousin Vinnie, a bail bond agent. Despite keeping her gun in the cookie jar and not a holster, Stephanie jumps right in and tracks down some of Trenton's shadiest characters. Her adventures in crime fighting are matched only by her colorful family, the sexy men in (and out of) her life, and her faithful companion, Rex, the pet hamster.

The author of the Stephanie Plum series of books is also a Jersey girl: South River's Janet Evanovich. She used to write romance books until she "ran out of positions" and then took a leap into crime (novels). In 1994 Evanovich launched her first Stephanie saga, *One for the Money*. The book's mixture of serious crime, humor, and romance won a slew of devoted fans, who quickly gobbled up each new volume. Evanovich's books are all worldwide best-sellers. One of the latest, *To the Nines,* shipped 750,000 hardcover copies and made it to number one on the *New York Times* best-seller list.

You Can Go Burg Again

Evanovich has stated that the setting of Trenton contributes both to the comedy and the gritty crime elements in her novels. Jersey food, Jersey traffic, Jersey folks, and Jersey energy in general are, she feels, a key to Stephanie Plum's success. Life in Plum's neighborhood can be difficult, but according to Evanovich the important thing is that it's never bland—since bland is the kiss of death to an audience.

Still it's something of a puzzle to those who know her life story why, of all the places in Jersey, Evanovich set her story in the Chambersburg section of town (called the Burg for short). Janet's first connection to Trenton's old Italian-German neighborhood wasn't a happy one. After her family moved to Mercerville, Janet's father became very ill. He spent a lot of time recovering at St. Francis Medical Center, located on the edge of the Burg, and Janet would take the train to visit him. As she sat with her dad she could look out from the high hospital windows down into the neighborhood.

Janet liked what she saw. The area between Hamilton Street and Chambers Street contained well-kept houses with lots of delis, bakeries, and Italian restaurants. It didn't exactly look like South River, but it reminded her of it just the same. As Evanovich spent more time strolling through the area and meeting the people, she felt comforted and comfortable. This was a place where the residents knew each other and watched out for each other. Memories of the Burg stayed with her long after she graduated Douglass College, married Pete Evanovich, and raised a family of two children, daughter Alex and son Peter.

When Evanovich began to write about a bounty hunter who worried about hair, her weight, and her makeup, she looked for the setting of a tight-knit community with strong values and traditions. Janet was living in a suburb in Virginia at the time but didn't feel it had enough character. Instead she figured that "you can't go wrong with New Jersey," and turned back to Chambersburg. The rest is history.

Hangin' at the Cop Shop

Writing a mystery series required research, so Evanovich returned to Trenton and did her homework. When she wasn't eating vodka rigatoni at Marsilios Restaurant, she was visiting the Clinton Avenue police station to learn the ropes. Three-quarters of the way through her first mystery book, Evanovich was stumped by her fictional crime—until one of her Trenton friends in blue stepped up to solve it so she could finish the book.

Meanwhile, Back in New Hampshire

Evanovich's connection with Trenton runs so deep that fans are often surprised to learn that she writes the series from her home in bucolic Hanover, New Hampshire. There, Janet's novels are the foundation of a family company, Evanovich Inc. Janet writes the novels; daughter Alex is the Webmaster for her successful Web site (which gets about 5 million hits a month). Janet's husband, Peter, is general manager, and her son, Peter Jr., handles the company's finances.

Will Evanovich move back to Trenton? Not in the near future. The creator of Stephanie Plum has explained that though her heart belongs to Jersey, if she lived there, she'd never get any writing done. She'd always be at the mall.

DID YOU KNOW?

Janet Evanovich gave horses to the Trenton police department to show her appreciation for their help with her books. The department now has  three horses, a mare named Stephanie Plum and two handsome bays named for Plum's romantic interests, Ranger (the mysterious bounty hunter) and Joe Morelli (one hunk of a cop). Mare Stephanie can often be seen patrolling the Chambersburg section of town.

Things That Go Bump in the Night

Don't be afraid, it's only Uncle John's collection of spooky specters, awful apparitions, and haunted high jinks in the Garden State.

Jenny Jump

Who's That Ghost? Jenny, a young colonial girl

Haunted Hangout: Hope, Warren County

Spooky Sights: A young girl floating around the lakes and cliff, crying out for her father

The Spectral Scoop: There are several versions of the story, but the most popular comes from a 1747 account of a Swedish missionary, Sven Roseen. Nine-year-old Jenny lived in a house beneath a high cliff that overlooked a lake. One day Jenny accompanied her father to the high cliff to pick berries while her father collected wood. When Jenny noticed the approach of some unfriendly Lenape tribe members, she cried out in warning to her father. Possibly afraid that his daughter's virtue (and her life) might be in danger, Jenny's father yelled, "Jump, Jenny, jump!" An obedient child, Jenny leaped off the rocky cliff and fell to her death. While her body was crushed by the fall, her spirit stayed on. To this day her plaintive voice can be heard and her ghostly figure seen around the surrounding cliffs in the Jenny Jump State Forest that was named for her.

Flute-Lovin' Traitor

Who's That Ghost? William Chaplain

Haunted Hangout: New Monmouth, Monmouth County

Spooky Sights: A young soldier, dressed in Colonial attire, playing mournful ballads on his flute.

The Spectral Scoop: Local legend has it that William Chaplain, a 17-year-old flute enthusiast, was a Revolutionary War soldier who was also a spy for the British. The patriots discovered his treachery and shot him in the back before a skirmish, within the sight of the British troops. Many thought those bullets had been the end of young William. But in the late evenings in New Monmouth, residents claim to hear sad ballads and tunes tooted on a flute by this ghostly traitor.

Surveying Specter

Who's That Ghost? Robert Erskine

Haunted Hangout: Ringwood State Park, Passaic County

Spooky Sights: A ghostly figure who sits on his grave, waves a lantern, follows people around, thumps around in his mansion, and holds a ball of blue light.

Spectral Scoop: It's not just the chills and clammy sensations or the doors that lock themselves that persuade many visitors that Erskine haunts the Ringwood property. In life Erskine had managed the American Iron Company's facilities in Ringwood. He was appointed by George Washington as the Surveyor General for the Continental Army during the War for Independence. Sadly, in 1780, he died young after he caught a cold while working on New Jersey maps.

In death, the ghost of General Erskine has been seen, but what has caused this spirit to linger in his manor remains somewhat of a mystery. Some say the appearance of ghostly Erskine is related to the possibility that the manor and iron ore mines may have defaced the nearby sacred Native American lands and cursed his spirit.

The Original Headless Horseman?

Who's That Ghost? A decapitated Hessian soldier
Haunted Hangout: Kenilworth, Union County
Spooky Sights: A galloping headless rider on horseback
Spectral Scoop: Washington Irving may have made Tarrytown famous with his ghost story, "The Legend of Sleepy Hollow," but some say that his inspiration for the menacing Headless Horseman came from a New Jersey legend. During the War for Independence, a Hessian soldier had his head taken off by the Continental army. Some say it was sliced off, while others say a cannonball did the foul deed. Ever since then his headless form and his horse continue to gallop across what is now the Galloping Hills Golf Course. The story of the Headless Hessian was popular during Irving's time, so perhaps he took a little literary license and relocated the story.

I've Been Haunting on the Railroad

Who's That Ghost? An unnamed, one-armed railway worker
Haunted Hangout: Chester, Morris County
Spooky Sights: Green light bobbing up and down over the railroad tracks.
Spectral Scoop: One of New Jersey's most famous ghost stories is of the Hookerman: a nameless railroad worker who lost his life while repairing the tracks at night. When his arm became stuck and could not be freed, an unexpected train mowed him down. A morbid tale indeed, but what makes his story even eerier is that

the man's body was found, but his arm and lantern had completely disappeared.

Since the accident, people have reported a bobbing green light that hovers over the Central Railroad of New Jersey's former tracks. Some say the Hookerman's body is looking for his lost arm; others say it's his ghostly arm that still clutches a lantern while looking for his body. Both sound perfectly reasonable. No matter what body part you prefer, the tale of Hookerman is so popular that he even has a beer named after him. The Long Valley Pub and Brewery created Hookerman's Light, an American wheat ale, in his honor.

It's Never Time to Leave the Party

Who's That Ghost? Esther Allen, "The Partying Ghost"
Haunted Hangout: The Southern Mansion, Cape May County
Spooky Sights: Phantom female who dances, laughs, rustles her petticoat, and leaves behind traces of her perfume.
Spectral Scoop: While many ghosts possess tragic pasts, here is the story of a ghost who stayed behind because she missed having a good time. As the niece of wealthy industrialist George Allen, Esther was able to enjoy all the privileges of affluence. Her uncle spared no expense in constructing a palatial seaside mansion in 1863, primarily for entertaining guests with extravagant parties. When Esther died she wasn't ready to stop her good time so she hung around her old home, now a bed and breakfast called The Southern Mansion. Esther currently entertains the owner and guests alike with numerous sightings of her lively spirit. Occasionally laughter can be heard from several empty rooms, and if observers are lucky, they can catch a glimpse of her dancing from room to room.

On the Banks of the Old Raritan

University of New Jersey would be so much simpler. But Rutgers, the State University of New Jersey sounds so much more official. Rutgers's school song tells you where it is, but it doesn't tell you much about the university itself. Uncle John is happy to offer a crash course on the great academic institution.

When it was first founded, Rutgers was located in New Brunswick, along the Raritan River in Middlesex County. Originally chartered on November 10, 1766, as Queen's College, Rutgers is the eighth-oldest institution of higher education in the United States. Since then the university has expanded to 29 divisions, 12 undergraduate colleges, 11 graduate schools, and 3 schools offering both undergraduate and graduate degrees. In all, the school offers more than 100 bachelor's, 100 master's, and 80 doctoral and professional degree programs.

What's in a Name?

Queen's College was named for Charlotte Sophia of Mecklenburg-Strelitz, queen consort (that is, wife) of King George III. The name was changed to Rutgers College in 1825 to honor Colonel Henry Rutgers, a hero of the Revolutionary War and supporter of "benevolent causes." He donated a bell and $5,000, which was enough to keep the school from closing its doors. *College* became *University* in 1924, and an act of the state legislature in 1954 put on the final touches, designating all its divisions as Rutgers, the State University of New Jersey.

One University, Many Colleges

Today Rutgers University has approximately 65,000 students on three campuses. The main grounds are in New Brunswick and Piscataway, which is home to Rutgers, Douglass, Cook, and Livingston Colleges. There are additional Rutgers campuses in Camden and Newark.

Rutgers College is the flagship institution, with an enrollment of more than 11,000 undergraduate students. Douglass College, with approximately 3,000 students, dates back to 1918 and is the largest women's college in the United States. Cook College is a land-grant college with 3,200 students and a focus on agriculture and environmental sciences. It became a separate branch in 1973, having evolved from the Rutgers Scientific School (1864). Livingston College was founded in 1969 as the first coed liberal arts college at Rutgers. It currently has 3,900 students and is committed to diversity, equality of opportunity, and educational innovation.

R.U. Trivia

- In the 1770s classes were held at a tavern called the Sign of the Red Lion. Oddly enough, the original focus of Queen's College was to produce ministers for the Dutch Reformed Church.

- William Franklin, New Jersey's last colonial governor and the illegitimate son of Benjamin Franklin (his mother is unknown), signed the Rutgers charter.

- Henry Rutgers's most famous quotation was, "Don't let your studies interfere with your education."

- The Rutgers motto: *Sol iustitiae et occidentem illustra* (Sun of righteousness, shine upon the West also). Rutgers's founders modified the motto of the University of Utrecht (in the Netherlands), "Sun of righteousness, shine upon us," to embrace the New World.

- In 1793 a resolution to merge Queen's College with the College of New Jersey (now Princeton University) lost by one vote.

- A Rutgers professor "discovered" Cheez-Whiz at the Center for Advanced Food Technology.

Alma Mater

The Rutgers alma mater, "On the Banks of the Old Raritan," dates from 1872. It opens as follows:

> *My father sent me to old Rutgers,*
> *And resolv'd that I should be a man;*
> *And so I settled down,*
> *In that noisy college town,*
> *On the banks of the old Raritan.*
>   (Chorus)
> *On the banks of the old Raritan, my boys,*
> *Where old Rutgers ever more shall stand,*
> *For has she not stood since the time of the flood,*
> *On the banks of the old Raritan.*

Rutgers College went coed in 1972 and is now 52 percent female. The "my boys" in the first line of the chorus was changed in 1990 to "my friends," yet the opening wish "that I should be a man" remains.

Famous Alumni

- Mario Batali (class of 1982): Iron Chef and restauranteur
- Kristin Davis (class of 1987): actress (*Sex and the City*)
- Calista Flockhart (class of 1988): actress (*Ally McBeal*)
- Louis Freeh (class of 1971): director of the FBI
- Milton Friedman (class of 1932): Nobel laureate
- James Gandolfini (class of 1983): actor (*The Sopranos*)
- Alfred Joyce Kilmer (class of 1908, did not graduate): poet
- Oswald "Ozzie" Nelson (class of 1927): actor (*The Adventures of Ozzie and Harriet*)
- Paul Robeson (class of 1919): athlete, actor, political activist
- Selman Waksman (class of 1915): Nobel laureate
- Mr. Magoo (class unknown): fictional cartoon character whose creators chose Rutgers because it was "the embodiment of the 'old school tie' in America."

DID YOU KNOW?
President George W. Bush's Scottish terriers, Barney and Miss Beazley, were both born in New Jersey.

This Land Is My Land

From California to Ellis Island . . . New Jersey, that is.

You may think that Ellis Island is in New York, right? Well, think again. The main immigration building on Ellis Island, now a museum, does have a New York address. But since 1998 the kitchen and laundry facilities of the main building and the rest of the island, including the docks where tourists arrive, are actually located in New Jersey. How did this place come to have such an identity crisis? It's just the last stage of a centuries-long border dispute between the two states.

Drawing a Line in the Sand

The Hudson River forms the border between New York and New Jersey as it flows through New York Harbor into the Atlantic Ocean. But just where in the river does one state turn into another? The first border battle started in 1801, when Alexander Hamilton built a pier in Jersey City pointing out into the Hudson River toward New York. New York City informed Hamilton that his pier, and anything else extending into the Hudson River, was part of the state of New York, not New Jersey.

The dispute kicked off 30 years of squabbles and court battles. Finally, in 1834, the two states signed a compact agreeing that the border between the states runs down the middle of the

Hudson, with the exception of a few now-famous islands in the river—namely, Liberty and Ellis Islands.

The 1834 agreement gave New York jurisdiction over Ellis and Liberty islands even though they clearly fall on New Jersey's side of the river. At the time, it didn't much matter. Ellis Island was three acres of rock with an army installment on it. Bedloe's Island (renamed Liberty Island in 1956) was a completely uninteresting lump until 1886, when the Statue of Liberty was placed there.

Ellis Island Expansion

The federal government set up its main immigrant-processing center on Ellis Island in 1892. Between then and 1954, when it closed, some 12 million immigrants came through this facility; 40 percent of all Americans can trace their heritage back through this rock in New York Harbor.

To accommodate that number of immigrants, the U.S. Army Corps of Engineers built up the island, which gradually expanded between 1892 and 1954 to its present size of 27.5 acres. The additional land gave room for a ferry slip, a hospital, and various administrative buildings. Since this land was not part of Ellis Island in 1834, it wasn't all that clear which state could officially lay claim to it later on down the line.

Tag, You're It!

Where the official state line was didn't seem to matter all that much until 1992. Terry Collins, a national park ranger, lost part of his leg while working on the landfill area of Ellis Island. He sued Promark Products, the makers of the equipment he was using, who turned around and sued the federal government for not properly training Collins. Here's where it gets tricky: the state of New

York allows such a countersuit; the state of New Jersey does not.

In order to avoid liability, the government said that the part of Ellis Island Collins was working on was actually in New Jersey, not New York. The 1834 pact said Ellis Island belonged to New York, but it also said that all the underwater land surrounding it was New Jersey's. Therefore the expanded island, since it was not part of the original exemption, *must* be in New Jersey. The Federal District Court of Manhattan didn't buy it. They ruled that all the dry land on Ellis Island was New York's, and all the underwater land was New Jersey's. With this logic, you could sit on a pier in New York and have bits of New Jersey wash up over your ankles.

Hey, Wait a Minute . . .

Perhaps incensed by the Collins ruling, New Jersey filed suit against New York in 1993 for custody of the 24 added acres of Ellis Island—a case that made it all the way to the U.S. Supreme Court in 1996. New Jersey's case rested almost entirely on the pact of 1834, while New York claimed that Ellis Island was, and always had been, a *cultural* part of New York. To support its claim, New York's lawyers argued that the immigrants going through Ellis Island were going to New York, not New Jersey. The way you could tell, they said, was that the immigrants on the boats coming to Ellis Island were facing New York, so the island was therefore part of New York. (Ah, yes, the famous but-they-were-looking-at-New-York argument.) Since no poll was taken of the immigrants at the time, the court dismissed both of these claims.

Solomon's Wisdom

Instead of rendering a decision, the Supreme Court assigned an arbitrator to evaluate the case and make a recommendation. The arbitrator, New Yorker Paul Verkuil, issued his decision on April 1, 1997. In light of the evidence, he decided that New York had no legal claim to the landfill areas of Ellis Island. In the interest of fairness, he recommended that New York be awarded approximately five acres since the original island is now landlocked. The compromise pleased nobody. Both states wanted all of the additional land. (One annoyed citizen wrote the *New York Times* suggesting that since New York and New Jersey were being so immature, the court should give the island to Connecticut instead!)

Welcome to the State of New Jersey

So back to the Supreme Court it went. On May 26, 1998, the Court voted 6–3 to divide the island, and to award New Jersey all of the landfill acres. (State loyalty played no part in this case. Antonin Scalia, the only New Jerseyan on the Court, voted to keep the island in New York.) Based on this decision, the official state line runs smack through the middle of the main immigration building.

Triumphant, New Jersey's governor, Christine Todd Whitman, sported a T-shirt saying, "Ellis Island, NJ" in bold letters. The U.S. Postal Service added a New Jersey zip code for the island. New Jersey raised its flag on Ellis Island on the Fourth of July that year, thumbing its nose at New York.

A Moot Point

So what's the upshot of all this legal wrangling? What does it mean for the island now that it's (mostly) in New Jersey? Absolutely nothing. Ellis Island is owned by the federal government and has been since 1800. It's a national park. Other than a few thousand dollars a year in sales tax, all New Jersey really got from the ordeal was bragging rights.

Famous Turnpike Stops

As most Jersey Turnpike drivers know, that efficient roadway's 12 rest areas are all named after famous New Jersey residents. To find out who four of them are, just solve the puzzle!

ACROSS

1 Hoof it
5 Common coffee-break time
10 Passing notice?
14 Peak figure: Abbr.
15 Wonderful smell
16 Sheet of stamps
17 Sicilian hot spot
18 Actress Sophia
19 Old gas brand
20 Rest stop named for a football coach
23 "Don't worry about me"
24 Killer serve
25 Global positioning meas.
28 "___ sakes!"
29 Bok ___
32 Psychic energy, to Freud
34 Rest stop named for a famed inventor
36 Seesaw sitter in verse
39 Atlanta Braves div.
40 Charts of hearts
41 Rest stop named for a Revolutionary War heroine
46 Vampire feature
47 Rat-___
48 Einstein birthplace
51 Take to the slopes
52 RV refuge
54 Stereotypical Beemer driver
56 Rest stop named for the 28th U.S. president
60 Brewski topper
62 Shadow
63 Isn't wrong?
64 Crew member
65 Dove, for one
66 Original thought
67 Grass houses
68 What's happening
69 Big name in computers

DOWN

1 Cotton-eating beetle
2 Nissan model
3 "Imagine" writer
4 Comic-strip duck
5 Fox-hunting cry
6 Ending with switch or smack
7 Hefty regular at Cheers
8 Critter on a slide
9 Shackle
10 Newspaper feature
11 Serpent of myth with a lethal glance

| 1 | 2 | 3 | 4 | | 5 | 6 | 7 | 8 | 9 | | 10 | 11 | 12 | 13 |

12 November winners
13 Auto racer ___ Fabi
21 Every partner
22 Tim who played Venus Flytrap
26 "My Life as ___"
27 Oodles
30 Former Atlanta arena
31 Big Three conference site in 1945
33 Casket
34 Rock's Jethro ___
35 Shakers, e.g.
36 Caligula and Napoleon: Abbr.
37 Take to the cleaners
38 1971 Joni Mitchell song

42 ___ Ono
43 Merchandise item
44 Oscar-winning actress Susan
45 Sewing case
48 Positive aspect
49 Big name in small trains
50 Kind of telepathy
53 Knight wear
55 Scot's pattern
57 Bookie's numbers
58 Reed instrument
59 Perky songbird
60 LBJ's veep
61 ___ de vie (brandy)

Turn to page 317 for the solution.

The Real Rocky
A New Jersey Legend

Sylvester Stallone's Rocky movies were based on a real-life person. But he wasn't from Philadelphia like in the movies. He was from New Jersey. And now he's going 12 rounds with Sly's lawyers.

Meet the Real Rocky

Everyone's heard of Rocky Balboa. But only true boxing fans know about Chuck Wepner, the real-life Rocky upon whom the movie was based. Born in Bayonne, New Jersey, in 1939, Wepner cut his teeth as a Jersey nightclub bouncer. He was a tough—just ask the upstarts unfortunate enough to require his services—and he soon gained a reputation for his fearlessness, determination, and high tolerance for pain.

As a young man Wepner belonged to the Marine Corps, where he first learned to box to earn him extra time off. When he finished his time in the military, Wepner fought in the amateur boxing circuit on the weekends and evenings. He could never quit his day job to box full-time and could train only at night. At a friend's suggestion, one year he threw his hat into the ring for a Golden Gloves match—and won. He went on to fight professionally in 1964, but making ends meet was hard. While other boxers could spend their days training, Wepner still had to earn a living at regular jobs: he worked as a bouncer, liquor salesman, and security guard during his career. His professional career was one of quiet distinction. He fought tough, up-and-coming contenders but always remained in the background.

The Bayonne Bleeder

But eventually Wepner became famous for his ability to take a beating. So famous, in fact, that he earned the nickname the Bayonne Bleeder. He wasn't about finesse; he was about being the last one standing. And after a respectable number of wins, he finally got a huge opportunity in 1975: Chuck Wepner would take on Muhammad Ali for the world heavyweight title. This was his big chance, and he leaped at it. But the rest of the world laughed—no way was this nobody going to last against the Champ! The consensus was that Wepner was a joke. Some experts predicted that the fight would last only three rounds, if that long at all.

Well, the crowd was right in one respect: Wepner did lose to Ali. But he was no joke. Wepner shocked the boxing world by going 15 rounds with Ali—even sending the Champ crashing to the canvas with a wicked right hook in the 9th. The referee stopped the fight out of concern for Wepner's health, with only 19 seconds to go. Despite taking a dangerous beating from Ali, Wepner simply wouldn't give up on his own.

He retired in 1978, after having fought not only the great Muhammad Ali, but also Sonny Liston, George Foreman, and Andre the Giant. Wepner wrote an autobiography entitled *Toe to Toe with Any Foe* and was eventually inducted into the New Jersey Boxing Hall of Fame (with a professional record of 35–14–2; 17 of his wins were by knockout).

Yo, Chuckie?

Every real boxing fan in the country caught that 1975 fight between Wepner and Ali, if only to see Wepner get creamed. And New York actor Michael Sylvester Enzio Stallone was no exception. A dropout of the University of Miami's drama program, Stallone made his living acting in off-Broadway plays and the occasional small film; but he also liked boxing. Stallone wound up at the Wepner-Ali fight and was inspired by the underdog's performance in the 15-round brawl to write a screenplay that would become the hit film *Rocky*, the story of a down-on-his-luck tough guy who makes it big in boxing. Stallone sold the screenplay for $150,000 and played the lead role in the movie. The movie was a smash: *Rocky* won the Oscar for Best Picture in 1976, and Stallone himself was nominated for his performance. Many say this film was the best work of his career. The film became a franchise and launched five hit sequels.

Still Fighting—in Court

Everyone knows Sylvester Stallone as Rocky. But how is it that Wepner never saw a cent of the reported millions of dollars the *Rocky* movies generated? That's just what Wepner is trying to find out in the lawsuit he's filed against Stallone. When Stallone sold the script, he called Wepner to tell him about it. Over the years, Wepner claims that Stallone promised compensation in a variety of forms, including a bit part in *Rocky II* that wound up on the cutting-room floor. But Wepner claims that after years of promises and the use of his name to promote the *Rocky* series, he has been cheated. He told the *Philadelphia Inquirer* that "after 28 years, even an ex-fighter starts to figure maybe this guy is not going to keep his word."

The real-life tough guy, now 65, wants compensation for all the times Stallone used Wepner's name during the promotion of the films that made Stallone's career. So in 2003 the inspiration for *Rocky* filed suit against the writer of *Rocky*. Wepner's lawyer told *CBS News* that "Stallone has been using Chuck's name—and continues to this day—in promoting the *Rocky* franchise without any permission or compensation." Today Wepner still lives in Bayonne and still holds down a steady job as a liquor salesperson. But he says he'd like to use the settlement money for his family now that he's entering his golden years. In September 2004 Stallone's lawyers tried to have the case thrown out of court, but they were unsuccessful. Keep your eye on the news for the next round.

DID YOU KNOW?

New Jersey is home to the National Marbles Championship. Since 1960 Wildwood has hosted the event where eight- to fourteen-year-olds compete in a game called Ringer.

Hometowns
A Tale of Two Cape Mays

Located at the southernmost tip of the state, Cape May's beaches and Victorian buildings have made it a great place to get away from it all for centuries now.

The Town: Cape May
Location: Cape May County
Founding: That's a little tricky. Cape May County was officially chartered in 1692, but settlers had been living there since the 1630s. The resort of Cape May, a separate city within the county, became a popular resort in the early 19th century and was officially incorporated in 1869.
Current Population: 4,034
Size: 2.3 square miles
What's in a Name? Cape May County was named after the Dutch captain who first explored the territory in the 1620s, Cornelius Jacobsen Mey. So it's not clear if the city is technically named after the county, the explorer, or both.

Claims to Fame
- Cape May remains the oldest seashore resort in the United States.

- Presidents Pierce, Buchanan, Grant, and Benjamin Harrison vacationed in Cape May.

- A beachcomber's delight, Cape May diamonds are milky quartz pebbles that wash up on the beaches. When polished, they can be cut and faceted like gemstones. While the majority of the stones are pebble-sized, a Cape May diamond that weighed more than three pounds was discovered in the 19th century.

- Every Labor Day weekend, the International Clamshell Pitching Club of Cape May holds its annual tournament, where competitors try to toss shells into 5½-inch-wide holes that are 25½ feet apart on hard-packed sand.

- For more than two decades the New Jersey Audubon Society has hosted the World Series of Birdwatching in Cape May. This annual ornithological competition is always held on the second Saturday in May. Thousands of avid birders fly in from around the world to compete and determine which team can find and identify, by sound or sight, the most varieties of wildfowl in a 24-hour period. The current record is 201 sightings in the day-long search.

Looking Back
at Nassau Hall

Called the most famous college building in the United States, Princeton University's Nassau Hall also played an important role in colonial history.

Visit Princeton University and you can't miss stately old Nassau Hall. Situated in the middle of the campus, this building has been the heart and soul of the university since it was built in 1756. For many students it symbolizes the university itself. Today the building houses mostly administrative offices, but its history is much more colorful—it played an important role in our country's early years.

Situated and Celebrated

Before Nassau Hall, the College of New Jersey (as Princeton University was then known—it officially changed its name in 1896, but that's another story) had convened in the Elizabethtown home of Reverend Jonathan Dickinson, its first president. Then it moved to the First Presbyterian Church in Newark. The college's trustees, however, were uncomfortable with these arrangements—they were concerned that Elizabethtown and Newark were too exciting, and that the students would be distracted from their studies by the temptations of big-city life. They wanted the college situated in a sleepy, bucolic hamlet, far away from temptation. Princeton fit the bill just fine.

What's in a Name?

So how did Nassau Hall get its name? The building very nearly came to sport the inharmonious moniker Belcher Hall, after New Jersey's provincial governor, Jonathan Belcher, a keen supporter of the fledgling college. Heaven only knows what students would have made of this name. But fortunately Belcher declined the honor and suggested that the building be named instead in memory of "the Glorious King William the Third who was a Branch of the Illustrious House of Nassau." (King William was also known as William of Orange—hence Princeton's school colors, orange and black.)

On December 3, 1755, college president Aaron Burr Sr. wrote, "We have begun a building at Princeton which contains a [h]all, library, and rooms to accommodate about one hundred students." When completed in 1756, Nassau Hall was the largest stone structure in the colonies.

For the first 50 years of its existence, the college was housed entirely in Nassau Hall. On its three main floors were a library, a two-story prayer hall, and 42 rooms for classes, offices, and student housing. The dining hall, kitchen, and steward's quarters were housed in the basement—which later also included additional rooms for students. According to Thomas Jefferson Wertenbaker, a chairman of Princeton's Department of History, "So closely did the building become identified with the college, that for many years it was customary to speak of graduating, not from the College of New Jersey, but from Nassau Hall."

Bowling for Scholars (and Tutors)

There is little doubt that Princeton's earliest graduates were serious and sober young men—men destined to serve the professions, the church, and the state. Roused each morning to mandatory prayer by a bell at 5:00 a.m., the students were expected to behave in exemplary fashion and occupy their time with study, discussion, and other scholarly pursuits. They were subject to strict rules of conduct and a rigid pecking order. Even the use of nicknames was forbidden.

But like college students throughout history, Princeton's undergraduates were partial to blowing off steam with pranks and practical jokes. In his book, *Princeton,* Varnum Lansing Collins (secretary of the university in the early 20th century) writes of the rambunctious relationship between students and tutors that manifested itself in all-out prank wars. To thwart the efforts of tutors checking up on them, students would build barricades of wood on stairways and entrances to keep them out. Tossing the occasional firecracker out a window startled college authorities—and amused undergraduates to no end. Students would often coax reluctant animals (calves, donkeys, and even horses) to climb to the upper floors of the hall, where authorities had to struggle to get them back down again.

Probably the most dangerous source of fun was the rolling of heated cannonballs down Nassau Hall's long central corridor. Presumably, any unwary tutor who didn't run away and attempted to stop the noisy projectile would find himself surprised, if not burned, by the hot metal.

But Seriously

All was not fun and games in colonial Princeton, especially as the War for Independence brewed around the college. In January

1774, to show their allegiance to the patriots, students stole an entire year's supply of tea and, as the college's bell tolled, used it to fuel a large bonfire in front of Nassau Hall.

John Witherspoon, president of the college at the time of the Revolutionary War, was also a signer of the Declaration of Independence. In November 1776, as the fighting approached Princeton, President Witherspoon sent all the students home. It wasn't a moment too soon, because the British took control of Nassau Hall on December 2. For a month control of the building shuffled back and forth between the British and the Continentals. It was variously used as barracks, a hospital, and a prison for the armies of either side. The British even used the basement for stables.

During the Battle of Princeton, the Continental army retook Nassau Hall early in the morning of January 3, 1777. American cannons fired two balls at the building. One ball bounced off the thick exterior stone wall, leaving it pockmarked to this day. Legend has it that the other ball crashed through a window into the prayer room and struck King George II's portrait (some say right in the face). With glee the Continentals later installed a portrait of George Washington in that very spot, where it remains prominently displayed today.

Both armies proved to have been poor houseguests, and when they finally left, Nassau Hall was a mess. It took about a year for even rudimentary repairs to be completed. The fixes were apparently good enough to allow the building to serve as the nation's capital when the Continental Congress relocated there after fleeing Philadelphia in 1783. From July to November, the Continental Congress met in Nassau Hall's library and used the prayer hall for state occasions.

It was in Nassau Hall that George Washington, sitting with the Congress, received the first news of the definitive treaty of peace with Great Britain, which effectively ended the Revolutionary War and recognized the colonies' independence. Among the congressmen who received the good news with Washington were six Nassau Hall alumni.

Nassau Hall Today

When visiting Princeton University today, Nassau Hall is one of the top attractions and a main part of the Orange Key tours of campus. On the outside you can still see the scar on the building's facade made by the British cannonball. It is located on the south wall of the west wing and the ivy is carefully clipped so that everyone can still see it.

DID YOU KNOW?

New Jersey has more nail salons per capita than any other U.S. state.

100,000,000 Bon Jovi Fans Can't Be Wrong

It's hard to remember a time when Bon Jovi wasn't a household name, but these Jersey boys from Sayreville weren't always the hair metal gods they are now. It's the Bon Jovi basics.

Starting Out

The story of Bon Jovi the band naturally begins with Bon Jovi the man: Lead singer Jon Bon Jovi—or, as he's known on his birth certificate, John Francis Bongiovi—was born March 2, 1962, in Perth Amboy, and raised in Sayreville. From an early age Jon was more interested in music than just about anything else (by the time he graduated from Sayreville War Memorial High School in 1980, he'd accumulated more than 100 absences). In the eighth grade he was in his first band, called Raze, and in high school had another band called Atlantic City Expressway with future Bon Jovi member David Rashbaum (better known as David Bryan).

Jon's first job in the biz wasn't exactly glamorous. He swept floors at New York's Power Station music studio, which was co-owned by his cousin Tony Bongiovi. As he swabbed up after famous musical acts, he also started cutting demo tapes with the musicians using the studio, including members of the E Street Band and Aldo Nova. Some of these demos would surface in a

1997 quickie CD: *1980–1983—Power Station Years,* credited to
John Bongiovi.

It was one of these demos that would become the breakthrough for him. A catchy rocker with a hooky synth line,
"Runaway" (emphatically *not* the Del Shannon song) found its
way to a New Jersey radio station in 1983, where it was an
instant smash. Bon Jovi quickly assembled a full band with Richie
Sambora, Tico Torres, David Bryan, and Alec John Such. They
signed to Mercury Records, which released the band's self-titled
debut album in 1984. "Runaway" performed reasonably well and
cracked the Top 40.

Hair Metal Poster Boys

The band's follow-up, *7800 Fahrenheit* (allegedly named for the
temperature at which rock melts), went gold. Most young rockers
would be pleased to achieve this level of fame, but Bon Jovi felt
that they could be bigger, *much* bigger. So, they organized a plan
of attack. First they got together with songwriter Desmond Child
and produced more than two dozen poppy, yet still rocking,
tunes. Then they auditioned the songs live for New Jersey and
New York fans, to find out which ones had "curb appeal"—that
is, which ones the kids thought were good. Those songs were the
ones that made the next album.

This methodical approach wasn't exactly rock and roll, but the
resulting album in 1986, *Slippery When Wet,* did exactly what Bon
Jovi intended. It rocketed the band into superstardom and sold 8
million copies in the United States alone. Two #1 hits, "You Give
Love a Bad Name" and "Livin' on a Prayer," became Bon Jovi's
anthems (sort of their own "Born to Run," if you will). Despite the
loud, fun songs, there's another key factor to Bon Jovi's success: Jon

Bon Jovi's good looks and long hair both helped ensure his mug and his music were in high rotation on MTV. Hair metal—an amalgam of blistering rock and sugary pop—had found poster boys.

Having established a winning formula, the band stuck with it for the next album, 1988's *New Jersey*. Like its predecessor, *New Jersey* was a smash with two #1 hits, but the critics were less than impressed. One of the most charitable reviews came from *Rolling Stone* magazine, which noted: "Jon Bon Jovi is brilliant . . . at what he does. *New Jersey* has all the virtues and drawbacks of a popular record, hitting all the marks yet remaining thoroughly unidiosyncratic." Other critics, less kind, compared it to the toxic dumps the album's namesake was infamous for. Nevertheless *New Jersey* sold 5 million copies, and Bon Jovi wrapped up its tours and called a hiatus in 1989. At that time it was the biggest band in the world.

A Slight Decline

While his band took a break, Jon Bon Jovi branched out into new things. When movie star Emilo Estevez wanted to use the Bon Jovi hit "Dead or Alive" for his 1990 movie *Young Guns II,* Jon offered him a new song instead: the Western-themed "Blaze of Glory." The song provided him with his first solo hit, as well as Golden Globe and Oscar nominations for the song (it won the Golden Globe; it missed out on the Oscar).

The biggest challenge to Bon Jovi occurred in 1991, when Nirvana's *Nevermind* album blasted out of Seattle and the new grunge style all but killed hair metal. Grunge couldn't quite stop Bon Jovi, but it put a dent in the group's superstar status. The band's 1990s albums, *Keep the Faith* and *These Days,* performed well but not to the megaplatinum level to which the band had become accustomed. Bassist Alec John Such left the band in 1994 (he would go on to run a motorbike shop and manage other bands), and the group took another hiatus in 1996. Jon Bon Jovi kept himself occupied by making movies, beginning with 1996's *Moonlight and Valentino* (in which he played a hunky handyman). He also released a solo album in 1997, which generated little attention.

You Can't Keep Bon Jovi Down

But you can't keep a good band down, even if in this case "down" means "a base level of popularity and celebrity most musicians would kill for." By the year 2000 grunge had leveled off, pop was back in, and the band had fine-tuned their music to encompass the fact that their teenage fans from the 1980s now had families but still wanted to rock out in their minivans. The result was the album *Crush*. It featured the massive hit anthem "It's My Life" that referenced both fellow New Jersey native Frank Sinatra and the love-struck teens (Tommy and Gina) from "Livin' on a Prayer." It gave the band and its fans musical continuity from one music era to the next.

"Livin' on a Prayer" would take on a special emotional resonance after the 9/11 attacks, when Bon Jovi played a slowed-down elegiac version of the song, with a gospel choir, at an October 2001 benefit for New Jersey families affected by 9/11. The attacks would also serve as a theme for the band's 2002 album *Bounce*, whose title track—yet another anthem—told the story of a guy who "takes the hit, but not the fall," a metaphor for the country in an uncertain time. The Jersey guys who started out just wanting to rock were still rocking—now just in a slightly more mature fashion.

"Why Aren't You Dead?"

With their comeback cemented, Bon Jovi has felt comfortable tweaking their musical legacy and their critics: 2003's *This Left Feels Right* album took some of the band's biggest hits and reimagined them in various ways: "Livin' on a Prayer" as a torch song, for example, and "Dead or Alive" as a loop-filled remix. The band's 2004 box set of previously unreleased tracks stated their greatness right there in the title: *100,000,000 Bon Jovi Fans Can't Be Wrong*. Critics, who have never warmed to the band, may ask Bon Jovi the question from the opening track of the box set: "Why Aren't You Dead?" The answer is in the rootsy, rocky music of the song itself: Bon Jovi is too catchy and fun and New Jersey tough to die.

DID YOU KNOW?

Jon Bon Jovi's first credited vocal performance was for *Christmas in the Stars: A Star Wars Christmas Album*. He sings lead vocals on the supersweet "R2-D2, We Wish You a Merry Christmas," C-3PO's gift of song to his silver sidekick, with timeless lyrics like "If the snow becomes too deep/Just give a little beep/We'll go in by the fire/And warm your little wires."

Lighthouses Along the Shore

New Jersey's waterways have been used for trade for over 300 years, and for just as long, ships have had to navigate the tricky coastline. These are just six of the many lighthouses that dot the coastline and make Jersey a safer harbor.

Absecon

Location: Atlantic City
Built: 1857
Height: 171 feet
This 16-story lighthouse is the tallest in New Jersey. Its light is visible 19 miles out to sea. The first keeper, Daniel Scull, was paid an annual salary of $600 per year. Although not officially used today, Absecon is the only lighthouse that still has its original first-order Fresnel lens.

Barnegat

Location: Barnegat Light
Built: 1858
Height: 165 feet
Located on the northernmost tip of Long Beach Island, this famous red-and-white landmark used to flash once every ten sec-

onds in every compass direction. Barnegat stopped serving officially in 1927. Luckily it reopened to the public in 1991 after extensive renovations.

Cape May

Location: Cape May City
Built: 1823
Height: 157 feet

Some say that the English laid a foundation for this lighthouse in the 1700s, but hard evidence has yet to be found. The Cape May lighthouse is the second oldest in the state and has been rebuilt twice—in 1847 because of erosion and in 1859 because of poor construction. This red-roofed lighthouse still serves as a navigational aid. Its 1,000-watt bulb and curved mirrors project a beam of light 24 miles out to sea.

Hereford Inlet

Location: North Wildwood
Built: 1874
Height: 49.5 feet

Now listed on the National Register of Historic Places, this lighthouse had to be moved inland 150 feet in 1913 after a severe storm damaged its foundation. In 1964, the lights were put out when a skeleton tower took over its job. Luckily, in 1986, they put the lights back on, and now the Coast Guard maintains the site. Visitors can take in the tower and the lovely gardens that surround it.

Sandy Hook

Location: Middletown Township
Built: 1764
Height: 103 feet

The waters leading into New York Harbor can be treacherous, and the Sandy Hook Lighthouse was built to safely guide trading vessels in to the harbor. During the American Revolution, Loyalist forces occupied the lighthouse while patriots tried but failed to put the light out. It is the oldest lighthouse in New Jersey and the oldest still in use in the United States.

Twin Lights

Location: Highlands
Built: 1828
Height: 40 feet

Originally built in 1828 and rebuilt in 1862, this unique complex has two towers, one octagonal and the other square. Both towers can shine their lights up to 22 nautical miles. In 1841 this lighthouse was the first in the United States to use Fresnel lenses. It also served as the site of the first test of the wireless telegraph by inventor Guglielmo Marconi.

DID YOU KNOW

New Jersey has more horses per square mile than any other state.

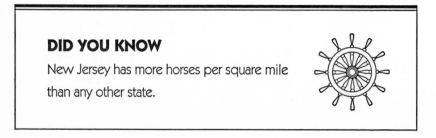

Trenton Makes,
the World Takes

Ever wonder where the slogan on Trenton's bridge comes from? We did too.
Here's the story behind the slogan.

If you've driven through New Jersey, you probably know the slogan of Trenton, its capital city: Trenton Makes, the World Takes.
How do you know the slogan? Well, it's hard to miss the giant
neon letters emblazoned on the side of the Trenton-Morrisville
Bridge that spell it out. The Trenton Makes bridge, as it is known
to locals, runs parallel to the commuter train tracks, so it is seen
by thousands of passengers every day. Where did the slogan come
from? the curious commuter might ask. Today Trenton has been
superseded by Taiwan as a manufacturing dynamo, but it turns
out that it was quite a powerhouse in the past.

Golden Age

Strategically located between New York City and Philadelphia on
the Delaware River, Trenton was once a booming center of commerce and industry. Connected to the coalfields of Pennsylvania
and the iron mines of New Jersey, Trenton became famous for its
ironworks. John Roebling, a German immigrant, set up a wire-
rope factory in Trenton in 1849. The Roebling company supplied

wire for aqueducts and suspension bridges all over the country—and some quite nearby.

In fact, John Roebling designed the Brooklyn Bridge, in a fit of pique after waiting too long for a ferry. He convinced New York to finance the bridge and in addition suggested the construction of the Williamsburg and Queensboro bridges, which were later also built over the East River. Roebling's foot was crushed while inspecting a tower site for the bridge; he later died of tetanus from the injury. His son Washington took over construction of the Brooklyn Bridge, which is held up with—what else—Roebling wire, made in Trenton. Literally built with the sweat and blood of Trentonians, the Brooklyn Bridge is a testament to the valuable contributions of New Jersey's capital.

By the middle of the 19th century, Trenton was the nation's center of iron manufacture. Other industries also grew up in Trenton: It was the center of American ceramics manufacturing, creating $50 million worth of goods in 1910.

Trenton Makes

It was with no sense of irony that the city fathers chose the slogan, "Trenton Makes, the World Takes." The winning slogan was picked out of 1,477 submissions in a contest held by the Trenton Chamber of Commerce in 1910. Future state senator S. Roy Heath coined the slogan. His daughter, Dartha, described her dad as "one shrewd Quaker. He knew he could get ahead if he worked hard. That's why people came to this city, for the opportunity." In 1917, the sign was updated with 2,400 electric bulbs—the largest slogan sign in the world, according to the *Trenton Daily State Gazette*. The sign was replaced again in 1935, the new neon slogan 7 feet high and 330 feet long.

Sadly the sign became something of a joke. In the move to nationalize industries, Trenton suffered as one after another of its businesses left. John A. Roebling's Sons Company moved out in 1952 and it was official. Trenton didn't make much of anything anymore.

The World Takes

The sign is still there, though it went dark in 1973 due to the oil crisis. The city couldn't afford the electric bills. Local businesses paid to have it replaced in 1980, and it blazes on, today the quintessential symbol of Trenton.

In May 2004 a local newspaper suggested that the bridge be updated with a new, different slogan. Trentonians hated the idea. Citizens wrote hundreds of angry letters. Mayor Douglas Palmer vowed to fight any efforts to change the beloved sign. After seeing how much the Trenton Makes sign was loved, the Delaware River Joint Toll Bridge Commission, the agency that owns the bridge, decided not to change the slogan at all. But they did decide to give it a freshening up. When its new look is complete, the sign will be able to flash and change colors, still proclaiming "Trenton Makes, the World Takes" to the world.

DID YOU KNOW?

Clarence Birdseye, the father of frozen food, first studied cooking when he was a student at Montclair High School.

Living Large
in New Jersey

New Jersey itself may only be 7,417 square miles (only four states in the United States are smaller), but it's still got some big-league claims to fame.

World's Largest Wine Bottle, Tenafly

A chocolate and wine shop in Bergen County called Wine Ventures owns the Guinness Book–verified, world's largest bottle of wine. The business paid $47,500 for it at London's Sotheby's auction house in November 2004. The 340-pound bottle was manufactured in the Czech Republic by Beringer Vineyards for Morton's, the Steakhouse to commemorate the restaurant's 25th anniversary. The bottle holds the equivalent of 1,200 glasses of Beringer Vineyards 2001 Private Reserve Napa Valley Cabernet Sauvignon.

World's Largest Elephant Building, Margate

No, it's not the secret headquarters of the Republican Party. It's Lucy, the world's tallest elephant-shaped building. Located a couple of miles south of Atlantic City, the six-story tall pachyderm was initially built in 1881 as a real estate office. In her lifetime Lucy has also been a functional home and neighborhood pub. Her ears are 17 feet long, her body 38 feet long, and her head 16 feet high.

Made of sheet tin, the oceanfront elephant is now the only elephant registered as a National Historic Landmark. Today visitors can get a guided tour of its interior.

World's Largest Clock, Jersey City

Fifty feet in diameter, the Colgate Clock was built in 1924, the largest single-faced clock on the face of the Earth at the time. Facing Manhattan on the New Jersey Waterfront, the clock was a tribute to the Colgate-Palmolive Company, which had been a Jersey City native since the turn of the century. Even though Colgate left Jersey City in 1985, the clock still graces the urban landscape. It's been said that you can see its 50-foot-wide face as far away as the Bronx. Its minute hand is taller than a *Tyrannosaurus rex*. And its hour hand is over 20 feet long.

World's Largest Concrete Monument, Jersey City

Despite its name, the Lincoln Park Fountain is not in the town of Lincoln Park. It is in a park—in Jersey City—called Lincoln Park. It was built in 1911 by sculptor Pierre J. Cheron, who gave the fountain a 10-year guarantee (which it well outperformed). The spot where the fountain sits used to be a baseball diamond for the city's first baseball league. The 53-foot fountain weighs a total of 365 tons: That's equal to the weight of 75 rhinoceroses.

World's Largest Collection of Spoons, Paterson

Bertha Koempel loved spoons. In fact she lived when the spoon-collecting craze was at its craziest (1890s–1900s). And collect she did. Visitors to Paterson's historic Lambert Castle can see the fruits of her labors at the Bertha Schaeffer Koempel Spoon Collection. From czarist Russia to your typical spoon-peddling

American tourist traps, the collection holds more than 5,000 collector spoons dating from the 1890s to the 1950s. And after getting the scoop on spoons, you can check out Lambert Castle's other cool collections such as the Hester Cappio/R. J. Walter Postcard Collection.

World's Largest Model Railroad, Flemington

Like many model-train enthusiasts, Bruce Williams Zaccagnino started a model railway in his basement. But unlike most others, Zaccagnino's hobby grew into what is now the world's largest model railroad. He named his attraction the Northlandz and opened it to the public. Today people can wander through three floor's worth of his exhibit that features more than 100 model trains, 8 miles of track, 10,000 freight cars, hundreds of bridges, and sculpted mountains over 30 feet tall! Today it's a popular attraction that also features the world's largest dollhouse and a 5,000-pipe theater organ.

World's Largest Theme Park, Jackson

Six Flags Great Adventure, Six Flags Wild Safari, and Six Flags Hurricane Harbor take up over 2,200 acres in Central Jersey. The entire park has 14 roller coasters, including the new Kingda Ka, the world's tallest, fastest roller coaster—456 feet tall and 126 miles per hour out of the chute! It's got the world's largest drive-through safari (outside of an actual safari in Africa). Whether you want to learn about tigers, cool off on some water rides, or ride the merry-go-round, there's something for everyone in Jackson.

World's Largest Collection of Wine Glasses, Egg Harbor

In the mid-1800s the phylloxera aphid was making vintners' lives miserable in western Europe. Frenchman Louis Nicholas Renault fled to the United States. He eventually settled in New Jersey in 1864 and brought his family's heritage of fine champagne making with him. The winery he started is still active today (in fact, it's one of the oldest continually working wineries in the United States). In addition to New Jersey's finest bubbly, it also houses the Antique Glass Museum. The museum sports glasses older than the Republic of France itself, dating back to the Middle Ages. Go at the right time, and you can catch a champagne brunch.

World's Largest Collection of Fluorescent Minerals, Franklin

In 1810 Dr. Archibald Bruce, founder of the *American Mineralogical Journal,* discovered large deposits of zincite in Franklin—compelling lots of geological investigation in the Sussex County region. Franklin and the surrounding area soon became a hot spot of geological research because of the variety of minerals; so many fluorescent minerals were eventually found there that the government officially deemed it the Fluorescent Mineral Capital of the World in the 1960s. Mineral collectors can find dozens of fascinating mineral types in the area including garnet, pyrite, and rhodonite. And its crown jewel is the Franklin Mineral Museum, which houses thousands of mineral specimens and a life-size mining exhibit. In addition to the 42-foot by 8-foot, glow-in-the-dark rock exhibit in the Fluorescent Room, the Franklin offers lectures, fossil rooms, and a team of scientists who can identify any mineral on earth.

World's Largest Organ, Atlantic City

Boardwalk Hall, the old Atlantic City Convention Hall, houses the Midmer-Losh pipe organ. This pipe organ has more than 33,000 pipes inside and more than 400 ranks (a complete set of pipes on an organ is called a rank). The biggest pipe of all is 64 feet tall. The organ's blowers have more horsepower than a Ferrari, and a complete tour of the organ takes more than four hours.

World's Largest Cat, Jersey City

It's not the world's largest living cat, but it may be the world's largest statue of a cat—made of fiberglass, 19 feet long, and weighing 500 pounds. Created in the 1950s for the Macy's Thanksgiving Day Parade, this big cat has moved around a bit since then. It lived on the roof of a truck stop in the 1960s and moved to its present location on top of a Jersey City garage (it's on private property) in the 1970s. From the street, you can still see the jolly giant tabby as it peers out from behind a locust tree behind a 10-foot-high fence near the Holland Tunnel viaduct.

World's Biggest Pickle Bar, Edison

Harold's New York Deli and Restaurant claims to have the world's biggest pickle bar. It's eight feet long with a nice selection of kosher dill, sour, half-sour, and tomato pickles. But the pickle bar ain't the only thing that's big. The portions at Harold's are huge, too. Pancakes are "monster-size." A foot-high, triple-decker sandwich can easily serve four to six hungry people. A hero sandwich serves at least two. As Harold himself says: "Being that our sandwiches and dinners are of humongous portions, we encourage you to share at no extra charge." Thanks!

The Garden State Goes Hollywood
Lights, Camera . . . Jersey!

Jersey and Hollywood: made for each other? You'd be surprised—a number of classic (and some, well, not-so-classic) films have New Jersey as their stomping grounds. Here's a small sampling from the last half century.

On the Waterfront (1954)

"I coulda been a contender!" Well, Marlon Brando was a contender, not a palooka, with his gripping performance as Terry Malloy, a former prizefighter turned hood who goes up against a crooked mobster (is there any other kind?) on the docks of Hoboken. The film was in fact shot on location in Hoboken, with actual local longshoremen as extras. Indisputably the most honored New Jersey film, *On the Waterfront* won eight Oscars, including awards for Brando as Best Actor, Best Director for Elia Kazan, and Best Picture.

Atlantic City (1980)

Burt Lancaster plays a washed-up numbers runner who is under the impression he used to be more important than he really was; Susan Sarandon is a young woman who dreams of dealing blackjack in the casinos of Monaco. The two of them together make for a bittersweet film about "things that should have been but weren't" and "things that could be but probably won't." Lancaster and Sarandon both notched Oscar nominations for the film. More memorable: what Sarandon does with lemon wedges in the film is likely to make men wish they could be a tart yellow fruit—even if only for a few minutes.

Return of the Secaucus 7 (1980)

The debut film of writer/director John Sayles concerns the trials and tribulations of baby boomers coming to grips with the fact that they're getting older and becoming the adults they swore they'd never trust. Sound oddly like *The Big Chill?* Yeah, well, this film was done first and done cheaper. It only cost $60,000 to make—cheap even by 1980 standards (Sayles paid for it by writing scripts for cheesy horror flicks like *Piranha*). Sayles would return to New Jersey as a setting for later films such as *Baby It's You* and *City of Hope,* and he would also direct videos for Jersey's own Bruce Springsteen.

Cop Land (1997)

Hey, remember when Sylvester Stallone was known as an actor? No, really, he was! In *Cop Land,* Stallone put aside his outer action hero and reconnected with his inner actor. He put on over 40 pounds (mostly by eating pancakes) to play the beaten-down Sheriff Freddy Heflin, the head cop in a little northern New Jersey town that's home to a large and corrupt group of New York City cops. They belittle Sly's character for being small-town, but when a rookie cop shows up dead, Sly's character is inexorably drawn in to action. Stallone's performance received some solid critical reviews and held its own against a very talented cast, including Robert De Niro, Harvey Keitel, and (New Jerseyan) Ray Liotta.

Harold & Kumar Go to White Castle (2004)

Two high-achievers, uptight investment banker Harold and laid-back medical school candidate Kumar, are on a quest. Thanks to some marijuana and the resulting munchies, their mission is to find a 24-hour White Castle to buy some sliders (also known as burgers). This journey into the heart of darkest New Jersey confronts our heroes with Princeton students, creepy wife-swappers, extreme-sports freaks, and Neil Patrick Harris (of *Doogie Howser, MD*) as himself. As stoner films go, this is pretty darn funny—even if you're not totally baked.

Garden State (2004)

Zach Braff is a TV actor from New Jersey who, in this film he wrote, directed, and stars in, plays—you guessed it—a TV actor from New Jersey. The actor goes back home for his mother's funeral, deals with family resentments, meets up with old friends from high school, and meets a really great girl (played by Natalie Portman). This unassuming little film took a lot of folks by surprise with its wit and depth, which of course makes it a perfect New Jersey film: one that gets underestimated and then just sneaks up on you.

It's Official

A quick guide to New Jersey's state symbols and the dates they became official.

ANIMAL	Horse	1977
BIRD	Eastern Goldfinch	1935
COLORS	Jersey Blue and Buff	1965
FISH	Brook Trout	1991
FLOWER	Violet	1971
FOLK DANCE	Square Dance	1983
INSECT	Honeybee	1974
MEMORIAL TREE	Dogwood	1951
MOTTO	Liberty and Prosperity	First used on the state seal in 1777
NICKNAME	Garden State	First imprinted on a license plate in 1954
SHELL	Knobbed Whelk	1995
SOIL	Downer Soil	2004
TREE	Red Oak	1950

A Sticky Situation

Salt water taffy is a favorite boardwalk treat. We were curious about just who came up with this confection. It turns out that it's not really clear who—if anyone—has the exclusive right to call himself the inventor of this Atlantic City Boardwalk favorite.

First things first: Belying its name, salt water taffy contains no salt water. Not a drop! Nor do recipes for the soft, smooth, glossy, airy, chewy, pastel-tinted candy call for any more salt than do recipes for other candies. And that's just the tip of an iceberg of confusion surrounding this candy's sticky story.

Sweet Home, New Jersey

It seems that nobody can agree on who, if anybody, can truthfully claim his salt water taffy to be the "original." Just *when* this candy was first created is also still debated. Less at issue, however, is *where*. Though some insist that Midwestern county fairs first touted the confection, New Jersey's Atlantic City and its famous Boardwalk are generally thought to be its home.

From the Mouths of Babes

Though the story of this taffy's origin varies a bit from source to source, the most popular tale claims that the term salt water taffy came about as the silver lining from some dark clouds.

David Bradley, an Atlantic City candy merchant, kept his inventory on a cart on the Boardwalk, which was only a few steps above the sand at that time. One night in 1880 or 1883 (sources disagree on the year), a storm blew in and the waves soaked the cart with—you guessed it—salt water. When a young customer asked for some taffy the next day, Bradley sarcastically told the girl that she must mean *salt water* taffy instead. Undeterred, she bought the candy. Later the girl was coincidently overheard by (according to some tales) both Bradley's mother and his sister: she was telling beach buddies that hers was *special* taffy—*salt water taffy*.

The Bradley women knew a good gimmick when they heard one; they encouraged David to keep the moniker as a sales tactic. The candy that weathered the storm produced a name that has now weathered more than a century. A Bradley brand taffy, however, seems not to have.

Taffy Wars

Though by most accounts savvy entrepreneur Joseph Fralinger doesn't claim to have been the first to sell the sticky sweets, he is generally acknowledged as the Salt Water Taffy King. Joseph started selling the taffy on Atlantic City's Boardwalk in 1885, and his family business is still doing so today.

Once Enoch James moved to Atlantic City from the Midwest, Joseph Fralinger had a mighty battle on his hands. The so-called Taffy Wars had officially begun between the two companies and would last well over a 100 years. A worthy opponent, James was already an experienced candy man (the company's logo claims "Established 1880"). Some say he was even already making taffy when he relocated his family to the East Coast.

Making a Federal Case out of It

By the early 1920s, Fralinger and James had lots of competition: More than 400 others were also making and selling the seaside confection. Legend has it that the question of any one company's being the only one to use the name "original salt water taffy" even went to the Supreme Court. The Court declared that taffy was "born of the ocean and summer resorts and other ingredients that are the common property of all men everywhere." Its answer was—in Atlantic City lingo—"no dice." According to the Court, too many people had been using the term for too long for just one company to claim the "original" rights to the name.

Though some taffy purveyors skirt the issue entirely and opt for the word "traditional," both the Fralinger and James companies still use the "O" word on some of their boxes. In January 1930 and again in September 1993 "Fralinger's Original Salt Water Taffy" received a trademark. Both times, though, the disclaimer section of the registration made clear that no claim was made to the *exclusive* use of those words, apart from their "stylized form" within the company logo.

The Competition Continues

Can a truce in the taffy wars be far off? Not on your life. A current taffy catalog features selections from both Fralinger's and James's companies. Together. On the same pages. Customers can easily do a taffy-by-taffy comparison. The Fralinger company touts 16 flavors, including root beer and teaberry. James's advertises 17 flavors to choose from, including licorice and wintergreen; 15 flavors are available sealed in chocolate. (Choices sure have expanded in the past 100 years, from when molasses, vanilla, and chocolate were all one could enjoy.) Neck and neck, these competitors continue.

Westfield's Murder Mystery

One of New Jersey's most notorious murder mysteries occurred in 1971. The quiet town of Westfield was shaken by what happened to the List family. The patriarch, John List, had disappeared and his family lay dead in their home. Just what had happened?

When the Westfield Police Department received a call to check out the List family's Victorian mansion on Hillside Avenue, they figured it would be a pretty routine call. The Lists were supposedly away visiting a sick relative in North Carolina, but neighbors and friends had grown concerned. For a month there'd been no communication from anyone in the family. Even though all the lights were on, there were no obvious signs of people in the house. So police went to check out the situation, not expecting anything unusual. Westfield in 1971 was a quiet, upscale suburb that hadn't seen a murder in eight years.

But when the police entered the residence through an unlocked window, they were in for a bizarre discovery. Inside the vast, cold mansion, loud organ music played over an intercom system. Officers went into the mansion's vast ballroom, where they discovered four bodies. The victims were Helen List and her three teenaged children, Patty, John Jr., and Fredrick. Upstairs, Helen's mother-in-law, Alma List, was found dead in her attic apartment. But where was John List, Helen's husband and the three children's father? The man of the house was nowhere to be found.

The Mystery

Authorities soon discovered exactly what had happened; they found John List's confession left behind in a note for his minister. On November 9, in between raking leaves and going to the bank, John had used an automatic pistol to shoot and kill his wife, his mother, and his children. The victims had never gone to North Carolina; instead their bodies had lain in the unheated house for a month.

Two big questions remained. First, why had John List done it? He was a polite, church-going accountant who'd never had so much as a traffic ticket. Second, where was he? A massive man-hunt turned up no trace of John List.

The Killer Next Door

As the community of Westfield tried to come to terms with the murders, neighbors realized how little they'd known about the family in the three-story mansion called Breeze Knoll. The beautiful 19-room house even featured a signed Tiffany stained-glass ceiling over the ballroom. Outwardly the Lists fit into the community. Helen was a stunning woman who'd made homemaking her career; she liked to cook and collected cookbooks. The List boys played sports and daughter Patty wanted to be an actress. The kids' grandmother, Alma List, was a pillar of the local Lutheran church. As for John List, he was quiet, hardworking, and the Lutheran Sunday school teacher to boot.

Only after the murders did the people of Westfield learn how much was going wrong inside Breeze Knoll. Brought up by his strict father and domineering mother to be obedient and religious, John List had tried to raise his own family in the same rigid mold. That—to put it mildly—hadn't worked out. His wife was an alcoholic and suffered both mentally and physically from syphilis, which she'd contracted from her first husband. Sixteen-year-old Patty was in the throes of teenage rebellion. Fifteen-year-old John Jr. was unruly in school; both he and 13-year-old Freddy were ditching their religion classes. Except for his mother, John's family was straying from the path ordained by the Lutheran church, and John was too mild mannered to rule with the firmness he thought they needed.

Financial problems were growing too. By 1971 the accountant had lost his job and was heading into bankruptcy. Everything in John List's life was crumbling around him, including his showy house. Once he'd hoped to renovate Breeze Knoll; now he could barely afford to furnish the house and faced foreclosure. Raised to be proud and self-sufficient, List refused to seek counseling or public welfare. After much consideration and planning, he formed his own solution to his problems. On November 9, 1971, he killed his family and left town to start over.

Vanished!

Though police and FBI immediately set up an intensive search for John List, one week after the bodies were discovered the authorities admitted that the trail was cold. Having told everyone that the family was leaving town, List delayed the discovery of the bodies for 28 days. That gave him plenty of time to disappear.

Though police didn't then know it, List had moved to Denver, Colorado, and established a new identity with a phony social security number and the alias Robert P. Clark. A careful, methodical man, List (aka Clark) stayed under the radar. He worked as a night-shift cook where his fake ID wasn't scrutinized. Eventually he returned to his profession as an accountant, and he gradually acquired more phony identification, including a driver's license. In 1975 he finally felt safe enough to join a church again. There he met and married his second wife, Delores, who had no idea of his true identity. At the time of his second marriage, it was 1985. List had been a fugitive for nearly 14 years.

Down a Cold Trail

But Westfield police never forgot what happened at Breeze Knoll and never closed the case. Detectives were sure that List was still alive—if they could just get his image out to the public, someone would turn him in. Finally the department turned to a new and popular TV show, *America's Most Wanted*, to help them get their man.

In 1989, with the trail 18 years cold, *America's Most Wanted* decided to run a show that featured the List case. But since no one had seen List for nearly 20 years, the problem was figuring out what he might look like. They turned to forensic sculptor Frank Bender, asking him to make an "age-progression bust" of 64-year-old List.

To make the bust, Bender explored every aspect of how List would age. He researched how the neck scar from List's mastoid operation would look over time. List's diet, posture, and likely facial expressions were considered as factors in how his face would change. Bender believed that List would make himself look authoritative behind heavy, thick-framed glasses. He was also certain that List—who used to mow the Breeze Knoll lawn in a suit and tie—would be wearing a suit and tie when found.

When the bust was televised on *America's Most Wanted*, friends of a man called Bob Clark were astounded to see how much he resembled the murderer from New Jersey. The show brought in a tip that Bob Clark had moved from Colorado to Virginia. Eleven days later John List was finally arrested for murder.

The Nation Watches

List was extradited to New Jersey for trial. The nation followed the seven-day event, fascinated with the final mystery of why List had done it. List's attorney, Elijah Miller, used his client's own explanation as part of his defense. List had killed his family to save them. Financially he couldn't support them, and he didn't want them to suffer poverty or know the shame of living on welfare. Also, if he killed them before they could reject Christianity (as he believed they soon would), they would all go to heaven. According to the defense, a complicated mental disorder prevented List from seeing any other possibilities or truly understanding the horror of what he'd done.

Prosecutor Eleanor Clark, on the other hand, put together a more monstrous motive. List was a cold-blooded killer who decided to rid himself of his financial and emotional burdens. Ms. Clark pointed out that List had carefully plotted his own escape and never turned himself in. He went on with a new life showing neither sorrow nor remorse. The jury agreed with the prosecution and found List guilty. The accountant was sentenced to life in prison. (In 1989 New Jersey had no death penalty, so this was the most severe punishment that could be meted out.)

The Tiffany Solution

No one lived in Breeze Knoll after the Lists. In a mysterious act of suspected arson, the house burned down nine months after the murders. Eventually another house was built on the site for new owners. The fire that demolished Breeze Knoll also destroyed the ballroom's Tiffany stained-glass ceiling—a signed original that was worth at least $100,000 in 1971. Ironically, had List understood its value, he could have sold the magnificent ceiling, kept his house, and solved his financial problems with cash left over to put in the bank.

DID YOU KNOW?

Rutgers University offers a course called "Jerseyana." Professor Michael Rockland teaches this interdisciplinary class on New Jersey culture that tries to get at the essence of the state. The course's goal is to determine just what *is* Jersey culture and how it "differs from that of other American states in its ideas, values, and assumptions, its way of thinking of itself." Students cover the academic stuff (geography, the environment, the economy), but they also get to watch *On the Waterfront* and read *Goodbye, Columbus*.

Quotes from the Chairman of the Board

Sinatra's got some homespun wisdom for all of us. Pull up a chair and listen.

Frank on Women

"I'm supposed to have a Ph.D. on the subject of women. But the truth is I've flunked more often than not. I'm very fond of women; I admire them. But, like all men, I don't understand them."

"Never yawn in front of a lady."

"I like intelligent women. When you go out, it shouldn't be a staring contest."

"You treat a lady like a dame, and a dame like a lady."

Frank on Vices

"Alcohol may be man's worst enemy, but the Bible says love your enemy."

"Fresh air makes me throw up. I can't handle it. I'd rather be around three Denobili cigars blowing in my face all night."

"If I had as many love affairs as you have given me credit for, I'd now be speaking to you from a jar at the Harvard Medical School."

"I feel sorry for people who don't drink. When they wake up in the morning, that's as good as they're going to feel all day."

Frank on Music
"Whatever else has been said about me personally is unimportant. When I sing, I believe. I'm honest."

"You can be the most artistically perfect performer in the world, but an audience is like a broad—if you're indifferent, Endsville."

"Throughout my career, if I have done anything, I have paid attention to every note and every word I sing—if I respect the song. If I cannot project this to a listener, I fail."

Frank Gets Philosophical
"I'm like Albert Schweitzer and Bertrand Russell and Albert Einstein in that I have a respect for life—in any form. I believe in nature, in the birds, the sea, the sky, in everything I can see or that there is real evidence for. If these things are what you mean by God, then I believe in God."

"When lip service to some mysterious deity permits bestiality on Wednesday and absolution on Sunday, cash me out."

"Basically, I'm for anything that gets you through the night—be it prayer, tranquilizers, or a bottle of Jack Daniels."

"Fear is the enemy of logic. There is no more debilitating,

crushing, self-defeating, sickening thing in the world—to an individual or to a nation."

Frank on Frank

"I am a thing of beauty."

"I would like to be remembered as a man who had a wonderful time living life, a man who had good friends, fine family—and I don't think I could ask for anything more than that, actually."

"People often remark that I'm pretty lucky. Luck is only important in so far as getting the chance to sell yourself at the right moment. After that, you've got to have talent and know how to use it."

"You only live once, and the way I live, once is enough."

Frank on Life and Death

"Stay alive, stay active, and get as much practice as you can."

"Dare to wear the foolish clown face."

"You gotta love livin', baby, 'cause dyin' is a pain in the ass."

"May you live to be 100 and may the last voice you hear be mine."

The Genius on Mercer Street

When Albert Einstein moved to Princeton, he became just your friendly neighborhood genius.

Albert Einstein had become a symbol of man's ability to understand the world through science by the time he moved to Princeton, New Jersey. To his neighbors he became the embodiment of an absentminded professor and just one of the locals. Here's the story behind how this intellectual giant came to live in the Garden State and what happened when he got there.

First-Time Visitor

Einstein had first visited the United States in 1921, when he accompanied Chaim Weitzman on a fund-raising trip to benefit the medical school of the Hebrew University in Jerusalem. During the three months Einstein spent here, he gave a series of lectures on relativity at Princeton University (his talk was in German, and translated into English afterward). He was reported as saying, "I also found Princeton fine. A pipe as yet unsmoked. Young and fresh." Apparently the town made quite an impression on him.

The Road to Jersey

In the 1930s Einstein, while living and teaching in Berlin, was keenly aware of his precarious status as a Jew in Germany. "If relativity is proved right," he once said, "the Germans will call me a German, the Swiss will call me a Swiss citizen, and the French will call me a great scientist. If relativity is proved wrong, the French will call me a Swiss, the Swiss will call me a German, and the Germans will call me a Jew." Einstein's theory of relativity, of course, was accepted, and the world acclaimed the man and his work. But many in Germany demeaned his work, calling it "Jewish physics." As the Nazis rose to power, they burned Einstein's treatises and seized his belongings, including his violin.

It didn't take a genius to see the writing on the wall. Einstein left Germany in 1932, just before Hitler's takeover, and never returned. Although many countries offered him asylum, he remembered the little town of Princeton—also the location of the Institute for Advanced Study, whose philosophy of providing a comfortable setting for serious academic research impressed him. Einstein arrived in Princeton in October 1933 to become the Institute's first permanent faculty member. Germany's loss was certainly New Jersey's gain.

Albert Einstein brought his second wife, Elsa, her daughter Margot, and his devoted secretary, Helen Dukas, along for the trip to the Garden State. They spent their first few weeks in New Jersey at the Peacock Inn, before moving to a rented house at 2 Library Place. Eventually they bought a small Victorian wooden house at 112 Mercer Street, about a mile and a half from the Institute's campus. His telephone number was "PRINCETON 1606."

Lost: One Fuzzy-Haired Genius

It was clear that Einstein loved his new home. He once described living in Princeton as "banishment to paradise." And it turns out that his neighbors thought fondly of him too—especially since the genius next door was as down-to-earth as he was absentminded. He loved to walk to and from work, greeting neighbors and stopping to talk to children along the way. The trouble was that Einstein had a knack for getting himself lost when he went for a walk—even in the most familiar of circumstances. Legend has it that the Einsteins painted their front door bright red because Albert regularly failed to recognize his own house; he would frequently appear at his neighbors' front doors looking sheepish and confused.

Jon Blackwell, writing in the *Trentonian,* recounts how someone once called the dean's office at the Institute for Advanced Study to ask for directions to Einstein's house. When told that this information couldn't be given out, the caller sighed. "This is Albert Einstein," he said. "I got lost walking home from campus."

Mr. Einstein's Neighborhood

Einstein also really enjoyed being around the neighborhood children and seemed to regard them with a mixture of amusement and fascination. In the summer these children would provide him with water pistols, and he would engage them in spirited water fights. He was said to have been an exceptionally good shot (maybe because he was able to factor in the curvature of space when taking aim?).

The neighborhood kids weren't too slow to figure out that they lived near some kind of genius. A famous story tells of an eight-year-old neighbor girl, Adelaide Delong, who rang Einstein's doorbell, a plate of homemade fudge in her hands, asking for help with her addition and multiplication homework. After accepting the chocolate gift and reciprocating with a cookie, Einstein reportedly told her that his helping her wouldn't be fair to the other girls in her class. "She was a very naughty girl," he is reported to have said years later, recalling the incident. "Do you know she tried to bribe me with candy?"

Sailing, Sailing, on Lake Carnegie

Aside from physics, Einstein's two favorite pursuits were playing the violin and sailing. He would sail his boat, which he called *Tineff* (German for "worthless thing") on Lake Carnegie. He couldn't swim, and by all accounts he was a mediocre sailor. Unlike most sailors, however, Einstein actually enjoyed getting caught in sudden calms or running aground, which seemed to happen with a certain regularity. He would always carry a notebook with him, and when becalmed, he would sit quietly, working out his complicated proofs while waiting to be rescued. "I like sailing," he once said. "It is the sport that demands the least energy."

Life and Death in New Jersey

Einstein lived the rest of his life in Princeton until he died at age 76 on April 18, 1955, in Princeton Hospital. Reportedly he murmured a few words in German just before he died. The nurse who was attending him did not speak German, and so the world will never know the Man of the Century's last words.

It was typical of Einstein's humility that he left specific instructions that his house not be turned into a museum or shrine. In accordance with his wishes, it has remained a private residence for members of the Institute, with no public visitors allowed. He didn't want people "worshipping at his bones," and his will stipulated that his body be cremated and scattered in a secret location.

An autopsy was performed before the cremation. In an act that has been steeped in controversy, the pathologist, Dr. Thomas Harvey, removed Einstein's brain for study. It was sliced into 240 pieces and kept in jars in Harvey's house. "It looked like any other brain," Harvey said. Since Einstein's death Harvey has given several pieces of the brain to different researchers in California, Alabama, and Ontario. Harvey remained in charge of Einstein's brain until 1998, when he gave what remained of it to Princeton Medical Center.

DID YOU KNOW?

Every February thousands of Jerseyans charge into the chilly waters of the Atlantic Ocean for a swim. They're not masochists, they're fundraisers. It's all part of the annual Polar Bear Plunge in Point Pleasant Beach. New Jersey Law Enforcement sponsors this annual event to raise money for the Special Olympics. In 2005 over 2,700 plungers participated. The event has raised over $3 million since its inception in 1993.

Hometowns
Falling for Paterson

Alexander Hamilton literally put Paterson on the map.

The Town: Paterson
Location: Passaic County
Founding: Europeans first moved to the Paterson area in 1678, but the town got its official start when Alexander Hamilton and his Society for Establishing Useful Manufactures (SUM) spied the waterfalls near the original settlement. Knowing these falls could be a power source for factories, SUM bought the land and created the first planned industrial community in 1701. The city itself was incorporated in 1831.
Current Population: 150,000 (est.)
Size: 8.73 square miles
What's in a Name? Paterson is named for New Jersey's resident patriot, William Paterson. He was New Jersey's representative to the 1787 Constitutional Convention, governor of New Jersey, and an associate justice of the Supreme Court.

Claims to Fame
- Samuel Colt built his first gun factory in Paterson in 1836. They made handguns, rifles, carbines, and revolving shotguns.

- Passaic Falls, also called the Great Falls, is located in Paterson and is the second-highest waterfall east of the Mississippi. Seventy-seven feet tall and 280 feet wide, this waterfall's energy was harnessed to power local textile, silk, and locomotive industries.

- Nicknamed Silk City, U.S.A., Paterson wove more than 50 percent of the country's silks in 1870.

- Paterson was home to funnyman Lou Costello. Today there's a life-sized statue honoring the comedian. Entitled *Lou's on First,* the bronze figure carries a bat and wears his trademark derby.

- Bob Dylan immortalized the city in his song "Hurricane," about the infamous boxer Ruben "Hurricane" Carter, accused of four shootings in a Paterson bar in 1966.

DID YOU KNOW?

New Jersey is home to over 10,000 colonies of bees. The Garden State's official insect pollinates more than $140 million worth of crops every year.

For anyone who wants to see a beehive up close without the risk of getting stung, just head to the New Jersey Agriculture Museum, located on the Cook College Campus of Rutgers University. There, visitors can see a huge live colony (25,000 bees!) in the Giant Observation Beehive.

Pirates of the Jersibbean

Avast, me hearties! There's gold down that there shore!

Get out your metal detectors, Jerseyans! It's time to go treasure hunting. There was no need to travel to the Caribbean to find legendary cutthroats like Henry Morgan, Blackbeard, and Captain Kidd. When things got hot for pirates in southern waterways, they put in time in Jersey, where the jagged coastline offered plenty of creeks, inlets, bays, and marshes to hide in. Buccaneers prowled New Jersey waters along the northern tip of Sandy Hook and infested the 110 nautical miles that led south to Cape May, where they stopped for fresh water. Another popular spot, Ocean Beach, offered a great place to scout out approaching merchant ships and launch surprise attacks.

Pirates were often welcome in colonial New Jersey. Local politicians and businessmen were quite happy to protect them when they could also profit by them. Many wealthy Jersey colonists invested in pirate expeditions and traded in plundered goods. Pirates knew they were welcome, or at least tolerated. And some say that two of these legendary pirates left buried treasure behind them. So there's a chance that today's Jerseyans can get rich from the plunder even now!

Henry Morgan

Born in Wales in 1635, Henry Morgan became one of the most successful pirates to sail the high seas. In the 17th century Captain Morgan made his name plundering Spanish galleons and Cuban cities, the Caribbean, and Central America. While other pirates were hunted or executed, Morgan used his wealth and highborn relatives to escape capture and become Sir Henry Morgan, governor of Jamaica. In fact, he became so respectable that when he was called a pirate in print, he sued for defamation of character—and won.

Although he's most famous for his exploits in the Caribbean, local legends say that Morgan liked to hang out in New Jersey, where he also had friends and relations. The Morgan section of Sayreville is allegedly named for his relatives that set up their homestead near that favorite pirate hangout, Raritan Bay. Sir Morgan liked to have a drink at the Old Spye Inn, which once stood at the foot of Old Spye Inn Road in Sayreville (it burned down in 1976). But that story is probably just wishful thinking: The inn was built circa 1703, and Henry Morgan died in 1688.

Blackbeard

No pirate's reputation for blood ever exceeded Blackbeard's. Born in England around 1680 as Edward Teach, he came to pirate power in 1717. His colorful nickname accurately described his extravagantly long black beard; sometimes he braided it, tied it up in ribbons, and stuck flaming pieces of hemp in it. Teach commandeered a French merchantman, turning it into a 40-gun pirate vessel that he named the *Queen Anne's Revenge*. He then launched a reign of terror along the Atlantic seaboard from Maine all the way to Trinidad.

One of Blackbeard's haunts was near Little Egg Harbor in Jersey. Legends say that he performed one of his impressive escapes from the British navy in the wetlands near Brigantine Beach. While the navy searched, Blackbeard hid underwater in a marsh, breathing through a reed until the coast was, literally, clear. In Blackbeard's case the settlers were probably sorry he escaped: Not even landlubbers were safe from Teach's thieving pirates who rowed up the creeks and rivers to attack and plunder farms. Jerseyans, in what is now Middletown, stood up to Blackbeard—who had raided their town for supplies—engaging his pirates in a fierce battle, refusing to give up their flour and smoked ham without a fight. The pirates are said to have then gone on to easier pickings.

During his career in crime the swashbuckler amassed a huge fortune and up to 14 alleged wives to help him spend it. Burlington tale-tellers swear that one stormy night in 1717 he sailed up the Delaware River to bury treasure chests near a saloon on what is now Wood Street. Blackbeard shot one of his men and a huge black dog, burying them both with the treasure to guard it. He never returned to get his loot, but the black dog's ghost has remained—prowling Wood Street to defend Blackbeard's stolen booty—which has yet to be found.

Captain Kidd

The most well-remembered participant of New Jersey's sea-loving crime organizations is Captain Kidd. The reason? Captain Kidd is the only buccaneer proved to have actually stored ill-gotten gains in the ground. All along the shoreline from Sandy Hook to Cape May there are stories that Captain Kidd—whose homeport was New York City—buried big bucks in Jersey.

William Kidd, the son of a minister, was born in Scotland around 1655. When he came to New York in the 1690s, he was a successful privateer. (A privateer was a legal pirate who worked for a government—in Kidd's case the British government authorized him to attack enemy ships in return for a share of the spoils.) Traveling to New York, the privateer married a wealthy widow and, for a time, enjoyed respectability and a high rung on the social ladder.

Then, in 1696, Kidd's fortunes changed. He left New York on the 34-cannon *Adventure Galley* with aristocratic investors and orders to attack pirates and French ships. He took a ship with French papers, the *Quedagh Merchant,* which carried a cargo worth a fortune (what would be millions in today's currency). But while at sea, he learned that his backers were in political trouble in England and that he was now considered a dangerous pirate with a price on his head. (Some historians claim the Scotsman actually had committed an act of piracy and deserved these charges.)

In 1699 Kidd sailed back to New York proclaiming his innocence and waving his papers to claim he was a privateer and not a scurvy pirate. He stopped along the way to bury booty on Gardiners Island near Long Island, New York, and used it as a bargaining chip to get himself off the hook. "A pardon for me, some treasure for you," he told authorities. Alas, the chip didn't work. Kidd was arrested, tried, and executed by hanging in London in 1701. His body hung in an iron cage above the river Thames as a warning to all considering piracy. The Gardiners Island treasure was recovered, and it was believed that the authorities got all there was to get.

But wait just a moment! Some treasure hunters and historians claim that the recovered Gardiners Island booty was only a quarter of Kidd's vast fortunes. They believe that Kidd went down the Jersey Shore to bury much of his treasure before he returned home to New York. To this day his buried fortune awaits an enterprising treasure seeker combing the beaches of Jersey.

Hide and Seek

Where could Kidd's treasure be? A beach near Brigantine Inlet is rumored to have buried treasure gleaned from one of Kidd's earlier voyages. Other likely sites have been offered as well. Sandy Hook and Cliffwood Beach are two often mentioned hot spots for treasure. Captain Kidd would have anchored at Sandy Hook—popular with smugglers in those days—before his final trip and arrest in New York. It's rumored that he buried three-quarters of his great treasure in a site marked with pine trees—but those markers are long gone.

Actual Spanish gold coins have been found near Cliffwood Beach. Some of those coins were found in a lake that was once ignominiously called Duck Pond, but now sports the moniker Treasure Lake. Visitors to Cliffwood Beach still bring metal detectors to search the area. So far they haven't found anything, but hope still exists that some of Kidd's fabulous treasure will be detected—unless, as some old documents indicate, the plunder is buried in Del Haven; there it would probably be located under pavement or an office complex. So if you see treasure hunters with their metal detectors out in a Del Haven parking lot, you'll know what they're after.

Can It!

Canned soup and beer have become so common that the cans themselves have become invisible. But these cans pack a lot of New Jersey history. From Maine to Mainland China, consumers of soup and suds take a little piece of Jersey innovation into their pantries every day.

The food processing industry in New Jersey generates around $9.6 billion in sales per year—enough money to buy approximately 12,151,898,734 cans of Campbell's Cream of Mushroom Soup. And canned goods make up a big chunk of that cash. French Chef Nicolas Appert invented the process of heating and preserving food in jars. And Englishman Peter Durand patented the first tin can. But it was in New Jersey that the practice of food canning really came into its own. And it all took off during the War Between the States.

Soups for the Troops

Canning existed in the early 1800s but hadn't been perfected. Early canisters (as they were called then) were made by hand in a painstaking process of cutting sheets of tin with circular scissors and then soldering them together. A factory could make only about 60 cans a day. Can making improved in the 1830s and 1840s, with Englishman Henry Evans's patent of a can-making machine. As similar technology spread, New Jersey canneries were soon cranking out thousands of cans per week.

But the foundation for New Jersey's canning claim to fame would be laid in 1847 when Harrison Crosby of Jamesburg had the bright idea to start canning locally grown tomatoes. During the Civil War in the 1860s these tomato canneries in New Jersey kept Union soldiers fed across the nation. At the end of the war, New Jersey was perfectly outfitted to keep cranking out the cans—this time to civilians who'd grown a taste for them on both sides of the Mason-Dixon Line.

Campbell's Condenses in Cans!

In 1869 Joseph Campbell of Camden also decided to try his hand at canning vegetables. After a few years of experimentation he formed Joseph Campbell & Company in 1876, along with a business partner, Abraham Anderson. He canned everything from mincemeat to jellies, but Campbell's first big seller was his beefsteak tomato—notable because a single tomato filled an entire can.

The magic would happen for Campbell's company in 1897, when one of the managers, Arthur Dorrance, hired his nephew, a chemist named Dr. John T. Dorrance. John devised a way of condensing soups that would slash shipping costs and lower prices for the Camden company. Because of this innovation, Campbell's just-add-water soups could be sold for only a dime (rather than 30 cents), and consumers ate it up—literally. The original Campbell's flavors were chicken, vegetable, consomme, oxtail, and—of course—tomato.

To spread the word, Campbell's began advertising. The company created dozens of types of soups and soon created a soup empire—as well as a market for lots of cans. In 1900 the soups took a medal at the Paris Exposition; that's the little gold seal you see on the can today. By 1922 Campbell's soups had become so popular that they made soup their middle name—changing officially to the Campbell's Soup Company.

The company continued to grow and grow. In the 1930s, chicken noodle soup came into the mix. In 1962 Andy Warhol painted his famous soup can art. But by the 1970s it was so popular it was a permanent part of Americana—people ate it because they had a taste for it.

After over 100 years of Campbell's soup making, 90 percent of American households stock 11 cans of Campbell's soup in their pantries at all times. With 105,000,000 households in America, that adds up to over a billion cans of New Jersey heritage around the nation at all times. Campbell's is still headquartered in Camden, and the once one-tomato-in-a-can outfit now sells around a billion dollars' worth of soup every three months.

A Cold One in a Can

Soup isn't the only thing that New Jersey put in a can. In the 1930s, the tiny Gottfried Krueger Brewing Company of Newark, New Jersey, was dying. Following more than a decade of Prohibition, its war chest for battling bigger breweries such as Anheuser-Busch and Pabst was all but empty. And to make matters worse, just as Prohibition was repealed, Krueger's workers went on strike! The company just couldn't get a break, until the American Can Company came to it with an offer: Let's put beer in a can.

American Can was another New Jersey company that was up-and-coming in the canning industry. Their offer to Krueger: to install American Can canning machines (free of charge, of course) that would can Krueger's beer. If the canned beer took off, Krueger could purchase the machines and keep on using them.

At the time, beer was sold only in bottles. Earlier attempts to can beer had been disastrous. Not only did they explode in trucks and stores from pressure, but the beer reacted poorly with canning metals and tasted awful. American Can engineers claimed to have fixed these problems, but it was still a tough sell. All of the big breweries had rejected American Can's initial offer, not wanting their brands associated with exploding cans and foul-tasting beer. But Krueger had nothing to lose. And the results shocked the nation.

As it turns out, American Can's engineers really had made canned beer work—and people loved it. The tiny brewer slashed huge chunks of the big breweries' market from beneath their feet. By 1935 the Krueger factory couldn't brew beer fast enough.

The majors quickly learned their lesson, and after 1935 more than 30 breweries offered canned beer. Krueger's gamble bought them more time on the market, but the brewery did eventually go out of business. The big boys finally beat it into submission in 1961 by investing over the years in more and more advanced manufacturing and canning, efficient distribution processes, and, of course, the marketing to sell those cans. Today Gottfried Krueger's mansion in Newark is in the National Register of Historic Places and what used to be the American Can Company is now a part of Citigroup. But Anheuser-Busch still brews beer in New Jersey. Last year, it made over 233 million gallons of beer in New Jersey alone.

Ivy League Antics

If undergraduates get soused and do something stupid, it's a mistake. If they do it again the next year, it's a tradition. And for Princeton University, which has been around since 1746, that's a lot of traditions.

A Tale of Two Cannons

If you're strolling across Cannon Green on the Princeton campus, you may notice a strange black nub poking out of a ring of gravel. Across a path from the green is another black nub. Believe it or not, these are both Revolutionary War cannons, buried nose-down in the ground.

Princeton was the site of a major battle during the Revolutionary War (but that's another story). The war left a few cannons lying around on campus that were brought back into play during the War of 1812. The Big Cannon, now in the middle of Cannon Green, was taken to New Brunswick, New Jersey, for the war effort then. In 1835 citizens of Princeton stole it back, or at least tried to. They ended up dumping it on the side of the road when their wagon broke. Four years later Princeton students hauled it the rest of the way, and it was planted nose-down behind Nassau Hall to make sure it remained in Princeton.

New Brunswick is the home of another prestigious school—Rutgers, the State University of New Jersey—and in 1875 some Rutgers students decided to steal back the cannon they thought belonged to them. Unfortunately they cannon-napped the wrong one—they took the Little Cannon, which had never been to New Brunswick. The War of the Cannons was on. Princetonians planned to steal the gun back, but Rutgers students kept watch and cagily moved the Little Cannon from location to location. Princetonians only managed to steal some Revolutionary War muskets in their raid, as hostages for the Little Cannon. The heads of both schools negotiated a truce, and the cannon and muskets were returned to their rightful owners. The Little Cannon was planted on Princeton campus as well, to prevent further raids. Rutgers still paints the Little Cannon red a few times a year, splashing "R.U." on the lawn around it, to remind Princeton that the war is not over.

Clapper Capers

Another Princeton tradition has its roots in the grand old practice of cutting classes. In the 1860s the bell in the tower of Nassau Hall ruled campus life. It rang at the start of the day, at curfew, and at the beginning of each class. One winter's night in 1863 an enterprising undergraduate snuck up the tower and stole the bell's clapper. The next morning the bell couldn't ring—no bell, no classes. After that it became a tradition for entering freshmen to steal the clapper as a symbolic gesture. Members of the administration resigned themselves to the thefts and kept a barrel of extra clappers on hand. The firm that made Nassau's bell said they got more orders for clappers for Princeton's bell than for any other in their history. The tradition finally ended more than a century—and many injuries—later: In 1991, the university removed the clapper permanently. The bell continues to toll on Princeton campus, though, due to a mechanical striker installed in 1955.

Princeton's a Riot

Around the time of the American Civil War, Princeton students followed national fashion by carrying walking canes. In 1865 the upperclassmen decided the freshmen should not be allowed to carry canes, and the sophomores decided to take these status symbols away from the freshmen. Sophomores waiting on Nassau Street one evening tried to grab the canes away from freshmen, resulting in a brawl. This was the first Cane Spree, a term that at the time meant a ruckus. Since then, every year the freshman and sophomore classes have faced off every fall in the annual Cane Spree. The contest gained an organized, if eccentric, set of rules in the 1870s. Cane Spree was to take place at midnight on the night of the October full moon, in front of one of the dorms. The contest, lit only by broom torches, started with three organized bouts between white-clad freshmen and the black-clad sophomores. After that, an all-out rumpus broke out as underclassmen wrestled for each other's canes. In the late 1920s a few new rules were added: no throwing of dangerous missiles and no "parading in the streets in an undressed condition" (that tradition would come later). Apparently firecrackers, rocks, and iron bedsteads were commonly thrown during previous brawls.

Over the years Cane Spree has become more sedate. In 1951 football and track events were added to the traditional wrestling matches for the canes. Women first participated in 1970. Nowadays Cane Spree is a set of organized athletic contests between the sophomore and freshman classes, with bragging rights going to the winners. But in the 140 years that Princetonians have been facing off in Cane Spree, the freshman class has won only four times!

Nude Olympics

Nothin' says intelligence like a sophomore running through the snow with only a hat, boots, and a smile. Nobody knows exactly how or why the Nude Olympics started. Sometime in the 1970s, just as the first female students entered Princeton (a coincidence?), it became tradition for sophomores to run naked through one of the campus courtyards on the evening of the year's first snowfall. Originally the streaking actually involved events—wheelbarrow and three-legged races—but it quickly degenerated into running laps and campus-wide antics, probably fueled by too much alcohol. In 1976 overenthusiastic Olympians ran into the University pool, where they interrupted a championship swim meet. During the next 20 years, the event became an established ritual, looked forward to by sophomores as a rite of Princeton passage.

Alas, a tradition so wholesome could not go on forever, and time was up for the Nude Olympics in 1999. During the 1997–1998 school year, not a single flake of snow fell on the Princeton campus, so the sophomore class missed out on the event. The following year, when snow came on January 8, 1999, the campus was in for some trouble. The current crop of sophomores had never seen how the event should go; meanwhile the packs of juniors who felt cheated out of their own Olympics joined these games. Things quickly got out of hand. Six students were hospitalized for overconsumption of alcohol, property was damaged, the press was all over it, and the university was embarrassed. The administration banned the event, threatening any student who participated in something even remotely similar to the Nude Olympics with a year's suspension. The ban stuck and the Class of 2003 was the first in a quarter century to never see nude Olympians running half-frozen through the snow.

Fountain of Knowledge

In front of the Woodrow Wilson School of Public Policy, called "Woody Woo" by the students who major in it, is a reflecting pool with a pinnacled sculpture called Fountain of Freedom in its center. Officially, there is no swimming allowed in the fountain. Unofficially, graduating Woody Woo seniors can take a dip on that glorious day when they turn in their theses in early April. They gather at 5:00 p.m. to hand in their papers, don a commemorative T-shirt, and dash into the fountain.

Seniors aren't the only fountain frolickers. After each home football game that Princeton wins, the Princeton University Band marches through the fountain, orange plaid jackets flashing, in celebration. The university seems to have resigned itself to this tradition as well: a recent renovation of the pool added steps descending invitingly into the water.

It's Not the Grades, It's the Gates

Since 1970, as the final act of graduation, Princeton students walk out through the FitzRandolph Gates, Princeton's main gates, into the Real World. Before 1970 the gates, erected in 1905, remained closed except for a few special occasions, such as the bicentennial of the university. When the gates were permanently opened that year, a superstition spontaneously emerged: If you walk out of those gates as a student, you will never graduate. Some students ignore the story, but most go out of their way to avoid the gates. As some students say, "Why risk it?"

State Tall Ship
A. J. Meerwald

"Enacted by the Senate and General Assembly of the State of New Jersey on April 21, 1998."

Everybody loves a comeback, and the story behind New Jersey's official tall ship is a good one. Once abandoned by its owners and left to rot in the tidal flats of a river, the now tall and stately *A. J. Meerwald,* a Delaware Bay oyster schooner, has come a long way.

Humble Beginnings

When Augustus Joseph Meerwald commissioned a ship in 1928, building a state symbol was the furthest thing from his mind. He just wanted an oyster dredge to expand his two-ship fleet. The oyster business was booming along the Delaware Bay coast in New Jersey, and Meerwald wanted his business to grow along with it. Being a working boat, it was anything but glamorous, but hopefully it would be profitable.

The ship was built in Dorchester, a shipbuilding center on the Maurice River in southern Cumberland County. The 112-foot *Meerwald* had no topmasts. Like most Dorchester ships, its sturdy construction of oak planks on oak frames made it a fine example of the hardworking schooners that were built specifically for sailing the shallows of inland and bay waters to harvest oysters.

Out of the Oyster Biz

Like so many hard working Americans, the *A. J. Meerwald* was called upon to serve its country in 1942 in World War II. Under the War Powers Act, the U.S. Maritime Commission drafted the schooner to help out the U.S. Coast Guard. During its stint in the armed services, most of the *Meerwald's* sails were removed in order to turn the oyster dredge into a fireboat.

Five years later the ship was sold to a businessman who once again put it to work in the oyster business. The *Meerwald* still went mastless and sailed under power. Sadly, in 1957, the parasite MSX wiped out the New Jersey oyster industry by killing an estimated 90 to 95 percent of the critters that year. In 1959 the old ship was sold again and transitioned to surf clamming. Finally, in the 1970s, the *Meerwald* was retired and abandoned by her owners.

A Schooner Is Saved

Luckily for the *A. J. Meerwald,* the Delaware Bay Schooner Project rescued the ship and restored it to its former glory. The 8-year, $1 million restoration only used historically authentic materials such as canvas sails, hemp ropes, and cedar planks (for the deck). The ship's dock, however, was made from recycled milk and beverage containers. The grayish-brownish composite is resistant to rot and stronger than wood. Another plus, the Cumberland County Improvement Authority estimated that the dock kept more than 240,000 gallon milk jugs out of landfills.

The ship took to the water again in 1996. It has since become a floating classroom where both young and old can learn about the history, natural environment, and local culture along the Delaware Bay. Now docked at the project's headquarters in Bivalve, the ship is available for public sails and schooner day camps, in addition to making the occasional appearance in tall-ship parades and schooner races.

Making It Official

An important symbol of New Jersey's oystering past and hopeful future, the *Meerwald* has a place on both the National Register of Historic Places and the state register. In 1998 New Jersey officially recognized the *A. J. Meerwald* as its official tall ship.

DID YOU KNOW?

The oldest standing log cabin in the United States is in Gibbstown in Gloucester County. The Nothnagle Log House was built by Benjamin Braman between 1638 and 1643. The county is also home to the oldest brick house in the country. Built in 1688 by John Ladd, who helped William Penn design the streets of Philadelphia, the house is called Candor Hall or Ladd's Castle.

Grover's Mill's Martians

How aliens invaded a small town in New Jersey.

L adies and gentlemen, I have a grave announcement to make
. . . observations of science and the evidence of our eyes lead
to the inescapable assumption that those strange beings that
landed in the New Jersey farm lands tonight are . . . an invading
army from the planet Mars." On October 30, 1938, when those
stunning words came over the radio, millions of Americans in
the audience believed they were hearing an official news broadcast from Intercontinental Radio News. Their regular program-
ming had been interrupted with live reporting from New Jersey,
where a strange meteorite had landed in rural Grover's Mill. The
meteorite proved to be a metal cylinder from another planet.
Quick as you could say flying saucer, New Jersey was facing
death and destruction; the American military fell back helpless
before the mighty Martian death rays.

Martians in New Jersey? Not exactly. It was all a part of
Orson Welles's famous *War of the Worlds* radio broadcast, one of
the greatest practical jokes ever played on an audience. Since it
was the night before Halloween, Welles and his radio theater
company adapted H. G. Wells's *War of the Worlds* (a story about
an invasion of hostile aliens from Mars) into a scary—and very
realistic—radio play. Though it seems silly today, at the time the

program sounded completely authentic, and Americans were in a panic over it.

The show began as a music program—peppered with "flash bulletins" that told the story of a Martian takeover. The use of real locations in the bulletins convinced unsuspecting listeners that what they were hearing was happening; it was estimated that more than a million people thought they were listening to an actual invasion. Concern and even panic spread as far west as San Francisco and north into Canada. People went to the hospital convinced that their dizziness and nausea were caused by Martian gas. Others were treated for rashes, rapid heartbeat, hysteria, and shock. Thousands of frightened citizens fled their homes or hid in their cellars. Some even loaded their guns and went hunting for Martians while they faced the end of the world.

But how did the locals in New Jersey act? Were they in a panic over the little green men from Mars?

They're Bombing New Jersey!

Yes, even Jerseyans believed their home state had actually been attacked. On a single block in Newark, more than 20 families fled their houses with wet handkerchiefs or towels over their faces to protect themselves from poisonous Martian gas. As folks packed up and fled the invasion, churches opened their doors to the newly devout who had come to pray for deliverance from the calamity. Those in West Orange who chose a more inebriated approach to dealing with the Martian invasion were out of luck when the bartender closed his tavern on Valley Road, believing that everyone had been ordered to evacuate the metropolitan area.

In Maplewood and Orange, newspapers and police were inundated with frantic phone calls such as the one from a caller who declared, "They're bombing New Jersey!" New York and New Jersey State Police had to send out messages via their Teletypes and shortwave radios that the invasion was fictional. But when Welles broadcast a "bulletin" about the mobilization of 7,000 National Guardsmen in New Jersey, the state armories were overwhelmed with calls from reporting officers and guardsmen.

It's easy to claim that only the gullible would be fooled by the broadcast, but how about the head of the Department of Geology at Princeton and another distinguished professor? Early in the program, when another "bulletin" described a meteorite landing near Princeton, the pair gathered up their equipment. They rushed toward Grover's Mill to search for the alien craft that had been described as "a huge flying object" flaming down to earth.

Beachhead Grover's Mill

But what of the tiny community of Grover's Mill? Surely, because its inhabitants could see for themselves that the Martians and the U.S. Army were nowhere in sight, *it* wasn't fooled by the broadcast. Not so fast. At the beginning of the broadcast that night, the town was nearly deserted. But by 8:30 p.m. crowds were everywhere, and it was difficult to tell what was going on. Local switchboards were jammed with worried callers. Some citizens brought guns to Grover's Mill for a standoff with the aliens. Fortunately the only casualty was a farmer's water tower that was mistaken for a Martian spaceship.

Many wondered why a sleepy rural site was chosen as the beachhead for the interplanetary war. The answer was simple. Playwright Howard Koch, who wrote the script, closed his eyes and aimed his pencil point at a map of New Jersey. When the pencil point landed at Grover's Mill, so did the Martians.

Post Invasion

Fifty years after the supposed invasion the story hasn't been forgotten in Jersey. In 1988 a bronze, six-foot-tall monument was erected in Van Nest Park, near Grover's Mill Pond in West Windsor Township, to mark the place where the aliens first "landed." The face of the monument includes depictions of a Martian craft, Orson Welles performing from his script, and a family listening to the radio. At the dedication Douglas R. Forrester, head of the War of the Worlds Commemorative Committee, gave a speech that touched on the reactions of the residents in Grover's Mill and West Windsor Township on the night that the Martians "invaded." They were, he explained, just like everyone else at the time: "some were perplexed, some were amused, and some were alarmed." Ten years later in 1998 a "Martian Ball" was held to celebrate the 60th anniversary of the War of the Worlds. And even in the 21st century, fans still flock to visit the monument that celebrates one of the scariest Halloween stories ever told—a story that even fooled the locals.

DID YOU KNOW?

M&Ms are made in a candy factory in Hackettstown. Every day, a white *M* is stamped on a candy shell 200,000 times per minute.

Sons of Jersey
A Quiz

The Garden State is proud of its Jersey Boys too. Can you match them up to what they were famous for?

1. Edwin "Buzz" Aldrin
2. David Copperfield
3. Lou Costello
4. Savion Glover
5. William Halsey Jr.
6. Ice-T
7. Alfred Kinsey
8. Ernie Kovacs
9. Ray Liotta
10. Zebulon Pike
11. Paul Robeson
12. Philip Roth
13. Amos Alonzo Stagg
14. Dave Thomas
15. Edmund Wilson

A. This son of Metuchen made his name doing magic, but his neatest trick was dating supermodel Claudia Schiffer for several years.

B. This Princeton native is a football All-American, a law graduate, an accomplished Shakespearean actor—and a target of Senator Joe McCarthy.

C. This Newark-born writer won a Pulitzer prize in 1998, and his 2000 novel, *The Human Stain,* was made into a movie starring Anthony Hopkins and Nicole Kidman.

D. This Atlantic City native took a chance on fast-food restaurants and created one of the biggest chains in the county. He was also a proponent of adoption.

E. The NCAA Division III football championship is named after this famous coach and West Orange native.

F. Born in Newark, this artist is better known as a West Coast rapper, and a star of a New York City–based detective show.

G. This inquisitive character from Hoboken found out more about sex than nearly any other person—purely as a matter of scientific interest.

H. This Paterson comic made sure the majority of the profit earned by his comedy team went to his partner, saying, "Comics are a dime a dozen. Good straight men are hard to find."

I. This deeply intellectual scion of Red Bank was the toast of literary society in the early- and mid-20th century—and yet had the unlikely nickname of Bunny.

J. This Newark-born actor is best known for playing gangsters and psychos, but he also played fellow New Jersey native Frank Sinatra in a TV film about the Rat Pack.

K. This Montclair son boldly went where only Neil Armstrong had gone before and became the second man on the Moon.

L Hailed as a pioneering talent during the golden age of television, this Trenton-born comedian frequently ad-libbed and broke the so-called fourth wall on his live show.

M. Born in 1779, this explorer grew up in Somerset County and set out in 1805 to explore the headwaters of the Mississippi. A peak in the Rocky Mountains is named for him.

N. This Newark hoofer danced his way to a Tony nomination in 1989 at the tender age of 16 for *Black and Blue* and won a Tony in 1996 for *Bring in 'da Noise, Bring in 'da Funk*.

O. This U.S. Navy Admiral from Elizabeth not only commanded the Third Fleet during much of the Second World War, but his name is also part of the title of one of Paul McCartney's solo pop singles.

Turn to page 317 for answers.

Cruising to Catastrophe

The last sailing of the Morro Castle *was a mysterious voyage to disaster.*

On September 8, 1934, crowds flocked to the boardwalk in Asbury Park, New Jersey, and strained to see the smoldering remains of the SS *Morro Castle*. A once-elegant luxury liner, the *Morro* now lay shipwrecked near the convention center. The captain had died mysteriously during the ship's final voyage from Cuba to New York. Only a few hours after his death, a terrible fire had raged through the ship, costing the lives of 134 people.

Few in the crowd knew that the luxury liner had problems long before it caught fire and foundered off the shores of New Jersey. During the following 70 years, the shipwreck would remain a controversial mystery, complete with tales of scandal and rumors of murder.

Trouble in Paradise

The *Morro Castle,* named for the 16th-century fortress on Cuba's Havana Bay, was a four-year-old, 11,520-ton steamship liner operated by the Ward Line. Known for its fine food, entertainment, and modern accommodations, the *Morro Castle* took wealthy tourists from New York to Havana, Cuba, and back. Carrying 316 passengers and 230 officers and crew, she was considered a state-of-the-art vessel and one of the safer ships at sea. But the glitzy *Morro* had a darker side.

While the passengers may have been sailing in the lap of luxury, the crew didn't have such a cushy arrangement in the 1930s. During the Great Depression workers were desperate for jobs, and the Ward Line needed to save money. Many of the crew lacked training, and rumors abounded that many of their seaman's papers had been forged. The crew complained of long working hours, low pay, and extremely poor working conditions. (One sailor reported that the officers and passengers ate gourmet, while the crew existed on "awful slop.")

Captain Robert R. Wilmott, who commanded the *Morro Castle,* often butted heads with junior officers and crew, especially since some crew members subsidized their low wages with a bit of smuggling on the side. They smuggled just about everything— from narcotics and Cuban rum to illegal immigrants and political asylum seekers.

Contraband hidden on the ship was profitably ferried from Havana into New York. Captain Wilmott constantly had to break up these mini-smuggling rings. According to some historians, the tension between the captain and his crew reached a dangerous pitch by the time the *Morro Castle* set out on her last voyage to New York.

A Brewing Storm

On September 7, when the ship was about six miles away from New Jersey, a storm blew up in the Atlantic and buffeted the ship with gale force winds. But Captain Wilmott wasn't at the helm. In fact Wilmott, who usually dined with the passengers, stayed in his quarters suffering acute distress from stomach pain. Later that night the ship's doctor declared that Wilmott had apparently died of a heart attack in his stateroom. Without its captain, the ship continued to sail. Meanwhile passengers—who thought they'd soon be docking in New York—danced at the traditional farewell ball.

After Wilmott's death, command of the ship passed to First Officer William Warms, who accepted the new title while he contended with the raging storm that continued through the night. To add to the new captain's problems, at 2:15 a.m. a passenger saw smoke coming out of a locker near the writing room on the promenade deck. The locker was on fire.

The crew rushed to extinguish the flames and failed; fire spread once the locker doors were opened and the storm's heavy winds fanned it. An hour later the blaze was burning out of control.

Ship of Shame

Acting Captain Warms seemed determined to get the ship to safe harbor at all costs. And he would later be criticized for failing to order an SOS for help. Radioman George Rogers, acting on his own initiative, battled heat and smoke to send out the first distress call at about 3:24. He was later hailed as a hero. There were other heroes among the crew, who worked to save lives and who—like Rogers and Warms—stuck to their posts. But their courage was overshadowed by the surfacing accounts of angry passenger-survivors.

Some in the underpaid and poorly trained crew apparently didn't hang around during the disaster. Warms, still trying to reach safety, had given no order to abandon ship. But crew members commandeered the lifeboats and rowed for the Jersey Shore, eight miles away. Chief Engineer Abbot was said to have ordered his crew to stay at their posts below decks—while he leaped into a lifeboat. Of the first 98 survivors to reach the shore, only six were passengers.

Most of the passengers—who'd never gone through a fire drill or a lifeboat drill on the *Morro*—had to fend for themselves. Supplied with so-called "Mae West" life preservers, many jumped into the deathly cold waters of the Atlantic. Some swam toward the shore; others tried to stay afloat until rescue ships arrived. For the elderly and weaker passengers, rescue didn't come soon enough. More than 100 of the 134 people who died that night were passengers who either burned to death or drowned.

Castle Controversy

When the smoke cleared, so to speak, the public investigation concluded that an "act of God" had destroyed the luxury liner. Investigators noted that highly flammable blankets were stored in the locker where the fire broke out. The blankets rested against a wall facing a smokestack, which could have overheated and started the fire. But rumors of crime persisted.

The rumors claimed that Captain Wilmott (remember his stomach distress?) was poisoned by a crew member who ran a smuggling ring and would have been fired—or even prosecuted—when the voyage was over. Then the arson was committed to hide the murder.

A Flaming Murderer?

The theory gained credibility when Radioman George Rogers, hailed by the Veteran Wireless Operator's Association as the maritime hero of 1934, later proved himself a deadly criminal. After the shipwreck George Rogers opened a radio repair shop, but the shop burned down in a fire as mysterious as that of the *Morro*. Rogers then joined the Bayonne police force, but he was convicted of attempted murder when (ironically to speed up his promotion) he mailed a bomb to his supervisor. After emerging from prison in the 1950s, Rogers was sent back for life for murdering two of his neighbors. Rogers also had a juvenile criminal record involving fire, and he was labeled by some authorities as a pyromaniac.

Did Rogers commit both murder and arson on the luxury liner? One crew member later recalled that Captain Wilmott disliked and distrusted Rogers, calling him a "bad man." Rogers might have been worried about being dismissed in disgrace, but after the disaster struck, the fire brought him medals and fame.

Thomas Gallagher, author of the history *Fire at Sea,* visited Rogers in prison to ask the convict if he had started the *Morro Castle* fire. Rogers refused to answer. More than 70 years after the tragedy, no version of what happened that night can prove that murder or arson occurred.

Out of the Ashes

More controversy surrounds the rapid spread of the fire, the failure to send out a timely distress call, and the lack of help getting the passengers into lifeboats. Acting Captain Warms was tried, convicted, and sentenced to two years in prison for negligence. But he claimed he did his best, and the ruling was later overturned. Chief Engineer Abbot got four years, with his sentence overturned, too. No one ever served time in jail for the deaths on the *Morro.* To escape bad publicity, the Ward Line changed its name and continued doing business as the Cuba Mail Line until 1959.

Not in Vain

Despite all the unsolved mysteries, one fact is clear: The *Morro*

Castle fire had an impact on cruise ship safety. After the terrible shipwreck, the United States government took notice and became convinced that more federal involvement in maritime training was necessary. Congressional hearings led to the Merchant Marine Act of 1936, which provided tougher safety regulations including lifeboat drills for passengers. *The Morro Castle* disaster also led to the creation of the U.S. Merchant Marine Academy, where seafaring men and women can be professionally educated and trained.

DID YOU KNOW?

Dogs aren't usually allowed on the boardwalk in Ocean City, but the town makes an exception every April for the Boardwaddle. Hundreds of costumed basset hounds (and their owners) congregate to take part in the event, which raises money for the Bassett Hound Rescue League.

The Boardwaddle is part of Ocean City's Doo Dah Parade, the parade for anyone who wants to be in one. The annual procession is made up of clowns, comedic impersonators (the Marx Brothers and Three Stooges are favorites), Brigades (like the beach chair drill association), and other assorted costumed characters. Past Grand Marshals include Soupy Sales, Mickey Carroll (the mayor of Munchkinland from *The Wizard of Oz*), and Larry Storch (of *F-Troop* fame).

North and South

To an outsider it may not be obvious that a state as small as New Jersey would have regional distinctions. But to misidentify from which region a Jerseyan hails could be a serious faux pas. So here are a few things to keep in mind when traveling throughout the Garden State.

Room with a View or Room to Move?

New Jersey is the fourth smallest state, but it has the ninth largest population, making it the most densely populated state in the nation. More than 40 percent of New Jersey's 8.4 million residents have squeezed into the five counties that surround New York City (Bergen, Essex, Hudson, Middlesex, and Passaic). These make up the bulk of the North Jerseyans. In comparison, the five largest counties in the south of the state (Atlantic, Burlington, Cape May, Cumberland, and Ocean) house just 1.5 million residents in four times the space. These are the South Jerseyans. There is also a rarely acknowledged group: the Central Jerseyans, hailing from the midsection of the state around Mercer, Middlesex, and Monmouth counties. But this group tends to blend in with its neighbors to the south or north.

There is no physical line of demarcation, but Jerseyans know which side they're on. How? By their TV channels. Those north and east of Trenton look to the Big Apple for their news, while the rest find Philly broadcasters on their screens.

Dialects

When confronted with a Jerseyan, the most obvious distinction is his or her accent. The popular idea of a North Jersey accent comes from *The Sopranos* ("Fuhgeddaboutit!"), but the Northern accent can be subtler in the real world. Listen for the short A's— that's what gives the North Jerseyans away. For instance, if you go to a park and hear someone "cawl" their "dawg" and throw them a "bawl," they're probably from the Northern half of the state.

A South Jerseyan twang reflects their slightly slower pace of life. Words can be lengthened and sometimes have an extra syllable: For example, you may say "home," but they say "hoe-m." Other giveaways: It's not a creek, but a "crick." "On the road" becomes "onna road." If you hear the term, "wooder," which means water, you've got a South Jerseyan on your hands.

Slang across both regions can be similar. For example, both groups take their summer vacations "down the Shore," although they flock to different areas. North Jerseyans tend to gather at the beaches from Belmar to Seaside Heights. South Jerseyans favor Long Beach Island, Avalon, Stone Harbor, and Cape May. With apologies to Rudyard Kipling, "East is East" but "never the twain shall meet"—at least not on the same beaches.

Divided Sports Loyalties

Long-suffering Jersey sports fans often have little choice but to pledge allegiance to teams from either New York or Philadelphia. Like Rodney Dangerfield, North Jersey football fans get no respect. Both the Jets and the Giants play at the Meadowlands Sports Complex but call New York home, in name at least. Only the New Jersey Nets (basketball) and the New Jersey Devils (ice hockey) admit to where they live.

As a result, New Jersey sports allegiances tend to favor the big city the fans live closest to. North Jerseyans like the New York teams and South Jerseyans prefer the Philadelphia ones. A wearing of the green on St. Patrick's Day is a sign that all are Irish for a day, but during football season confusing the greens can be dangerous. South Jerseyans put on green and cross the Delaware River, chanting "Fly, Eagles! Fly!" Jets fans are more famous for baring green-painted chests on cold Sunday afternoons at the Meadowlands. On alternate weekends, the chests are painted blue when the Giants are in town.

The Best Way to a Large Stomach

North Jerseyans love to dine on all things Italian, especially pizza and pastries such as cannolis and sfogliatelle. South Jersey regional cuisine contains such favorites as cheesesteaks (with Cheez-Whiz) and Tastykakes.

A true giveaway for spotting South Jersey baby boomers is if they admit to trying to break a lifelong addiction to a syrupy, caffeine-loaded liquid named Drink-A-Toast, but known as Take-A-Boost, or simply just Boost. They joke that it was in their baby bottles. Northerners who tasted Boost when visiting southern friends would politely describe it as flat Dr. Pepper (and quietly dump it down the sink).

You Say "Sub" and We Say "Hoagie"

Delineating North and South Jerseyans is a multistep process. Here are some additional things to look and listen for:

	North	**South**
SANDWICHES	Subs	Hoagies
SCRAPPLE	Taylor ham	Pork roll
ICE CREAM TOPPINGS	Sprinkles	Jimmies
DRIPLESS POPSICLES	Italian ice	Water ice
TRAVEL	"Going to The City" (New York City)	"Going into town" (Philadelphia)
CONVENIENCE STORES	7-11	Wawa
ENTERTAINMENT	St. Patrick's Day Parade	Mummer's Parade
PERIODICALS	*Newark Star Ledger, Bergen Record, Jersey Journal*	*Philadelphia Inquirer, Trenton Times*

The E Street Band
A Triple-Threat Quiz

We love the Boss, but most love him best when he's backed by the E Street Band, since together they created such incredible albums as Born to Run, Nebraska, Born in the U.S.A., *and* The Rising. *To honor the band, see how much you know about one of the best rock-and-roll bands in Jersey.*

Match these members of the E Street Band with these instruments...

1. Roy Bittan   A. Backing Vocals
2. Clarence Clemons   B. Bass
3. Danny Federici   C. Drums
4. Nils Lofgren   D. Guitar (1975–1984; rejoined in 1999)
5. Patti Scialfa   E. Guitar (joined in 1984)
6. Garry Tallent   F. Organ
7. Steven Van Zandt   G. Piano
8. Max Weinberg   H. Saxophone

And these bits of performance trivia...

I.   This E Streeter's 1985 solo album *Hero* featured a minor hit song with backing vocals by movie star Daryl Hannah. Why? Because she was the girlfriend of Jackson Browne, who sang lead with the E Streeter on the track.

II. Prior to joining Bruce and the band, this E Streeter recorded with Neil Young and Crazy Horse, including the album *Trans*, which Young's record company sued him for because it was "non-representative" of his earlier work.

III. Meatloaf, Bonnie Tyler, and Air Supply: What do these three artists have in common? Two things: Over-the-top rock songwriter Jim Steinman wrote hits for each of them, and this E Streeter has appeared on each of their albums.

IV. This Asbury Park High School grad used to perform in Greenwich Village's Sheridan Square for meal money before hooking up gigs with the Rolling Stones, Buster Poindexter, and Asbury Park faves Southside Johnny & the Asbury Jukes.

V. From Jersey Rock to Berlin Glam? This E Streeter did it by appearing on David Bowie's 1976 *Station to Station* as well as his 1980 album *Scary Monsters*.

VI. When not jamming with the Boss, this E Streeter has found time to champion human rights across the globe, a side gig that caused the United Nations to offer its kudos—twice!

VII. This E Streeter also tours with his own jazz band. He has released the same jazz album twice, with a different name for both releases (the first time, in 2001, it was called *Flemington*, after his New Jersey hometown).

VIII. This E Streeter summed up his role in the band by saying, "Nobody notices I'm there until I'm not."

Turn to page 318 for the answers.

New Jersey and Tomatoes
Perfect Together

Jersey tomatoes are just about the sweetest, most scrumptious, most delicious . . . Well, they're really good. So what's the story behind this special crop and the Garden State?

You might say it all started with Colonel Robert Gibbon Johnson back in July 1820, or so the legend goes. In those days, tomatoes were considered poisonous, but Johnson, on the steps of the Salem County courthouse, dared to eat one. Thankfully for us—and for him—he lived to eat another day. From then on, it seems New Jerseyans had a very special relationship with tomatoes.

Tomatoes, Tomatoes, Everywhere

With the rise of the Campbell Soup Company (in Camden), southern New Jersey became the center of the tomato industry in the early 1900s. In the 1940s approximately 50,000 acres of New Jersey farmland were dedicated just to growing tomatoes.

Today New Jersey is the eighth leading state in tomato production in the United States and is still known the world over for its sweet, juicy tomatoes. They're commonly known as Jersey Tomatoes but, just to be safe, the New Jersey Tomato Council trademarked the term to control what can and cannot be designated an official Jersey Tomato. Just being grown in native Jersey soil (all 150 types of it) is not enough. Official tomatoes are only produced on choice growing fields and shipped farm fresh within 24 hours of harvest.

To-ma-to, To-mah-to

So what makes these tomatoes so special? First, Jersey Tomatoes are vine ripened, meaning they are picked after they start to turn red (or 60 percent pink, as one farmer explains), not a common practice in other states. Vine ripening creates a firm tomato full of fiber, potassium, vitamin A, and vitamin C. Second, experts say a good Jersey Tomato should have a bruise or two, indicating that it was grown in a field and not in a greenhouse. Third, a Jersey Tomato should be sweet, meaty, and firm, giving in to gentle pressure. Larger than most varieties, they are sold with the stems off. Finally, the tomato season lasts for only four months, July through October. Once summer's gone, so are the Jersey Tomatoes.

Buy the Numbers

In 2002 New Jersey farmers harvested about 76 million pounds of the fresh red vegetable, planted on 3,300 acres, bringing in $27.3 million. The top four producers of Jersey Tomatoes are Atlantic, Cumberland, Gloucester, and Salem counties.

Attack of the Overripe Tomatoes

New Jersey continues to celebrate its special relationship with the tomato. In 2004 the first annual New Jersey Tomato Festival was held on the waterfront in Camden. It drew 5,000 attendees, who used the more squishy, overripe variety to stage a "tomato war" in honor of La Tomatina, an annual tomato fight held in Spain. (Over 130,000 pounds of tomatoes are donated for the fighting at La Tomatina: New Jersey only had 5,000 pounds of tomato-flinging fun.) The Jersey festival included a tomato-growing contest, gardening seminars, and chefs' demonstrations. People dressed as tomatoes and ate specially prepared tomato cakes and cookies.

Festival promoter and president of the Gloucester County Business Association, Ira Shaffer, now has plans to have the tomato named the official state vegetable. Although the tomato is scientifically categorized as a fruit (Shaffer calls it a "big berry"), it is legally a vegetable. In the late 19th century the Supreme Court decided that the tomato was a legal vegetable for tariff purposes. After the highbush blueberry became New Jersey's own state fruit, Shaffer and his followers set their sights on the vegetable crown. It's a no-brainer to Shaffer: "When people think of New Jersey, they think of two things: the turnpike and the tomato. It's time the Jersey Tomato got its due."

DID YOU KNOW?

At 18, Rodney Dangerfield played his first gig as a comedian in Newark. He was only paid $2. Ten years later and tired of living hand-to-mouth, he took a hiatus from comedy, got married, settled down, and sold aluminum siding in Englewood.

Hometowns
Stuck in the Middle

Not surprisingly, Middletown occupies a central place in Jersey's history.

The Town: Middletown
Location: Monmouth County
Founding: 1664
Current Population: 67,000 (est.)
Size: 41.11 square miles
What's in a Name? From the sounds of it, you would guess that Middletown is in the middle of something, right? Well, it was. When the English began to settle the area in the 1660s, they established three villages: Portland Point, Shrewsbury, and Middletown, located in between the other two.

Claims to Fame
- During the War for Independence, most of Middletown remained loyal to the British, which is probably why the Redcoats felt safe retreating through the territory. Today there are signs along local roads showing their retreat after the Battle of Monmouth.

- Middletown is home to the "Evil Clown" sign. The 30-foot-tall, colorful yet menacing clown towers over Route 35, where he promoted a Food Circus in the 1950s. Today the Food Circus is gone, but he still remains to glare at passersby.

- Wealthy Avenue sounds like a place where Middletown's rich and famous might reside. But that isn't necessarily so. Despite the haughty-sounding moniker, Wealthy Avenue's name comes from something much more humble: apples. Wealthy is a variety of apple (developed around 1860), and the land near Wealthy Avenue used to be an orchard. Other streets—Apple and Baldwin (another varietal)—also reflect the apple's legacy in Middletown.

DID YOU KNOW?

Deep Water, New Jersey, is the birthplace of Teflon—a substance known to fans of non-stick pans everywhere. While working at the DuPont lab in Deep Water, Roy J. Plunkett was trying to synthesize new refrigerator coolants when he stumbled upon this white slippery substance (formally known as polytetrafluoroethane) in 1938. Plunkett went on to invent many other things for DuPont, but Teflon was his most famous achievement.

Atlantic City's Own Miss America

Still reigning after all these years, Miss America continues to be Atlantic City's tribute to the bathing beauty. Sure she's smart, talented, pretty, and socially conscious, but maybe her best assets are her ability to go with the flow and change with the times.

There she is, Miss America." For a quarter of a century host Bert Parks sang that song while a newly chosen Miss America walked down the runway. The song, a crown, and tears of happiness are all part of the pageant, which has been loved, protested, mocked, and imitated for more than 80 years. Miss America may be an American institution, but she's a Jersey Girl by birth. The pageant got started in Atlantic City, where it was invented to sell hotel rooms, hot dogs, and salt water taffy.

A Good Gimmick

New Jersey's beautiful beaches and brisk sea air have always brought visitors from all over the world to the Atlantic City Boardwalk—in the summer. But profits fell off in the autumn, so in 1921 the Businessmen's League of Atlantic City came up with a gimmick to bring crowds in after Labor Day: beautiful girls in a bathing beauty contest!

From the beginning the contest was popular. In the first week of September Atlantic City held a competition for girls from different cities for a crowd of about 100,000. By 1925 Atlantic City's pageant was receiving radio coverage. In the 1940s millions of moviegoers watched Miss America crowned in newsreels at the movies. Miss America might have started as a local promotion, but by the mid-1950s she had become a national phenomenon, with every state in the Union represented by lovely contestants who were watched by millions on TV. Today the contest is the fourth longest-running live broadcast event on television. So how has Miss America managed to stay around for so long?

Making "Judge"ments

One secret of the pageant's success has been its ability to change the rules to emphasize talents other than looking good in a swimsuit:

- Newspaper organizations picked the contestants in the early days; they sponsored photographic popularity contests and sent the winners to Atlantic City. Today contestants compete in a network of state and local competitions before they can qualify for Miss America.

- In 1935, as a way to improve the pageant's public image, the pageant added a talent segment to the competition. Some of the more interesting "talents" included trampoline bouncing and trained pigeon acts.

- In 1947 scholarships became a big part of the pageant. To show that beauties could be brainy, an official fourth category called Intellect and Personality (based on judges' interviews) was added.

- 1989 was the first year of Miss America's "official platform," when each contestant was required to offer a commitment to service on an important social issue, such as increasing literacy, raising awareness of diabetes, and bringing attention to the problems of homeless veterans.

Prizes! Prizes! Prizes!

As the contest got bigger, so did the prizes:

- Margaret Gorman, the first pageant winner, took home $100 and a golden mermaid statue in 1921.

- In 1925 Fay Lanphier won a starring role in a Hollywood film from Paramount Pictures, *The American Venus*, which featured the pageant as a backdrop. Unfortunately *Venus* flopped at the box office.

- In 1926 Norma Smallwood shrewdly used her status as Miss America to make $100,000 in appearance fees, making her income higher than either that of Babe Ruth or United States president Calvin Coolidge.

- Winners in the 1930s were offered Hollywood screen tests. Contestant Dorothy Lamour (1935) made it to the silver screen in Bing Crosby and Bob Hope's *Road to* . . . film series.

- In 1945 Bess Myerson received the first scholarship award of $5,000. Sixty years later, in 2005, winner Deidre Downs received $56,000 in scholarship money.

Scandalous

But interestingly enough, scandals have plagued the contest since the early days. Luckily, the contest has always bounced back:

- In 1925 Howard Christy, a contest judge, unveiled a nude statue of Fay Lanphier, the current Miss America. He called his work, *Miss America 1925*. Christy later admitted Lanphier never posed for him, but the public remained shocked.

- When Pittsburgh's Henrietta Leaver won the pageant in 1935, Pittsburgh sculptor Frank Vittor unveiled a nude statue that he had created of her. Henrietta insisted that she wore a swimsuit to model for the statue, and besides, her grandmother was with her when she posed . . . but the press went wild.

- There was more excitement in 1937 when the newly crowned Miss America, Bette Cooper (from New Jersey), disappeared with her male chaperone in the middle of the night. Romantic rumors flew during a statewide police search. Actually Cooper had decided to give up the beauty queen life, and her chaperone had taken her home.

- The 1950 winner, Yolande Betbeze, declared she was no "pinup" and refused to wear bathing suits at appearances. The offended sponsor, Catalina swimwear, left the pageant and founded the Miss USA and Miss Universe contests.

- The talent contest took on a more adult tone when Mary Ann Mobley performed a mock striptease in 1959. She wore a gown, sang the start of an aria, and then did a "wholesome" striptease down to a pair of shorts and a slip, while grinding out "There'll Be Some Changes Made." She won, but "wholesome stripping" was later banned from the contest.

- In July 1984 nude photos surfaced of the winner Vanessa Williams. They were published in *Penthouse* magazine, and the pageant forced Williams to resign. The crown and title went to the runner-up, Miss New Jersey's Suzette Charles, who became the second African-American and the second Miss New Jersey to wear the crown.

There She Is . . .

From a seaside gimmick to the leading provider of college scholarships to women, Miss America has shown a remarkable amount of flexibility. The contest's ability to adapt to the changing times and weather the shocking scandals means that it will be making its home in Atlantic City for a long time to come.

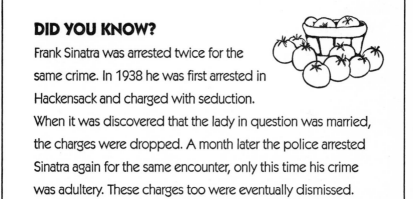

DID YOU KNOW?

Frank Sinatra was arrested twice for the same crime. In 1938 he was first arrested in Hackensack and charged with seduction. When it was discovered that the lady in question was married, the charges were dropped. A month later the police arrested Sinatra again for the same encounter, only this time his crime was adultery. These charges too were eventually dismissed.

Amazing Amber

Leave the "Tea" in Texas. California, keep your gold. Jersey's got its own underground treasure.

Translucent and mysterious, amber has been greatly valued as a precious gem since ancient times. Phoenicians roamed the seas to obtain it. The Romans considered it as valuable as gold. Folks in the Middle Ages sought its powers to fend off evil and black magic. But luckily for New Jerseyans, they've got an amber supply all their own in Sayreville in Middlesex County. But the jewelers are going to have to fight off the paleontologists to get their hands on these precious gems.

Interesting Inclusions

So why would scientists spend their time combing the Garden State for amber? Not surprisingly, the reasons behind their amber desire are more academic than materialistic. Because of how it is formed, amber droplets can hold a wealth of information that interests today's scientists studying the past. Amber starts out as a resin, the sticky stuff that a tree exudes to protect itself when it's injured or invaded by insects. When exposed to the air, tree resin usually dries out and crumbles. If the resin is protected from oxygen (like if it its buried under clay and silt), it will, over millions of years, fossilize into amber.

Before it hardens, the sticky resin sometimes traps bits from its environment. Feathers, animal hairs, plants, and insects become fossilized along with the resin. Called inclusions, these remnants of life on ancient earth, so fragile that they might not leave a fossil trace, are perfectly preserved inside bulbs of amber. Everything from flower pollen to the tiny hairs on insects can be seen just as it appeared millions of years ago.

Fast forward to the 1800s, when clay was mined in Sayreville. Large pits were dug to harvest the clay, and amber was found. But serious interest in Sayreville's amber didn't take off until the early 1990s, when a fossil hunter dug into an abandoned pit and discovered amber that held an ancient insect. Since that time New Jersey has proved to be a gold (better make that an *amber*) mine for science.

Science Goes Buggy

What makes New Jersey's amber so special? Its age. Most amber found today, like that in the Baltic or the Dominican Republic, was formed 30 to 50 million years ago during the Tertiary period, after dinosaurs had become extinct. Only a few places on Earth have amber from before that time—and one of those few is Sayreville. While New Jersey doesn't have the largest deposits of amber in the United States, it has the only substantial North American deposits that date back to the Cretaceous period, 65 to 135 million years ago.

During the Cretaceous period dinosaurs were still around, and flowering plants and modern insects began to emerge. Sayreville's amber and its inclusions contain perfectly preserved specimens of life from that time. David Grimaldi, curator and chairman of entomology at the American Museum of Natural

History, has found New Jersey amber with inclusions that date back as far as 95 million years. He and other paleontologists have discovered more than 100 species of insects and plants trapped inside the petrified resin. Sayreville's amber has housed the world's oldest

- Ant—the first proof that ants lived during the age of dinosaurs.

- Mosquito with a mouth tough enough to bite a dinosaur!

- Mushroom, *Archaeomarasmius leggetti*. It's 90 to 94 million years old.

- Bee—*Trigona prisca*—that flew for the last time about 65 to 80 million years ago.

Do You Dig Amber?

For anyone interested in seeing the amber up close, there are two options. First, the American Museum of Natural History in New York City has some of these specimens on display. Looking for a more hands-on experience? Then check out Kennedy Park, located near Sayreville, where there are sand pits that still hold bits of amber just waiting to be discovered. (Remember, adventurers, be sure to heed all posted signs and don't trespass!)

Amuse Yourself!

Jersey's chock-full of family fun and a wide variety of amusement parks!

Don't feel like schlepping all the way to Disneyland this year? No worries, since New Jersey has plenty of homegrown attractions for the kiddies—and adults, too.

Fairy Tales Can Come True

STORYBOOK LAND, EGG HARBOR TOWNSHIP

Storybook Land has been entertaining kids with rides for over 50 years. Owned and run by the Fricano family for three generations, this is the place where kids can have a tea party with Alice, take a ride on Bubbles the Dragon Coaster, and spend Christmas in July with Santa. Storybook Land is located in Egg Harbor Township, just 10 miles west of Atlantic City.

A City Running Wild

WILD WEST CITY, NETCONG

New Jersey's own version of the West can be found in Netcong, where Wild West City has been running wild since 1957. Owned and operated by the Stabile family, Wild West City is a living, breathing replica of an old Western town that features 22 live shows a day! Visitors can pan for gold, participate in a stagecoach holdup, or just play some mini-golf.

A World of Pure Imagination

THE LAND OF MAKE BELIEVE, HOPE

This Jersey treasure has been entertaining families for more than 50 years. Founder Hermann Maier purchased a former dairy farm to design the first park where parents could participate in the fun alongside their kids. Still run by the Maier family today, the park blends new and old attractions: Colonel Corn, the talking scarecrow, still chats with visitors, who can ride the Red Baron airplane ride or be the stars of the show at the Middle Earth Theater.

Farms in Space?

SPACE FARMS ZOO & MUSEUM, SUSSEX

Space Farms isn't named in honor of upper-atmosphere agriculture. It's named for founders Ralph and Elizabeth Space, who turned their gas station and general store into a museum and zoo that houses more than 500 animals. The Space Museum also features a large collection of Americana—check out the antique toy barn, the doll museum, the car barn, and the ever-popular farm tool collection.

DID YOU KNOW?

The world's largest bear, Goliath, used to live at Space Farms. Standing 12 feet tall and weighing over a ton, Goliath was the biggest Kodiak bear ever. He died in 1991, but Space Farms stuffed the bear, so people can still see him today.

The Lindbergh Baby
Part II: The Trial of the Century

Inside the courthouse in Flemington, New Jersey, the jury was selected while a grieving father and the accused murderer sat close enough to touch each another. Forget O. J. Simpson. In New Jersey, the Trial of the (20th) Century will always be the Lindbergh trial.

The Trial Begins

On January 2, 1935, the trial began and residents of Flemington realized that a media circus was in town. Celebrities such as comedian Jack Benny, novelists like Damon Runyon, and influential journalists such as Walter Winchell were among 60,000 spectators. State troopers had to form a human chain to protect the courthouse. Street vendors hawked souvenirs—everything from forged autographs of Charles Lindbergh Sr. to phony locks of hair supposedly from little Charlie's head.

Making a Case

New Jersey's attorney general David T. Wilentz was a confident, dapper man known to be fond of a good cigar. The prosecutor Wilentz made the case that greed was the motive for the crime; Hauptmann had lost a significant amount of money in the stock market and kidnapped the baby for the sizable ransom the wealthy Lindberghs could pay. He used a homemade ladder to break into the Lindbergh home, took the baby, and left behind a ransom demand. Wilentz asserted that Hauptmann killed little Charlie in his crib so he wouldn't cry out, though admitted the baby could have died from a fall when the ladder broke as the kidnapper fled. After the baby's death, Hauptmann buried the body in nearby woods on the side of the road.

Colorful Edward "Big Ed" Reilly was the defense attorney, dramatic in his striped trousers and rumored to be overly fond of martinis. He had a different version of events. Paid by the Hearst newspapers, the highly successful attorney made the case that Hauptmann was home with his wife, Anna, on March 1, 1932. The kidnapping was actually a conspiracy between Hauptmann's shadowy business partner, furrier Isidor Fisch, and someone on Lindbergh's staff.

Witness for the Prosecution

The prosecution's strong case rested on a few things:

- **Hauptmann's Criminal Record:** In Germany, Hauptmann had served time for burglary. In one of his crimes he had used a ladder.

- **Clues in Hauptmann's Garage:** The Lindbergh bills were found there. The ladder used in the kidnapping was partly constructed from a beam in the garage attic. Jafsie's phone number was also written inside a closet.

- **Ransom Notes:** Handwriting experts testified that samples of Hauptmann's writing matched the writing on ransom notes— including one in the nursery. Hauptmann's private papers also revealed some of the same grammar mistakes and misspelled words that the kidnapper used.

- **Witnesses:** A taxi driver and Jafsie had both seen Cemetery John. Lindbergh had heard his voice. All three testified that Hauptmann was Cemetery John.

- **Money:** At the same time that Cemetery John picked up his money, Hauptmann quit working as a carpenter and started living off "stock investments."

Sowing Reasonable Doubt

The defense argued that Hauptmann was the wrong man for the following reasons:

- **Planted Evidence:** The defense attacked police, claiming that police had written Jafsie's phone number on the garage wall and stolen the board from Hauptmann's garage to claim it was part of the kidnapper's ladder.

- **Police Intimidation:** Hauptmann was roughed up by police and forced to imitate the handwriting on the ransom notes for the prosecution's handwriting experts.

- **It Was an Inside Job:** Hauptmann wouldn't know how to pick out the nursery window at Hopewell, a huge house with 20 rooms. And he couldn't know that the Lindbergh baby would be at Hopewell since the family usually spent weekdays in Englewood. And Lindbergh's dog never barked—as it surely would have if a stranger were on the grounds.

- **The Kidnapper Was Fisch:** Isidor Fisch, a German immigrant, became Hauptmann's friend and business partner in 1932. The pair agreed to equally split the profits of Hauptmann's stock investments and Fisch's fur business. According to the defense, Fisch left for Germany in 1933 and gave Hauptmann "papers" in a shoe box for safekeeping. Hauptmann discovered that the box was actually full of (the ransom) money. Since Fisch owed him money, Hauptmann kept and spent it. The defense claimed Fisch conspired with Violet Sharpe and other members of the Lindberghs' staff to kidnap the baby. Fisch died in Germany in 1934, so he couldn't deny the accusation.

- **Hauptmann's Alibi:** Anna Hauptmann testified that she'd been with her husband the night of the kidnapping.

A Rush to Judgment?

Historians agree that the Lindbergh trial went better for the prosecution than the defense. Some on the jury took Reilly's flamboyant manner for arrogance. The defense brought in witnesses that had credibility problems. And a decision to have Hauptmann testify in his own defense backfired when he failed to convince jurors there were reasonable explanations for the ransom money found in his garage. (Reporters and Wilentz called Hauptmann's explanation a "Fisch story.") Hauptmann's testimony allowed the prosecution to admit evidence of his character, including his crimes in Germany.

The jury took only 11 hours to declare Hauptmann guilty. The prisoner was taken to the New Jersey State Prison in Trenton, where he was executed in the electric chair on April 3, 1936.

Is the Jury Still Out?

Though prosecution and defense have long since rested their

cases, history never rested. Hauptmann never confessed even though he was told it was his best chance to avoid the death penalty. A newspaper promised to give Hauptmann's family $75,000 in return for details of the kidnapping. Yet Hauptmann still insisted on his innocence. The Lindbergh family, however, believed that at the trial justice was served.

Months before Hauptmann's execution, Lindbergh took his family and left the country to live in seclusion in England. Meanwhile Anna Hauptmann campaigned tirelessly to clear her husband's name. Many began to believe her. Books and movies appeared arguing that police had in fact manufactured evidence against Hauptmann and that the baby was killed either by someone on the staff or even in the family. One revisionist theory claims Lindbergh himself accidentally killed the baby. To this day authors, historians, and crime buffs continue to debate the verdict in Flemington's Trial of the Century.

The Scene of the Crime

The Lindberghs deserted their beautiful Hopewell estate, donating it to New Jersey. Today their airstrip is woodland again. The estate, including the house, is now the Albert Elias Residential Group Center, a residential home for juveniles. Visitors still occasionally arrive to view the window that once looked in on the Lindbergh nursery. For those interested in a different kind of memorabilia, the kidnapper's ladder and the long-retired electric chair that executed Hauptmann are on display at the New Jersey State Police Museum in Ewing.

Turn to page 279 for more information on Flemington's role in the Lindbergh trial.

The Bride of Rotten Tomatoes

Even more of the worst Jersey jokes around

Can't get enough of lame humor at the Garden State's expense? Here are more Rotten Tomatoes.

New Jersey and Driving: Perfect Together

FAILED STATE MOTTO: "New Jersey: A Turnpike Runs Through It."

ANOTHER FAILED STATE MOTTO: "New Jersey: Not Pumping Our Own Gas Since 1949."

Scientists at the New Jersey Insurance News Service have determined that 50 percent of the state's drivers have road rage. It is not known whether this condition is caused by a defective gene or by New Jersey itself.

More Garden State Groaners

The New Jersey state bird is the Eastern goldfinch—the only bird that lives out of state and commutes.

What did Delaware? Her New Jersey.

What Exit?

According to a popular joke, if you ask a Jerseyan where they live, they don't tell you the town name. They tell you the exit number. But the Garden State Parkway is so much more than a series of lanes and exit numbers.

The Garden State Parkway (just called the Parkway by locals) may have gotten a bad rap. Like its sister highway, the New Jersey Turnpike, the Parkway was designed with the most modern highway innovations in mind in order to be the smoothest ride in the state. When it first opened, it was called the Parkway with a Heart and was supposed to make life easier.

All Points South

After World War II, New Jersey's roads were clogged with cars trying to get from New York City down to the resorts on the Shore—the spot for weekend getaways from the city. The state legislature decided in 1945 to build a superhighway to ease some of the congestion. They were planning to pay for it in tax dollars, but in the next five years, they only managed to build 18 miles of road. And those miles weren't even connected! Something had to be done to speed things up and bring in more funds for the project.

The brilliant solution the legislators devised was tolls. Using the New Jersey Turnpike as an example, the legislators would issue bonds to pay for the construction. Payments on interest and the principal would then be covered by the tolls. With the new plan of a self-sustaining toll road, they were able to finance the construction with more than $300 million of government bonds. In less than three years the Garden State Parkway was ready for business.

Vital Stats

The Parkway officially opened on July 1, 1955, when Governor Robert Meyner paid the first toll at the Paramus toll plaza. The Parkway's first chief engineer, Harold Giffin (inventor of the traffic circle, the cloverleaf, and the reflecting curb), featured his innovation, the "singing shoulder," on the Parkway (they're better known as rumble strips, the grooves on the shoulder that rattle your car when you drift out of your lane). The road was built for safety, comfort, and speed—an important feature for tourists who can't wait to get to the beach. The Parkway now stretches from Cape May, Jersey's southernmost point, up the shore 173 miles to the New York border, where it connects with the New York Thruway.

On its most congested stretch, the Garden State Parkway hosts 200,000 vehicles a day. When it was built, the Parkway had four lanes in most places. But as traffic congestion worsened, the government added a lane by building onto the shoulder and shaving a foot or so off existing lanes. This makes driving the Parkway a white-knuckle experience for most out-of-staters. It's a good thing no trucks are allowed, or it might get truly scary. The roadway curves gradually back and forth on its entire length, whether it has to or not. This design is to prevent drivers from being lulled to sleep by the monotony of a straight road. If you drive it end to end in a car, you'll fork over $3.85 at 11 toll booths: $0.35 each as of this writing.

Taking Its Toll

Unlike most toll roads where you pay at the on-ramp or exit ramp, on the Parkway there are tollbooths plopped in the middle of the road, in some places as little as six miles apart. These barrier tolls cause traffic jams as far as the eye can see, especially during rush hour. Why would anyone design a road with inherent traffic jams? For the drivers' benefit, of course. According to the designers of the road, "One criticism of today's expressways is the tedium and hypertension they create within the driver. A short 'break' en route . . . relieves the monotony." That's right; those tolls are there to *prevent* road rage.

Unbeknownst to most travelers, the Garden State Parkway toll plazas operate on the honor system. If you don't have enough money when you pass, you can pick up an envelope to mail the toll in later—and nobody takes your license plate number to ensure that you make good. Only 4 percent of these envelopes are ever returned, costing the state $125,000 a year in lost tolls.

It's So E-Z

But there's always the E-ZPass option, which was first used on the Garden State Parkway in December 1999. Using this program, you install a tag in your car. When you pass through a toll plaza, an antenna picks up the tag information and automatically records the toll. This allows drivers to get through a tollbooth without stopping—you can't fault what it's done for traffic.

My Bedroom for a Horse!

One of America's first liberated women came from New Jersey. Her patriotic duty was inspired by her love for her horse.

As legend has it, one of America's first liberated ladies lived on a farm near Morristown's Jockey Hollow, which had been the winter encampment for George Washington's army for several years during the Revolutionary War. Temperance Wick, known as Tempe (rhymes with *Shempy*), was the youngest of five children of Captain Henry Wick. A wealthy farmer and cavalryman, Captain Wick owned 1,400 acres of woods and fields that he gladly let the Continental army use as needed, including Major General Arthur St. Clair in the winter of 1779. Visiting officers would often stay with the Wick family in their large, wood frame home.

Pennsylvania Mutiny

The most popular version of Tempe's story starts out in January 1781, when the Morristown area around the Wick farm was home to the soldiers of the Pennsylvania Line under the command of General "Mad" Anthony Wayne. The men had endured freezing weather, inadequate food, and no wages for more than a year;

frankly, they were getting tired of it. But the men became infuriated when news arrived that new recruits were being given a handsome bounty to sign on while they shivered and starved away with no money to show for it. The soldiers decided to mutiny on New Year's Day. They abandoned their Morristown posts and vowed to return to Pennsylvania to take up their cause.

Horsey Heroine

Born in 1758, Tempe was an accomplished rider and thoroughly familiar with the local countryside. One January morning she was sent out on her large, white steed to fetch medicine for her ailing mother. On the way home Tempe was stopped by a half-dozen of these mutinous Pennsylvania soldiers who demanded she give them her horse. She had no intention of letting them steal it. So while pretending to dismount, she instead slapped the reins and the two of them took off, leaving the startled men behind. One fired a shot in their direction, but the pair was soon out of sight.

With the soldiers in pursuit, Tempe knew that it would be but a matter of time before the men would arrive at her farm. If she took her beloved steed to the barn, they would surely find him and take him. So the quick-thinking Tempe brought the horse to the back door and coaxed him into the house, through the kitchen, and into the guest bedroom. She closed the one small window in the room, plunging it into darkness, and muffled the sound of the horse's hooves with her feather bedding. There the pair would remain until her horse was safe.

Pay No Attention to That Horse Behind the Curtain

The mutinous soldiers soon arrived at the family farm and thoroughly searched the barn and pastures. No horse. They waited for

Tempe and the horse to return, never thinking to look in the house. Eventually they gave up and moved along. How long Tempe and the horse remained inside cannot be verified—some say three days, others say three weeks. Hoof marks were supposedly visible in the house for quite some time after the war had ended. Fact or fiction, the news of Tempe Wick's courageous act spread throughout the colonies, and she is remembered as one of the first Revolutionary War heroines.

Tempe married Captain William Tuttle a few years later, had five children, and lived until 1822. She is buried in her hometown at the Evergreen Cemetery in Morristown. The Wick house was restored to its original condition in 1934 and can be visited today as part of the Morristown National Historic Park.

DID YOU KNOW?

Howard Stern once had a rest area on Route 295 named after him. Fulfilling a campaign promise to Stern, Governor Christine Todd Whitman christened the Springfield Township rest stop in his honor in 1995. A $1,000 plaque commemorated Stern and depicted him peering out from an outhouse. Sadly, the rest stop is no more. It was flushed in 2003 due to budget cuts.

Sinatra's Early Years
True or False?

Before he was Ol' Blue Eyes, before he was the Chairman of the Board, Frank Sinatra was New Jersey's own Francis Albert Sinatra, a skinny kid with a big voice. How much do you know about Frank's Jersey connections? Take this quiz and find out!

True or False? Frank Sinatra is the most famous son of Jersey City.
False. And not only false, but a trick question, since Sinatra's original Jersey stomping grounds were in Hoboken. Sinatra was born at 415 Monroe Street, in fact, and was raised in the tenements near the Erie and Lackawanna railroads—the proverbial "wrong side of the tracks." He was the only child of Tony and Dolly Sinatra.

Sinatra and Hoboken didn't always get along. In 1947 Sinatra had tomatoes thrown at him as he participated in a parade in his hometown, and in 1949 he was heckled during a Hoboken performance that his parents were attending. Incensed, Sinatra refused to play in the town again. Legend has it that once, when informed that the airplane he was flying in was over Hoboken, he spat on the floor. His last official visit to the city came in 1985, when he received an honorary doctorate from Stevens Institute of Technology.

By the time Sinatra died, the hard feelings seemed to have

faded. Hoboken mayor Anthony Russo said, "Frank Sinatra has become beloved throughout the world. He's a success story from humble beginnings. But the people of Hoboken react to him more because he's our success story."

(*Pssst!* Jersey City citizens, you have a strong Sinatra connection too: The singer was married to his first wife in Jersey City and lived there immediately after. His daughter Nancy was also born in Jersey City.)

True or False? Bing Crosby inspired Frank Sinatra to become a singer.

True. Not personally, of course—it's not like Crosby appeared at Sinatra's door and anointed the young Francis. But in 1933 Sinatra took a trip to Jersey City to see Bing Crosby at the Loews Theatre in Journal Square and was blown away by the older crooner. "After seeing him that night, I knew I had to be a singer," Sinatra said. Shortly thereafter Sinatra began singing in earnest, as part of the Hoboken Four amateur singing group. He then went on to perform as the emcee and singer (and, when not onstage, also worked as a waiter) at the Rustic Cabin Roadhouse in Englewood. (There's a gas station at the site today with a commemorative plaque that honors the Rustic Cabin and Sinatra.)

Sinatra and Crosby would cross professional paths in 1956, in the movie *High Society,* in which they would sing the duet "Well, Did You Evah?"

True or False? Famed trombonist and bandleader Tommy Dorsey gave Sinatra his first big singing gig.

False. That honor belongs to Harry James, the famous trumpeter. In 1939 James had just put together his own big band (he'd recently left Benny Goodman's band) when he heard a radio performance of Sinatra at the Rustic Cabin. James was so impressed that he called Sinatra, auditioned him, and signed him to his band all in one day. Sinatra stayed with James until late 1940, when the Tommy Dorsey band stole Sinatra away from James by offering the singer the princely sum of $125 a week. Sinatra sang and toured with Dorsey through 1942, when he decided to step out on his own.

True or False? Sinatra found himself in a public relations scandal thanks to an appearance at a "tribute" to a mob boss.

True. These days Sinatra's relationships with the Mafia are well known, but in the singer's early years, these stories were scandalous. Probably the most famous mob story from Sinatra's early years involved bandleader Tommy Dorsey. It's alleged that when Sinatra wanted to go solo, Dorsey at first refused to let Sinatra out of his contract. He changed his mind only after New Jersey Mafia boss Willie Moretti had a gun put to his head. Dorsey himself repeatedly denied this version of events (but then, of course, why wouldn't he?). Perhaps it was an offer he couldn't refuse.

DID YOU KNOW?

The first cloverleaf in the United States was built in Woodbridge in 1929. The "Safety Engineered Super Highway Intersection" was built at the crossing of U.S. Route 1 and state Route 35.

Hometowns
Brooklyn, New Jersey?

Located on the shores of the state's biggest lake, Hopatcong made a smart move by changing its name.

The Town: Hopatcong

Location: Sussex County

Founding: Hopatcong was once part of another town, Byram Township; it seceded in 1898 to form the Borough of Brooklyn. The new borough was trying to make a name for itself as a tourist hot spot, but it seemed there might be some confusion with that *other* Brooklyn somewhere in New York. So in 1901 the town renamed itself Hopatcong to tie its fortunes to Lake Hopatcong, the state's biggest lake and tourist attraction. The gamble worked. Hopatcong became a popular resort town.

Current Population: 16,000 (est.)

Size: 12.29 square miles

What's in a Name? Hopatcong is believed to come from the Lenape word *hapakonoesson*. Scholars aren't sure if the Lenape used the word to refer to pipestone, a soft stone found in the area, or the jagged shape of Lake Hopatcong itself.

Claims to Fame

- Lake Hopatcong, the largest lake in the state, is located along the northwest side of the town. The lake holds 7½ billion gallons of water and is 58 feet deep.

- Prolific scientist and inventor Hudson Maxim lived in Hopatcong. He is best known for the invention of maximite, an explosive 50 percent more powerful than dynamite (it was used in naval guns). Thomas Edison called him "the most versatile man in America."

- The rich and famous of the early 20th century vacationed at Hopatcong—and the talented and funny came to entertain them. These superstars included Bert Lahr, Milton Berle, and Jerseyan Bud Abbott.

- You don't always have to head north for some good ice fishing. Lake Hopatcong first became a popular spot for ice fishing in the 1950s and 1960s. If it's not a mild winter, the best time to go is early January, when the ice starts to get at least 4–6 inches thick.

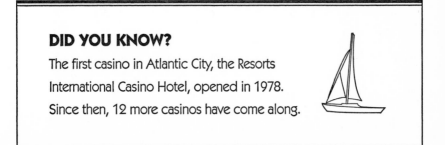

DID YOU KNOW?

The first casino in Atlantic City, the Resorts International Casino Hotel, opened in 1978. Since then, 12 more casinos have come along.

Oh, the Urbanity!

New Jersey was nicknamed the Garden State in the 1800s because of its lush greenery. But today, it's one of the most urban states ever. Which begs the question: How urban is it?

Shoulder to Shoulder

New Jersey is the most densely populated state in the country, packing in more than 1,000 people per square mile. That's greater than 10 times the national average! By comparison, New York has just over 400 people per square mile, California has 217, and Wyoming a lonely 5.1. It shouldn't come as any surprise, since the Garden State is such a great place to live. Don't believe us? Then just read on.

Thick with City Slickers

If you live in New Jersey, you probably live in a city. Sure, you can foxhunt in Sussex County or fly-fish the Musconetcong River. But around 90 percent of New Jersey residents live in an urban area, and every single county in the state is classified as a metropolitan area by the U.S. Census Bureau. Jersey is the only state with that distinction.

Going Mobile

New Jersey also has more vehicles per mile of roadway than any other state. Its central location between New York City and Philadelphia led to the development of the oldest and most heavily used transportation system in the nation.

Sporting Big-City Bucks

So there are a lot of people, a lot of cars, and a lot of money. New Jersey has the highest per capita income in the United States, an average of more than $27,000, as opposed to a national average of around $21,500. And median household income is more than $55,000 compared to the national average of a little more than $40,000. New Jersey also has less poverty and lower unemployment than the nation's average.

The Arts and Culture

Forget for a moment that New Jersey is a short drive from out-of-state attractions like Broadway and the Museum of Modern Art. New Jersey itself has hundreds of world-class arts organizations in every discipline—such as the New Jersey Theatre Alliance, Dance New Jersey, the New Jersey Chamber Music Society, the Newark Museum, and the Montclair Art Museum. The New Jersey Performing Arts Center, first opened in 1997 in Newark, has been praised as one of the world's greatest concert halls.

Crime, Mostly Disorganized

It's not that more criminals live here; it's just that more people in general live here. Although Camden was recently named the most dangerous city in the nation, Brick Township was rated the second safest in United States (two other Jersey townships, Dover and Hamilton, made the top 25 safe list). New Jersey gets a bum rap when it comes to outside perceptions about crime. In fact, the state's overall crime rate has been dropping according to the latest government reports.

Resident Diversity

New Jersey has been a true American melting pot since before World War II, when it was the immigration hot spot for Italian, African, Russian, German, Irish, Polish, Hungarian, Cuban, and Puerto Rican people. Even today, New Jersey residents are almost 20 percent foreign born.

High Technology

Jersey's been a high-tech haven since the days of Thomas Edison. Today, the state's second largest moneymaker is electronics manufacturing, with a high-tech payroll of over $12 billion. The New Jersey Commission on Science and Technology pumps $60 million a year into special Innovation Zones to help get tech businesses off the ground and to assist in research. New Jersey ranks as the state with the second highest concentration of broadband Internet connections, and 90 percent of public school classrooms in Jersey are online.

Perfect Together

So it looks like New Jersey has gotten a bad rap after all. But perhaps its reputation for smoke stacks and toxic waste is just a smokescreen to keep all the Jersey goodness to itself. But with so many new citizens moving in, it doesn't look like the bluff is working.

Family Secrets

You might think the cast of The Sopranos—the popular HBO series about a Mafia family based in New Jersey—has to be "connected." Their convincing portrayals feel so accurate and real that these actors and actresses must have had shady pasts themselves. Well, for the most part, it's just not so. Check out these very civilian facts about the cast members.

James Gandolfini (Tony Soprano)

In the show, Tony Soprano's not what you'd call book smart, but the man who plays him is. James Gandolfini holds a Communications degree from Rutgers University; he first got his big break on Broadway, costarring in *A Streetcar Named Desire* alongside Jessica Lange and Alec Baldwin in 1992. But don't take Gandolfini's talent for the arts to mean he's not a tough guy. Before he made it big on Broadway, he worked as a bouncer in both New Jersey and New York. In the series, his sister is a flaky, unstable murderer. In real life, Gandolfini's sister is an official in the New Jersey court system.

Edie Falco (Carmela Soprano)

On TV, her character forsook a career to assume her role as the First Lady of the New Jersey mob. Carmela lives a comfortable middle-class, if not tormented, suburban life as an unhappy housewife with ungrateful kids. In real life, Brooklyn-born Falco graduated from the State University of New York (SUNY) and has tread the boards in both Broadway and London. She racks up prestigious acting awards like bullet casings outside the Bada Bing. In fact she's the only actress ever to receive an Emmy, Golden Globe, and Screen Actors Guild Award for the same role in the same year.

Dominic Chianese (Corrado "Uncle Junior" Soprano)

Chianese plays Tony's uncle, who's had a successful—yet thoroughly illegitimate—local Mafia career. In the real world, Chianese has been a prolific actor since the 1950s, with a long list of Broadway and film credits, including Gilbert and Sullivan's *The Mikado*. *The Sopranos* isn't his first brush with the mob either— Chianese played Johnny Ola in *The Godfather: Part II*. Not limiting himself to acting, Chianese also moonlights as a musician; he released two CDs, *Hits* and *Ungrateful Heart*, and still performs live. Fans can catch him playing guitar at Sofia's in New York City every Monday night.

Steven Van Zandt (Silvio Dante)

On the show, as Silvio Dante, Steven Van Zandt owns the Bada Bing nightclub. Dante is a failed lounge singer who now manages strippers and serves as Tony's level-headed *consigliere* (that's an *adviser* for you civilians). He keeps a low profile, focusing the gang on profit rather than pride. But in real life, Van Zandt is all about high profile. He plays guitar for Bruce Springsteen & the E Street Band. He's an accomplished record producer and songwriter. And now "Little Steven" Van Zandt is one of the hottest radio DJs on the air, specializing in garage rock.

Tony Sirico (Paulie Walnuts)

On the show, Sirico plays a tough hothead with a long criminal history that includes hard jail time, violence against authorities, and the illegal use of firearms. As a young man in real life Sirico was a tough mob-connected hothead with a long criminal history that included hard jail time (in Sing Sing), violence against authorities (running a police car off the road), and the illegal use of firearms (he always carried a pistol). But acting changed his life. These days he's a new man; hardworking and respected, Sirico only plays criminals on TV. He's been in dozens of (gangster) movies and is an active supporter of the New Jersey Republican Party.

Federico Castelluccio (Furio Giunta)

On screen, Castelluccio played brutal mobster Furio, a recruited strongman from Naples. Like his character, Castelluccio was also born in Naples, but that's about all they have in common. Castelluccio's parents moved to Paterson, New Jersey, when he was three, and throughout childhood he knew the arts were his calling. He became a brilliant painter—eventually winning a full scholarship to New York's School of Visual Arts, where he received a BFA in Painting and Media Arts. His works hang in several renowned galleries. In the 1980s he took up acting and learned from top teachers. But acting has not replaced his desire to paint—it looks like it's inspired him! In 2002 he painted a portrait of characters Tony and Carmela Soprano, entitled *The Duke and Duchess of North Caldwell.*

Joe Pantoliano (Ralph Cifaretto)

Pantoliano played Ralph Cifaretto—a man who could really

only connect on a personal level if he were holding a Louisville Slugger or some brass knuckles. But in real life, Pantoliano's ability to connect with audiences on stage and screen has made him a Hollywood heavy hitter. A native of Hoboken, he made his first mark off-Broadway in a traveling production of *One Flew Over the Cuckoo's Nest.* His talent and hard work led to dozens of new projects—and eventually to the big screen, where he's starred in movies such as *The Fugitive, The Matrix, Midnight Run, Empire of the Sun,* and *Risky Business.*

Michael Imperioli (Christopher Moltisanti)

On the show, Imperioli plays Tony Soprano's nephew, who's been groomed by the boss to become a "made man." In real life, Imperioli had no boss to pave the way. To become a successful actor and writer, he first had to wait tables, work as a messenger, and work as a telemarketer. All these odd jobs helped make ends meet before his big break, which you may remember from *Goodfellas.* Imperioli played Spider, who was shot in the foot by Tommy DeVito (Joe Pesci). In an homage to Imperioli's earlier part, Christopher shoots a guy in the foot on a *Sopranos* episode.

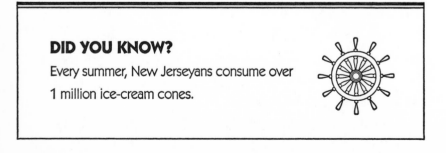

DID YOU KNOW?
Every summer, New Jerseyans consume over 1 million ice-cream cones.

The Wizard of Menlo Park
A Pop Quiz

Think you know all there is to know about Thomas Alva Edison, the most prolific inventor of the late 19th and early 20th centuries (if not of all time) and one of New Jersey's greatest citizens? Care to test that theory?

Getting Personal

1. *True or False?* Thomas Edison was born in New Jersey.
2. *True or False?* Thomas Edison's Canadian father, Samuel Edison, participated in a rebellion against the Ontario government.
3. *True or False?* In Thomas Edison's youth, family and friends called him Tom.
4. *True or False?* Edison had three wives.

EXTRA CREDIT

5. Edison's nickname for his son Thomas Alva Jr. was:
   A. Tom
   B. Junior
   C. Al
   D. Dash
   E. Buster

A Park by Any Other Name?

6. *True or False?* Menlo Park is a city in New Jersey.

7. *True or False?* To honor Edison's invention factory, Henry Ford relocated the entire original Menlo Park facility to Dearborn, Michigan, in the 1920s.

8. *True or False?* The Menlo Park Museum is located in Edison, New Jersey.

9. *True or False?* After Edison's team abandoned the Menlo Park Lab in 1884, it was used as a chicken farm.

EXTRA CREDIT

10. At Menlo Park, Edison and his team of inventors:
    A. Invented the Mimeograph machine
    B. Invented the phonograph
    C. Improved wax paper
    D. All of the above
    E. None of the above

Here a Patent, There a Patent

11. *True or False?* Thomas Edison had his name on more than 1,000 patents.

12. *True or False?* Edison's first patented invention was an electrographic vote recorder.

13. *True or False?* Edison filed for his first patent at age 21 and his last patent at age 42.

EXTRA CREDIT

14. Which of the following were among Edison's successful patents:
    A. Fruit preserving process

B. Magnetic ore-separator

C. Cement kiln

D. All the above

E. None of the above

Leading the Way

15. *True or False?* Edison invented the incandescent light bulb.

16. *True or False?* "Mary had a little lamb" were the first recorded words by Edison.

17. *True or False?* The first motion picture studio was built by Edison in Los Angeles, California.

18. *True or False?* The first copyrighted motion picture produced at Edison's studio is of a man sneezing.

19. *True or False?* Edison also invented a way to make houses entirely of concrete.

EXTRA CREDIT

20. Edison's addition of a carbon transmitter to the telephone made voices sound clearer. Which of the following greetings did Edison favor when answering the telephone?

A. Hello

B. Ahoy, Ahoy

C. Hey, Toots

D. What is the wish?

E. Greetings

Turn to page 318 for the answers.

State Dinosaur
Hadrosaurus Foulkii

"Enacted by the Senate and General Assembly of the State of New Jersey on June 13, 1991."

It's a little-known fact that the first nearly complete dinosaur skeleton was found in little old New Jersey in 1858. You could say that Jersey is the birthplace of dinomania (or vertebrate paleontology, if you were feeling bookish).

Duck-Billed Dino

Eighty million years ago, New Jersey and eastern Pennsylvania were home to the mighty Hadrosaurus. These duck-billed dinosaurs grew to approximately 10 feet tall, measured about 25 feet long, weighed from 6 to 8 tons, and dined on plants. One particular Hadrosaurus found his way to what is now Haddonfield, New Jersey, where his body came to be buried under lots and lots of marl, the perfect substance for preserving dinosaurs.

Hadrosaurus Hunting

In 1858 William Parker Foulke, a member of the Academy of Natural Sciences, spent a summer in Haddonfield. Twenty years earlier, local farmer John Hopkins had made news after uncovering some unusually large bones in a marl pit. Hopkins and his workers had no idea what they had stumbled on. They treated the bones like, well, bones, and gave them away to be used as doorstops and window jams. When Foulke heard about the 20-year-old discovery of the giant bones, he put together his own team to do some digging around in the area.

Foulke's team soon hit pay dirt—a big bone bonanza. They unearthed 49 bones and teeth that turned out to be the very first nearly complete dinosaur skeleton. For the first time, scientists could get a good look at what a whole dinosaur would look like (minus the skin and muscles, of course). Foulke knew it was time to call in the big guns; he contacted Dr. Joseph Leidy, a renowned vertebrate paleontologist and professor at the University of Pennsylvania, as well as a fellow member of the Academy of Natural Sciences. Astounded by the creature's structural similarity to both lizards and birds, Leidy immediately recognized it as a dinosaur and christened it *Hadrosaurus foulkii*, or "Foulke's bulky lizard." Thanks to Foulke and Leidy, scientists had the hard evidence they needed to prove the existence of dinosaurs. It was the breakthrough they had been looking for.

In 1868 the bones were the first to be mounted and put on public display at the Academy of Natural Sciences of Philadelphia, where they've been ever since. A mounted version made from plaster casts of the original bones can still be seen.

Making It Official

In 1988 students at Strawbridge Elementary School in Westmont (near Haddonfield) led the charge to make the Hadrosaurus the official dinosaur of New Jersey. It took three years of wrangling, but the students' efforts paid off in 1991, when the dinosaur was officially adopted by New Jersey. In 1994 the National Park Service designated the discovery site as a National Historic Landmark. Haddonfield itself has honored its ancient resident as well; it now has a Hadrosaurus Park, where Hadrosaurus Run courses through it. To top it all off, in 2003 the town erected a life-sized bronze statue of the terrible lizard, nicknamed Haddie.

DID YOU KNOW?

When thinking of Thoroughbred horse racing, make sure you consider your old New Jersey home. Why? Because two of the oldest races in the United States got their start right here—namely, the Derby and the Oaks. The Jersey Derby was the very first stakes race for three-year-old horses run in the United States. The event drew a crowd of 10,000 when it premiered in 1864. The Monmouth Breeders' Cup Oaks, a stakes race for three-year-old fillies, has been run for over 80 years; it's the oldest Oaks in the country. Both events now are held at Monmouth Park in Oceanport. Horses race there from May through September.

Are You There, New Jersey? It's Me, Judy.

Since 1969 Elizabeth-born Judy Blume has been the patron saint of the Awkward Years, otherwise known as puberty. Anyone who's grown up in America in the last 35 years has probably had a Judy Blume book on hand to explain something that parents often felt uneasy discussing.

J udy Blume, born Judy Sussman in Elizabeth in 1938, could have been one of the characters she wrote about in her own books, as she acknowledged in 2004: "I was a small, shy, anxious child with eczema, as fearful as Sheila the Great, as imaginative as Sally J. Freedman." As a girl, she was an avid reader—but not of children's books. The reason: "I never found my kind of reality in children's books. No child was anything like me. No child thought the kinds of things I did, leading me to believe I definitely wasn't normal." But with all that working against her, how did Judy Blume become the undisputed queen of all things preadolescent?

Become a Desperate Housewife

Inwardly normal or not, the young Ms. Sussman was determined to lead a "normal" life. She became Judy Blume in 1959 by getting married (while still in college), and she was a mother by 1961. But by the mid-1960s, the 20-something housewife was going nuts out in the Jersey suburbs. "I adored my children, but inside was an empty space, a gnawing, an ache that I couldn't identify, one that I didn't understand," she said. To fill that empty space, Blume went back to her childhood, resurrected her imagination, and began to write.

Her career didn't start auspiciously—the rejections piled up. One of Blume's earliest rejections was from *Highlights* magazine. The home of such immortal fare as "Goofus and Gallant" informed Blume that her work did "not win in competition with others." After that particular rejection, Blume literally hid in a closet and cried. It was two years before she sold her first book, *The One in the Middle Is the Green Kangaroo,* in 1969.

Be Able to Corner the Market

But it was Blume's third book that began her transformation into America's Muse of Puberty. *Are You There God? It's Me, Margaret.,* published in 1970, featured a girl dealing with both her confusion over religion (she was the result of an interfaith marriage) and her anxiety over being a "late bloomer." Neither subject had been frequently or directly tackled in adolescent fiction; to hit both at the same time made a definite impression.

What *Margaret* did for girls, Blume's *Then Again, Maybe I Won't* did for boys in 1971. Her other books touched on unpopularity, divorce, losing one's virginity, and the overall awkwardness of existence when you're in the space between pigtails and cocktails. Because she wrote in voice that kids could relate to, Judy Blume first cornered the market on adolescent angst.

Be a Target of Censorship

Naturally, all the frank discussion of touchy subjects in these books eventually ran afoul of some adults. One night Blume received a phone call from a woman who asked if she were the author of *Margaret*. When she answered yes, the woman called her a communist and slammed down the phone. "I never did figure out if she equated communism with menstruation or religion," wrote Blume. The principal of her children's elementary school refused to put *Margaret* in the library because he felt the topic was inappropriate, despite the high probability that some of his sixth-grade female students had already personally dealt with the subject at hand.

By the early 1980s, however, Blume's books increasingly became a target for organized censors, who complained her books were inappropriate for children because of language and subject matter. *Margaret* and *Then Again* weren't the only targets: Blume's 1974 book *Blubber*, which featured a girl being mercilessly teased by her classmates, was protested because it didn't show the girl's tormentors being punished. Blume's response was that in real life, sometimes tormentors aren't punished—which was a lesson in itself.

As a result of the push to get her books removed from school libraries, Blume found herself near the top of the list of America's most banned authors—the second most censored, in fact, according to the American Library Association (Alvin Schwartz, of *Scary Stories to Tell in the Dark* fame, is currently first).

Receive the National Book Award

Despite the best efforts of the censors, Blume's 22 books (including three books for adult readers) have sold more than 65 million copies combined. Blume's influence on entire generations of teens and preteens—and her fight against censorship—was enough for the National Book Foundation to present her with an honorary National Book Award in 2004, elevating her into the highest ranks of American letters with previous recipients such as Eudora Welty, Toni Morrison, John Updike, and Philip Roth. For those still not convinced of Ms. Blume's importance, a 1998 article in the *Boston Phoenix* weekly puts it best: "Presumably, puberty would have happened without Judy Blume books, but there's no way to know for sure."

BOOKS BY JUDY BLUME

A short list of some of Judy Blume's famous works.

Books for the Pre-Awkward Years

Tales of a Fourth Grade Nothing (1972)
Otherwise Known as Sheila the Great (1972)
Superfudge (1980)
Fudge-a-Mania (1990)
Double Fudge (2003)

Books for the Awkward Years

Iggie's House (1970)
Are You There God? It's Me, Margaret. (1970)
Then Again, Maybe I Won't (1971)
It's Not the End of the World (1972)
Deenie (1973)
Blubber (1974)
Starring Sally J. Freedman As Herself (1977)

Grease Is the Word

These sandwiches are not for the weak of heart. Literally.

A s any undergraduate can tell you, college life is nothing without good, greasy food. Luckily for Rutgers University students, New Brunswick does not disappoint. This haven for deep-fried food is home of the infamous Grease Trucks located on the corner lot of College Avenue. This collection of mobile sandwich shops help freshman pack on the pounds by devouring their famous fat sandwiches, entire meals shoved into a sub roll. In fact, the Fat Darrell became so well known that it won a major award—it was named *Maxim* magazine's number one sandwich in the United States.

Curious about what's on the menu? Here's just a small sample:

Fat Darrell Chicken Fingers, Mozzarella Sticks, French Fries, Marinara Sauce, Lettuce, Tomato, Onion

Fat Cat Two Cheeseburgers, French Fries, Mayo, Ketchup, Lettuce, Tomato

Fat Elbow Two Cheeseburgers, Cheesesteak, Bacon, Mozzerella Sticks, French Fries, Ketchup

Fat Sam Cheesesteak, Chicken Fingers, French Fries, Mayo, Ketchup, Lettuce, Tomato

Fat Koko Cheesesteak, Mozzarella Sticks, French Fries, Lettuce, Tomato, Onion

Fat Mom Cheesesteak, Bacon, Egg, French Fries, Mayo, Ketchup, Lettuce, Tomato, Onion

Fat Dad Cheesesteak, Gyro Meat, French Fries, White Sauce, Hot Sauce, Ketchup, Lettuce, Tomato, Onion

Fat Va Va Voom Cheesesteak, Bacon, Mozzarella Sticks, French Fries, Marinara Sauce

Fat Romano Cheesesteak, Taylor Ham, Egg, French Fries, Mayo, Lettuce, Tomato

Fat Sal Chicken Fingers, Mozzarella Sticks, Taylor Ham, French Fries, Scrambled Eggs, American Cheese, Lettuce, Tomato

Fat Mouth Chicken Fingers, Jalapeño Poppers, French Fries, Mozzarella Sticks, Mayo, Ketchup, Lettuce, Tomato, Onion

Fat Soprano Chicken Fingers, Bacon, White Sauce, Hot Sauce

Fat Mojo Chicken Fingers, Mozzarella Sticks, Honey Mustard, French Fries

Fat Moon Chicken Fingers, Bacon, Egg, French Fries, Mayo, Ketchup, Lettuce, Tomato, Onion

Fat Elvis Gyro Meat, Mozzarella Sticks, French Fries, White Sauce, Hot Sauce, Lettuce, Tomato, Onion

Meet the Locals

Jersey has a fine collection of well-known people, but the local characters are what give the state its depth, its color, and its charm. Some are famous, some are not so famous, but they're all Jersey originals.

Sam Patch: The Jersey Jumper

Evel Knievel has nothing on 19th-century daredevil Sam Patch. Patch first gained fame in 1827 when he took a flying leap over 77-foot-high Passaic Falls in Paterson. Patch's newfound celebrity convinced him to quit his day job in a cotton mill to devote himself full time to his career as the Jersey Jumper. Patch took his act on the road and jumped off of high places all over the country. In 1829 he became the first person to go over Niagara Falls—without a barrel—and survive. Patch's daring eventually caught up with him later that year, when he died attempting to dive over Genesee Falls in Rochester, New York.

Mark and Mark: The *Weird New Jersey* Guys

Once upon a time, there were two guys named Mark who shared a love for all things weird and wonderful about their state and its offbeat side. They got together and started printing all they could find about New Jersey legends, local characters, and mysterious places. Mark Sceurman and Mark Moran's *Weird New Jersey,* a semiannual magazine, has grown to a circulation of 60,000 and spawned both a Web site and a successful book series. "Weirdness is all around New Jersey," Moran says. "You just have to scratch the surface and it comes oozing out at you." It sounds like they'll have plenty of material for a long time.

Elsie the Cow: A New Jersey Jersey Cow

A Jersey cow named You'll Do Lobelia was christened Borden's first official Elsie in 1939 at the New York World's Fair. The newly dubbed Elsie went on to become one of the world's most famous mascots; she appeared in movies and even toured cross-country in her car, the Cowdillac. Sadly, after being seriously injured in a traffic accident in 1941, the first Elsie returned to her home at the Gordon-Walker Farm in Plainsboro, where she was put to sleep and buried under a headstone that reads, "A Pure Bred Jersey Cow. One of the Great Elsies of Our Time."

Red Mascara: The Would-Be State Song Composer

A New Jersey native who hails from Phillipsburg, 75-year-old Red Mascara penned what almost became the official state song. For over 38 years, Mascara has been fighting to have his bright little song "I'm from New Jersey" officially adopted. He wrote the song back in 1960, after the then governor complained that there was no song to play at official appearances. State senator Wayne Dumont introduced the song for adoption a year later, but it's been hung up in the legislature ever since. In 1972 both houses approved the song, but the sitting governor vetoed the bill. But that hasn't deterred Red Mascara one bit. He still leads the adoption effort every year and trolls the halls of the state-house to hand out candy to senators in the hopes that his song will make it after all.

Floyd Vivino: Who's Your Uncle?

This 54-year-old, Paterson-born Jersey native is a multitalented man: singer, piano player, puppeteer, actor, but best known as the porkpie hat–wearing host of the *Uncle Floyd Show,* New Jersey's longest-running television program. It's been on the air (in various forms and local stations) for more than 30 years. A low-budget collection of skits, gags, puppet co-hosts, and musical guests—including the Ramones, Jon Bon Jovi, and Cyndi Lauper—this variety show had lots of fans, including Richard Nixon, David Bowie, and John Lennon. Bowie even recorded a tribute song to Uncle Floyd called "Slip Away," on his 2002 album *Heathen.* In 1999 Vivino set the Guinness-verified world record for nonstop piano playing—24 hours and 25 minutes.

DID YOU KNOW?

Abraham Browning, of Camden, came up with the nickname Garden State. When speaking at New Jersey Day in 1876 at the Centennial Exhibition, Browning coined the name that has stuck to New Jersey and appeared on its license plates ever since.

Genius School

Imagine a New Jersey school without formal classes, without curriculum or degree programs, without exams or requirements. Oh, and without tuition or fees. Want to apply? There is just one teeny-tiny hitch, and that's the main criterion for admission: You have to be a genius.

Flexner's Folly

Noted educator Dr. Abraham Flexner had a vision. His idea involved an idyllic setting where the world's greatest minds would come together to share their genius-type thoughts and research. It would be a place where they would be free to lose themselves in the world of ideas, without the everyday demands of the world the rest of us live in.

Flexner was no slouch himself and knew a little bit about genius. The son of immigrants, he found himself uninspired by school in Louisville, Kentucky. But he discovered the world of books and was almost entirely self-taught. At age 17 in 1884 he entered Johns Hopkins University, then graduated in two years, and returned to Kentucky to teach at his old high school.

Some parents approached Flexner about educating their son, to give him a chance to gain admission to Princeton, even though he had been expelled from prep school. Flexner took the challenge—and succeeded. Soon other parents sent him their children to be tutored, with similar results: those students all gained admission to exceptional schools.

Flexner's teaching methods were highly unorthodox for their time. There were no homework assignments, exams, or other requirements. There was no pressure—students could come to their lessons or not, they could do as little or as much as they wished. Eventually the students found their own will to learn, and achieved more than anyone would have thought possible. These early educational experiences formed Flexner's core concept for the Institute for Advanced Study.

Luckily for geniuses everywhere, Dr. Flexner's reputation reached a pair of wealthy New Jersey siblings who happened to be looking for a deserving project in which to invest lots of money.

From Filling Cavities to Filling Great Minds

It was 1930, and Newark department store magnate Louis Bamberger and his sister Caroline Bamberger Fuld were in an enviable position. The siblings had been savvy enough (or lucky enough) to pull all their money out of the stock market just before the crash of 1929. Although their good fortune had more to do with shrewdness than geography, they wanted to do something nice (and expensive) to show gratitude to their home state of New Jersey. Their original impulse was to found a New Jersey dental school. And Abe Flexner was considered an expert on dental education, so it was natural that they should consult him.

But Dr. Flexner suggested another use for the Bambergers' generosity. He convinced them to consider providing a nurturing educational environment for genius to flower within New Jersey. And so the Institute for Advanced Study was born.

Genius at Work?

Dr. Flexner's idea was surprisingly simple. If the world's great thinkers could be freed of mundane concerns, they could devote all their time to thinking great thoughts and divining abstract ideas. The Institute would provide the academic setting—the classrooms and meeting rooms, libraries, and dining halls that all scholars require. And better yet, it would all be (and still is) entirely free of charge!

But that's not all. The lucky scholars who work and think at the Institute of Advanced Study have almost all their needs met without expending any effort. Their housing and food is subsidized by the institute (although, it must be assumed, they still need to chew their own food). There is even an on-campus nursery school to look after baby while parents slave over a hot theorem. At IAS pretty much everything is done for you. Except for laundry.

And in return, Institute scholars have to do . . . well, actually . . . nothing. There are no formal classes they have to attend or teach, no research projects they must complete, and no papers they must publish. Although most Institute members find their tenure there among their most productive years, the IAS never imposes on them or directs their research. Since they must be pretty hard workers to be admitted in the first place, members make optimal use of their time in Princeton.

Mathletes and More

The Institute began with just one department—mathematics—because it required the smallest investment in facilities and equipment. Over the years other departments have been added: the School of Historical Studies, the School of Natural Sciences, and the School of Social Sciences. The permanent faculty currently numbers 26 (plus 12 emeriti). Each year approximately 200 members (that translates to "students" at most schools) are accepted for terms of one to two years. All members have already received their PhD or an equivalent degree.

In Princeton, But Not of Princeton U.

When it first opened, the Institute for Advanced Study was housed in Princeton University's Fine Hall. Then, in 1939, Fuld Hall, the Institute's main academic building, opened, and the school moved to its own campus three miles away. In spite of the physical and spiritual closeness of the two institutions, they have always been, and remain, separate entities. But both schools benefit from the close relationship. Institute members are free to use the university's libraries and facilities, and they occasionally teach graduate courses there.

They're Not Considered Geniuses for Nothing

A list of the Institute's alumni reads like an international who's who in the natural and social sciences. Some names are instantly recognizable, while others enjoy glory in esoteric intellectual fields. Albert Einstein is probably the best known alum. He came to the Institute when he was at the peak of his fame and the entire world was wooing him. He spent the last two decades of his life there, becoming an instantly recognizable and much-loved fixture in the town.

Who's Your Daddy?

Other faculty members have included the brilliant mathematician John Nash, made famous in the movie *A Beautiful Mind*. Another veteran is another mathematician, John von Neumann, who is perhaps best remembered as the Father of Game Theory and the developer of many of the early concepts of computer architecture. J. Robert Oppenheimer, director of the Manhattan Project and widely known as the Father of the Atomic Bomb, was another. More than a dozen Nobel laureates number among the Institute's alumni, as well as winners of other prestigious awards.

Intimidated Yet?

Still think you're genius enough to apply? Just send your application to: Institute for Advanced Study on Einstein Drive. (Even the address sounds smart.)

DID YOU KNOW?

The band Fountains of Wayne named themselves after a local fountains and lawn decor store on Route 46 in Wayne. There you can find cement birdbaths, faux Roman statues, garden benches, and other decorations for your lawn. But Fountains of Wayne is probably best known for its ornate, animated Christmas display that goes up every year during the holiday season. People come from all over every year to see their Christmas Emporium, made up of animatronic figures and multiple Santas in myriad scenes, like Christmas in Venice, Santa at the Shore, and Santa in the Rain Forest.

Whitney Houston
By the Numbers

Born in East Orange and raised in Newark, Whitney Houston is indisputably one of the most successful musical artists of the last half century—but how successful has this Jersey girl been, really? Well, the numbers don't lie.

1

The top number on the U.S. pop charts; Whitney's reached it 11 times, starting with "Saving All My Love for You" in 1985, from her debut album, *Whitney Houston*.

2

The number of times Whitney's 1991 version of "The Star Spangled Banner" has been on the charts: first in 1991, right after she sang it at the Super Bowl during the start of the Gulf War. It sold over 500,000 copies, and raised money for the Red Cross. It was re-released in 2001, to benefit the families of firefighters and police officers who perished in the September 11, 2001 attacks. That release sold 300,000 copies and raised over $1 million.

4

The number of #1 albums Whitney's had in the United States: *Whitney Houston* (1985), *Whitney* (1987), and the sound tracks to *The Bodyguard* (1992) and *Waiting to Exhale* (1995).

7

The number of #1 hits Whitney notched in a row in the United States, starting with "Saving All My Love for You" in 1985 and ending in 1988 with "Where Do Broken Hearts Go," from Whitney's second album, *Whitney*. It's a record; the previous holders were the Beatles and the Bee Gees.

9

The highest chart ranking of "Love Will Save the Day," the song that broke Whitney's streak of #1 hits.

14

The number of weeks the Dolly Parton–penned hit "I Will Always Love You" stayed at the top of the U.S. charts in 1992—a record at the time. During the 14-week run, Dolly Parton reportedly joked to Houston to "let someone else have a turn, girl!"

47

The chart position of Whitney's first single, 1984's "Hold Me," a duet with Teddy Pendergrass.

75

The lowest chart position of any Whitney Houston single, achieved (as it were) by "One of Those Days," from 2002's *Just Whitney* album.

1963

The year Whitney was born, on August 9, in Newark.

1978

Whitney's first appearance on record, backing her mother, gospel singer Cissy Houston, on her album *Think It Over*.

1992

Whitney's film debut, in *The Bodyguard,* co-starring Kevin Costner. She also appeared in *Waiting to Exhale* (1995), *The Preacher's Wife* (1996), and the television film *Cinderella* (1997). This is also the year Whitney married singer Bobby Brown.

500,000

Units sold of *One Wish: The Holiday Album,* her album that's sold the least (it's still a gold record, by the way).

3,000,000

Units sold of *The Preacher's Wife* sound track, making it the most successful gospel record ever.

13,000,000

Units sold of *Whitney Houston,* making it, at the time, the most successful debut album for a female artist (it still holds the record for American female debut; Canadian Alanis Morissette holds the overall record).

17,000,000

Units sold of *The Bodyguard* sound track, making it the most successful movie sound track of all time. The sound track to *Waiting to Exhale* sold "only" 10 million units.

121,945,720

In dollars, the total lifetime North American gross of *The Bodyguard,* Whitney's most successful film. Houston's three films have a combined worldwide gross of over half a billion dollars (that's a lot of numbers!).

U-Who

*It was 1991. World War II had been over for more than 45 years. So what
the dickens was a German U-Boat doing off the coast of New Jersey?*

New Jersey may be the Garden State, but sailors have also
nicknamed it the Graveyard of the Atlantic. For hundreds of
years ships have come to grief because of the state's treacherous
shoals, inlets, and sandbars. With over 2,000 vessels lying on the
bottom of the Atlantic near Jersey, wreck divers find the state's
coastal waters one of the best places in the world for salvaging
artifacts and history. But few wrecks are as mysterious as the one
found off Brielle in 1991—it was a German World War II sub that
was never supposed to be there.

A Relic of War

In the fall of 1991 a fishing boat captain tipped off Captain Bill
Nagle to explore a mysterious steel wreck lying on the bottom of
the ocean about 60 miles east of Point Pleasant. The fishing captain warned Nagle that the site would be tough to explore. It
rested deep in freezing, current-swept waters that wouldn't give
up secrets easily.

Nagle and the divers had no idea what to expect that morning.
They might discover the *Corvallis,* a ship that was supposedly
sunk in the 1930s by a Hollywood film crew making a disaster

movie. Or they might find an old subway car, which officials sometimes deliberately dumped in the ocean because the metal hulks supported the growth of marine life. Then again, the wreck might just be an old barge filled with garbage that had been taken out to sea and scuttled—hardly glamorous stuff.

But on September 2, when lead diver John Chatterton explored the wreck, he saw a torpedo—not the sort of thing found on a sunken subway car. In fact, the divers had found a submarine: a Nazi U-boat resting right off the New Jersey coast. Nagle and his divers returned to shore, excited by their discovery. They were sure they'd soon know the identity of the sub and learn how it came to its final resting place.

U-Who?

Called *Unterseeboots* or U-boats, Hitler's submarines had been created to destroy Allied merchant ships during World War II. At the beginning of the war, the U-boats were a deadly success. Traveling alone or together in "wolf packs," U-boats inflicted terrible damage as they moved, silent and deadly, along the Atlantic coast of the United States and into the Gulf of Mexico. Winston Churchill, Britain's wartime prime minister, would later say that they were "the only thing that really frightened me during the war."

But by 1943 the U-boats had become less of a threat as the Allies developed methods to hunt them down. Sonar, radar, and, finally, the cracking of the Axis Enigma code, defanged the wolf packs and made the U-boats vulnerable to Allied sub hunters. By the end of the war Hitler had lost over 740 U-boats. So in 1991, which one of these had been found so close to New Jersey?

After some research the divers were amazed to find that maps, historians, and government records all agreed. No U-boat was ever attacked in the area where the wreck was found. The two closest U-boat sinkings (U-550 and U-521) were well verified and at least 100 miles away. The divers had a mystery on their hands, so they nicknamed the wreck U-Who.

Diving Can Make You a Wreck

With no official records to refer to, the divers needed to pull identifying artifacts from the mystery sub. But exploring the site was no easy job. Stepping into the rotting hulk, a diver swirled up enough rust and silt to put visibility at just about zero. Divers could get snagged in the wreck's cables, have their equipment cut on its sharp metal edges, or simply lose their way in dark narrow confines while their precious air supply ran out. Exploring the wreck also put the crew in danger from nitrogen narcosis and the bends. For safety's sake, recreational divers try not to go 130 feet below sea level. The U-Who rested 100 feet deeper than that.

On September 21 Nagle's trip to the sub turned into a tragedy when one of the divers died and was swept out to sea. In the first year after the U-Who was discovered, another diver had to be helicoptered to the hospital. Three more lost their lives exploring the U-boat, which still refused to give up its identity. Despite the danger, the team wouldn't give up.

A History Mystery

Two divers in particular, John Chatterton and Richie Kohler, refused to abandon the submarine puzzle. As Kohler explained to his friends, "This is a mystery like you read in a book. A German U-boat comes to our doorstep in New Jersey. It explodes and sinks with maybe sixty guys on board, and no one—no government or navy or professor historian—has a clue that it's even here."

The U-boat identity became an obsession for the two men until finally, on a dive in late 1991, they began to find some clues. Chatterton found a knife engraved with a crewman's name on the handle. Research showed that the crewman had served on the U-869 submarine. But, oddly enough, records showed that boat had been sunk near Gibraltar—half a world away from New Jersey. Then, later in 1992, Chatterton found a piece of metal inscribed with the words "Baurt IXC, Deschimag, Bremen." These gave them the origin and model of the sub. Checking out the fate of all the U-boats of that origin and model, Chatterton and Kohler, through a process of elimination, came to the conclusion that their submarine had to be U-869, even though written records said otherwise.

Unfortunately they could prove their theory only by returning to the wreck and finding corroborating markings. But though the divers found everything from dishes to gauges to a ship's clock to crew boots, not one artifact gave them the name of the U-boat.

Rewriting History

Finally, in 1994, Kohler's research led to a tip from a contact in Britain, who dug through mounds of official records and found that there was little conclusive proof that U-869 actually sank near Gibraltar after all. National Archives reports showed that the World War II code breakers in the United States had a better idea of where U-869 was located than the Germans did. The Allied code breaker knew that the U-869 was on its way to the New Jersey coast when it was given new orders to head for Africa instead; U-869 failed to receive those orders and kept cruising toward North America. Further research showed that the supposed sinking of U-869 at Gibraltar had never been thoroughly investigated or conclusively proved.

The Mood Was Electric

Finally, in 1997, advice from a shipwreck diver in another state led to a new plan. All U-boats carried spare parts tagged with the sub's identifying number. Find the tags and the proof was found, too. Boxes of spare parts would be in the electric motor room.

Chatterton and Kohler dove down to the wreck. Unfortunately, because of debris and twisted metal, the electric motor room was also the hardest place to reach and the most dangerous spot on the wreck. Chatterton had to swim through a small hole (without his air supply attached) to get into the motor room and hand out the boxes. It was a harrowing dive, but successful. Because of their daring and persistence, the sub was officially identified as U-869.

One Last Mystery

Both the video *Hitler's Lost Sub* and Robert Kurson's exciting book *Shadow Divers* chronicle Jersey's submarine mystery. Today one piece of the mystery still remains. Since the Allied records showed no account of attacking the sub, why did it sink? The accepted theory is that an acoustic torpedo (which followed the sound of enemy propellers) was fired from the U-869. Instead of heading to the enemy boat, the torpedo circled back and destroyed the U-869. Such accidents weren't unknown in World War II, but the official story will probably never be known.

Don't Be Afraid

New Jersey is home to some creepy crawly creatures that seem to inspire a lot of unnecessary fear. They can't hurt you. We promise.

Bats

There are nine species of bat found in New Jersey, but you don't have to worry about any one of them trying to bite your neck. They all eat insects. To test your bravery, the best place to see bats is the Hibernia mine in Rockaway. It houses up to 30,000 bats.

Dragonflies

Lots of dragonflies (over 175 species!) make their home in the Garden State. Even though their names are scary (e.g., devil's darning needle), they're perfectly harmless to humans. But they're deadly to other insects—especially mosquitoes, one of their favorite snacks.

Horseshoe Crabs

Every year in late spring, horseshoe crabs flock to the Jersey Shore for their mating season. And beachgoers are often frightened by the crabs' appearance: seven spidery legs, a hard domed shell, and a long spiky tail. (By the way, horseshoe crabs are really not technically crabs. Crabs are Crustaceans, and horseshoe crabs are Merostomatans.) But rest assured, horseshoe crabs have no claws to pinch and no teeth to bite. The worst they can do is startle you.

Hometowns
The Long Beach Island Gateway

Ship Bottom is the shore town with the funny-sounding name.

The Town: Ship Bottom

Location: Ocean County

Founding: Ship Bottom was originally part of Long Beach Township. It broke away in 1925 to form a borough named Ship Bottom–Beach Arlington. It shortened its name in 1947.

Current Population: The population of this little borough fluctuates wildly during the course of the year. During the summer you can find as many as 15,000 to 20,000 inhabitants, but during the off-season the population falls to approximately 1,400 people.

Size: 0.69 square miles

What's in a Name? A shipwreck and its mysterious survivor gave this town its name. The story goes that in 1817, as Captain Willets and his crew sailed off the coast of Long Beach Island, they came across a wrecked ship overturned and beached in the shoals. It appeared that everyone aboard had died, but a tapping noise seemed to be coming from inside the hull. Willets took an ax, chopped a hole in the wrecked boat, and found a young woman alive inside. She was removed unharmed, but she spoke no English and could not relate her travels to her rescuers. No one recorded her name or the name of her ship, but the location became known colloquially as Ship Bottom.

Claims to Fame

- Ship Bottom's nickname is Gateway to the Island. When going to Long Beach Island, drivers on Route 72 cross the bridge over the Barnegat Bay. And Ship Bottom is the first place they see.

- Ship Bottom was the site of another shipwreck in 1910. In a thick fog the Italian bark *Fortuna* ran aground and lay on its side for most of the year. It was eventually cut up for salvage.

DID YOU KNOW?

South Orange's William Allen invented standard time. A railroad man from the age of 16, Allen devised this timekeeping system to help synchronize train schedules across the United States. It was adopted at the 1875 General Time Convention, but the U.S. Congress didn't make standard time official until 1919.

Are You Game for Monopoly?

Did you know that the properties in Monopoly are based on the streets of Atlantic City—New Jersey's most famous shore town and casino spot? In honor of the great game and its place in Jersey history, we've put together a little wordsearch for you. You'll find most of the game's properties and utilities in this state-shaped puzzle.

ATLANTIC

BALTIC

B&O

BOARDWALK

CHANCE

COMMUNITY CHEST

CONNECTICUT

ELECTRIC CO

ILLINOIS

INDIANA

JAIL

KENTUCKY

MEDITERRANEAN

NEW YORK

ORIENTAL

PACIFIC

PARK PLACE

PENNSYLVANIA

ST CHARLES

ST JAMES

STATES

TENNESSEE

VENTNOR

VERMONT

VIRGINIA

Y
C L D
Y O V L X V
E W N K T R K B S
O M B A L D T S W V
P E N N S Y L V A N I A
U I D P A R K P L A C E U E
N R I G T A E R H X W V C M
B S S T J A M E S M Z O N E
H T E C I T N A L T A X D
Q J R L F C T D U H W G
Z X A R D E L Z V C M W Y
F S I A W Z C F K C D A
D W L N B A L T I C B
C G E D & K J R U   Q
B A X I O W U I T S   F
N L E A V G S C S W S
P T G N E H I C Y N
W T P Z H A A O R O M
C I F I C A P H W R V X
L B J V U Y V I R G I N I A
S E T A T S U R X E M T U
D W G O T I R O N T N E V I L
K R O Y W E N V K E N T U C K Y H
P Z T G O U S E L R A H C T S G
U M L G H M A N I L L I N O I S F
V E R M O N T E N N E S S E E
B O A R D W A L K W X T V
C O N N E C T I C U T
P H G J O E R A X
A D M Z
R X V

Turn to page 321 for answers.

Ghosts of Jersey Girls

One of the most popular ghost stories is the mysterious lady, usually dressed in a white gown, who appears along the side of a dark road. Other states have their own versions, like Resurrection Mary of Chicago, Illinois, and Hitchhike Annie of St. Louis, Missouri. Given that New Jersey is so densely populated, it's only fitting that this state has not one, but three ghostly ladies in white.

Lady Number One
Who: The Lady in White
Where: Branch Brook Park, Essex County
Why: A lovesick couple went for a drive one rainy night through Branch Brook Park in Newark. (The legends vary on whether they were newlyweds or just sweethearts.) As they drove, the slick road caused the car to skid and crash head-on into a big, old tree. The powerful collision threw the woman from the car and killed her. (Versions of the story differ on what happened to the guy; but since the ghost is a woman, nobody seems to mind.) Hours later, when the police arrived, all they found of her was a piece of white fabric hanging from some broken window glass.

Today witnesses, while driving through Branch Brook Park on rainy nights, report a haunting vision of woman in a bloody white dress near a large tree. She beckons to them, perhaps trying to warn them of a similar fate if they don't drive carefully.

Lady Number Two

Who: The Ghost of Annie

Where: Annie's Road (also known as Riverview Drive), Passaic County

Why: Annie's Road is the site of many popular New Jersey legends, the most famous being the ghost of Annie herself. Annie's apparition is a young woman, all dressed up on the side of the road. But that's about the only agreement you'll find in the Annie story. When it comes to explaining how Annie got ghostified, there are many different accounts. Here are just two of them:

Version 1: A teenage boy asked Annie to the prom. She happily agreed to go with him. On prom night, the boy didn't show. (No one knows why; but, as usual, what happens to the guy in the story is never all that clear.) Brokenhearted and suspecting some cruel joke, Annie decided to walk to the prom by herself. As she walked along the road, a car driven by drunk high school revelers ran her over and killed her.

Version 2: It's prom night. In this version, Annie and her date had an argument while on their way to the event. Her boyfriend became so angry that he kicked her out of his car and drove off. Annie was left to walk home by herself in her prom dress and high heels. Regretting his hasty decision, the boyfriend turned the car around, sped along a curve, but didn't see Annie. He ran right into her and killed her.

However Annie met her bloody end, her spirit still haunts the side of the road where she died. Some claim that Annie's bloodstains still remain on the road and guardrail and can never be removed. Another popular explanation is that her father, insane with grief, repaints the red stains every year to mark his daughter's death.

Lady Number Three

Who: The Lady in White

Where: Shades of Death Road, Warren County

Why: Legend has it that this location has had an eerie reputation going back to the local Delaware tribes of Native Americans, who believed that ghosts would wander in the area along what is now known as Shades of Death Road. The Lady in White may be just one of them.

Her story sounds vaguely familiar. It was prom night again. A young couple carelessly sped along the twisty road and got into a fatal accident. Now the spirit of the young girl haunts the side of the road. On dark nights you may see the girl's ghost in her bloody prom dress as she tries to cause another accident on that fatal curve.

By the way, Shades of Death Road didn't get its spooky name from the prom night ghost; the most likely explanation is that the road was named after the area had been the site of a deadly malaria outbreak in 1849.

DID YOU KNOW?

Franklin Township is home to one of the first concrete highways in America. Thomas Edison's plant created the makings of this "Concrete Mile" in 1912.

A Good Start for Sports

Despite not having many professional sports teams now, New Jersey was a hotbed for sports and their development. A lot of important athletic firsts occurred in the Garden State. Don't believe us? Then just read on.

The First Football Game

On November 6, 1869, students from Queen's College (now known as Rutgers) and from the College of New Jersey (now known as Princeton) played the first college football game. The rules were a little different and more closely resembled soccer. Each team had 25 players who wore no protective gear. That's right, no pads and no helmets. Touchdowns were worth only one point and were scored each time a player passed the opponent's goal line. The first match, Rutgers won 6–4. In the less famous rematch the following week, Princeton won 8–0. The two teams wanted to play again, but the schools' administrations canceled the game because football was too distracting and taking the players away from their studies.

The U.S.'s First International Soccer Match

British immigrants founded the first U.S. soccer governing body, the American Football Association (AFA), in Newark in 1884. The AFA team would play the first international match between the United States and Canada on Clark Field in what was then Kearny; Canada won, 1–0 (the U.S. would win the rematch in

1886). In 1885 the AFA also established the first National Championship, which was won by a team from Kearny. Sponsored by the Clark Thread Company (which also employed a lot of soccer-playing Scottish immigrants), the team was called ONT, which stood for Our New Thread.

The First Professional Basketball Game

The first professional basketball game was played in Trenton in 1898—when the game looked a whole lot different. Players wore velvet shorts, long tights, kneepads, elbow pads, and shin guards. Surrounding the court was a chicken wire cage that protected the players from the fans, who would often try to poke them with hatpins and cigarettes. The cage itself also proved to be quite hazardous to the athletes. "Players would be thrown against the wire and most of us would get cut. The court would be covered with blood," said 5-foot-4 Barney Sedran, an early basketball star. Thanks to the protective chicken wire in Trenton, we have the term *cager*, another word for basketball player.

The First Baseball Game

On June 19, 1846, at the Elysian Fields in Hoboken, the very first baseball game was played. The game had been played in earlier forms, but this was the first time that modern rules applied, such as 90 feet between bases, a diamond-shaped field, formal lineups, and 3 outs per inning, to name a few. Two New York clubs—the Knickerbockers and the New York Nine—squared off against each other. The result? The New York Nine clobbered the Knickerbockers, 23–1, thus starting the tradition of New York teams playing in the Garden State.

Starring Kevin Smith
... as Silent Bob

*When he started out, filmmaker Kevin Smith was just a Jersey guy
from the Highlands who worked in a convenience store. Now he's a
writer-director-actor who lives in California but whose artistic heart
still loudly beats for the Garden State.*

Since 1994 Kevin Smith has firmly established himself as a
chief film chronicler of life in New Jersey. All of his films are
set squarely within the confines of the Garden State. But the
thought of Smith as Jersey's preeminent filmmaker may offend
some, because his films are bawdy and profanity-laden. His
heroes are talky comic book geeks rather than mobsters or cops.
But in the midst of all the geekery and swearing, Smith also hits
on some serious issues like relationships, religion, and whether
the construction crews on the uncompleted second Death Star in
Return of the Jedi were innocent bystanders or Imperial drones.
(Okay, so that last one isn't so serious—unless you were on the
construction crew or a *Star Wars* fan.)

We've decided to take a look at Smith's first five movies,
which are all linked by a common characteristic—the appearance of two characters, Jay (Jason Mewes) and Silent Bob
(Kevin Smith himself). These two rather dimwitted characters

often provide the laughs, but they also have some valuable insights from time to time.

Clerks (1994)

Smith's first film followed a day in the life of two clerks, Dante and Randal, as they toiled away at dead-end jobs in a Quick Stop convenience store and a small video store. Smith could sympathize, since at the time he was holding down a dead-end job at the same convenience store (he got to use the Leonardo strip mall as a set on the condition that filming wouldn't be done during work hours). Filmed in black and white and starring Smith's friends and acquaintances, the entire film was financed for just a little more than $25,000, borrowed mostly from credit cards and from friends (the movie eventually made over $3 million in the theaters, so not a bad return at all). This film also introduces Jay and Silent Bob as two stoners who like to hang out outside the Quick Stop.

Fun fact: *Clerks* is so profanity-laden that it was initially given an NC-17 rating based on language alone—the first film to achieve that distinction. Miramax, the film's distributor, hired celebrity lawyer Alan Dershowitz to appeal the rating. It worked.

Mallrats (1995)

Smith's sophomore effort wasn't exactly a hit: Critics hated it and the movie did poorly at the box office. Generally regarded as Smith's weakest film, *Mallrats* was Smith's attempt to "breathe life back into a dead genre: the raunchy, R-rated teen comedy." This one features another pair of slackers (this time played by Jeremy London and Jason Lee), who lose their girlfriends (Shannen Doherty and Claire Forlani) and then travel to the mall in an attempt to win them back. Along the way there's a game show, a cameo by Marvel Comics founder Stan Lee, the first appearance of Ben Affleck in a Kevin Smith film, and Jay and Silent Bob interludes for comic relief. This film is set in New Jersey, but the interior shots were actually filmed at the Eden Prairie Center Mall in Minnesota.

Fun fact: The film's two main characters were named "T. S. Quint" and "Brodie Bruce"—an homage to three of the main characters in *Jaws*: salty sea dog Quint, heroic police captain Brodie, and the film's mechanical shark, who was referred to on the *Jaws* set as Bruce.

Chasing Amy (1997)

After the relative disappointment of *Mallrats*, Smith bounced back with an artistically successful film about a Jersey comic book creator (Ben Affleck) who falls in love with another comic book creator (Joey Lauren Adams) despite the fact she's a lesbian. And then she falls in love right back, which complicates things on many different levels, not the least of which is that they're both supposed to like girls. Smith's previous track record didn't suggest he was capable of subtlety—and indeed much of the film is gleefully unsubtle—but Affleck's and Adams's characters come across as real, conflicted, and complicated people. They're not the only ones: Silent Bob, heretofore confined to comedy, issues forth a surprisingly heartfelt speech on love and loss. A big step forward for Smith, who wrote that this movie "more than the other two, is me on a slab, laid out for the world to see. And believe me, that's scary."

Fun fact: Miramax offered Smith a $3 million budget for the film if he'd make it with people with "star power" (which at the time were Jon Stewart, David Schwimmer, and Drew Barrymore).

Smith made the film with the actors he preferred—for just $250,000.

Dogma (1999)

Smith's most controversial film featured two fallen angels (played by Matt Damon and Ben Affleck) who discover a way to get back into heaven when a New Jersey bishop (George Carlin) rededicates a cathedral and offers plenary indulgences to those who pass through its door (meaning all is forgiven). Problem is, if the fallen angels enter the cathedral, it proves God is fallible, and then there goes Creation. It's up to Linda Fiorentino to stop them. To aid her in her quest, she has Jay and Silent Bob (back in comic relief mode), as well as the lost 13th disciple, played by Chris Rock. Many conservative Catholics were not amused and called for a boycott. Their plan backfired, though, and *Dogma* became Smith's most financially successful film to date.

Fun fact: Smith infiltrated one of the groups protesting his film and protested the film himself—and was even interviewed by a TV reporter while incognito.

Jay and Silent Bob Strike Back (2001)

After serving on the sidelines in four films, Jay and Silent Bob get their own film, and it's a road film at that. After learning that a movie is being made of comic book characters based on their likenesses, the duo travel from New Jersey to Hollywood to stop the film from being made and have a series of ridiculous and juvenile adventures along the way. Smith called the film a "love note" to his fans—which means that if you haven't seen Smith's previous four films, you're going to miss about 90 percent of the jokes in this one.

Fun fact: Gay and lesbian groups protested this film because of Jay's incessant homophobic comments, prompting Smith to put a disclaimer on the film that said: "I'm not sorry, because I didn't make the jokes at the expense of the gay community. I made jokes at the expense of two characters who neither I nor the audience have ever held up to be paragons of intellect. They're idiots."

DID YOU KNOW?

New Jersey can be such a scary place that filmmakers really like to make their scary movies there.

Alice, Sweet, Alice (1976)

Starring a young Brooke Shields, this film (also called *Communion and Holy Terror*) was filmed and set in Paterson.

Halloween (1978)

This movie wasn't filmed in New Jersey, but the name of the town terrorized by Michael Myers is named for Haddonfield, New Jersey, where its producer Debra Hill grew up.

The Amityville Horror (1979)

You might think they filmed the movie on Long Island, but you'd be wrong. Several locations in Toms River played the part of Amityville in this movie.

Friday the 13th (1980)

Camp Crystal Lake, the spooky stomping grounds for Mrs. Voorhees and her son Jason, is actually Camp NoBeBoSco in Blairstown. The camp's odd name is an abbreviation of NOrth BErgen BOy SCOuts of America.

Jersey Boys and Jersey Girls

The natives' thoughts on their old New Jersey home

Jersey Boys

"I think when you come from a place that's made fun of your whole life . . . and you love it, you get defensive, and you want to sing its praises to people. I still love going up to New Jersey. I think it's made me who I am. . . . At home I could enjoy a nice beach, a great public school system, and I had a great time growing up there."

—Zach Braff, actor and director of *Garden State*

"You're in the shadow of New York, always trying to prove yourself. . . . It's like you're the redheaded stepchild."

—Kevin Smith, actor, writer, and director

"New Jersey's a pretty interesting place. . . . There are so many forces at work economically, culturally, and socially. I didn't realize it until I came back. It's kind of exciting seeing it through the camera. Now that I'm talking about it, I'm thinking maybe I should go make another movie there."

—Tom McCarthy, writer and director of *The Station Agent*

"It was really cool growing up in Asbury. . . . When I was a kid, it was the best of all possible worlds. In the summer all the city girls would come down, and in winter it was like a Bergman film."
—Danny DeVito, actor and director

"New Jersey has gone from a private shame to a juggernaut."
—Paul Rudnick, playwright

"[New Jersey seemed] very exciting and very mysterious . . . not dull and predictable as many New Yorkers like to believe. . . . There's something sophisticated about the place, strangely enough. . . . I think there's a certain savvy."
—David Chase, writer and director

"Being from New Jersey is great."
—Jon Bon Jovi, musician and actor

"I love Jersey. . . . I had a great time down there in Princeton doing *Anger Management*. Being a Jersey boy, you know [it] . . . was really something. I'm one of the few living people who can say they saw Dick Kazmaier play football live."
—Jack Nicholson, actor

Jersey Girls

"Your best bet when driving in Jersey: Move it or lose it. It's the pokey Pennsylvanians that tend to gum everything up, so step lively, and we're not kidding around with our left lane—if you can't hack it, move over."
—Sarah D. Bunting, writer and co-founder of *Television Without Pity*

"In this hotel I was talking to this woman from Germany and she began making fun of New Jersey. And I said: 'You're from Germany! How do you make fun of New Jersey?'"

—Diane Ruggiero, screenwriter

"I'm a Jersey girl and proud of it. . . . Out here (in Los Angeles) it's strange because everyone always says, 'You're totally from, like Jersey.' I'm like, 'What is that supposed to mean?'"

—Laura Prepon, actress

"New Jersey is the greatest place in the world. . . . It's close enough to New York, but you still have a backyard and some trees."

—Lauryn Hill, musician

"It's sort of funny that I've come around to this Jersey consciousness and appreciation of my Jersey background. . . . You come through all these stages of trying to be this and trying to be that, just to end up at a state of learning to appreciate what you really are."

—Deborah Harry, singer and songwriter

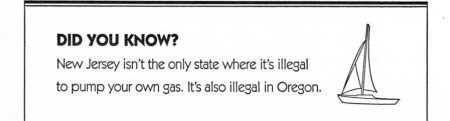

DID YOU KNOW?

New Jersey isn't the only state where it's illegal to pump your own gas. It's also illegal in Oregon.

The Play's the Thing

The most famous kidnapping trial in the world still takes place every year in New Jersey.

D id Bruno Richard Hauptmann kidnap the Lindbergh baby in 1932? Was he guilty or not guilty? Seventy years after the famous trial, these questions are still being asked in the Hunterdon County Courthouse, even though the defendant himself was declared guilty in 1935 and has long since been executed in Old Sparky, New Jersey's retired electric chair.

Famous Trials Theater created *Lindbergh & Hauptmann: The Trial of the Century* in 1990. This two-act play allows the audience to watch and listen, weigh the evidence, and then cast their own votes in the same Flemington courthouse where it all took place.

Way Off-Broadway

Getting picked for jury duty (otherwise known as buying a ticket) isn't always easy. This dramatic reenactment of the Lindbergh trial has been popular since its inception, making it one of the longest running plays around. Retired drama teacher Harry Kazman, who cowrote and coproduced *The Trial of the Century* with his wife, Reva, said they've both been amazed at the intensity of interest. Tickets for spectators or jurors are usually sold out in advance.

The theater (make that *courthouse*) has limited seating—especially in the jury box, which only holds 14. But it's the courtroom setting that helps make *The Trial of the Century* feel authentic. Flemington has grown since the original trial: It's now surrounded by shopping centers that weren't there in 1935. But the courthouse and the Union Hotel across the street (where the jury, the attorneys, many reporters, and celebrities stayed) have been preserved as historic landmarks.

During the weeks when the reenactment is playing, a vintage 1930s automobile parked in front of the courthouse lets the audience know that they are about to step back in time. The courthouse entry contains a case of memorabilia from the Lindbergh trial that can be viewed before proceeding to the second floor, where the trial and the jury deliberation still take place.

A Trial Run

The two-act play employs about 15 actors and is adapted from the original court transcript. The first part of the play depicts the prosecution of Hauptmann; the second act is his defense. Though the original trial took 32 days, the reenactment takes less than three hours. But audiences—who often include attorneys and Lindbergh kidnapping buffs—say that most of the famous highlights of the trial can be seen in the play.

The jurors not only listen to the prosecution's expert testimony about the famous ladder used to kidnap the 20-month-old toddler, but they also see a reproduction and can judge for themselves whether a carpenter such as Hauptmann would have built it. Defense testimony from Bruno Hauptmann and his wife, Anna, are also included, as jurors judge the defendant's alibi and his character for themselves.

Though the play is exciting, some of the heaviest drama at each performance happens in the jury room, when the play is almost over. In 1935 the trial was a slam dunk for the prosecution. But when the testimony is recreated decades later, with a different perspective, the verdict is no sure thing. Arguments have become heated and passions have run high as the jury debates. It's rumored that one couple in the jury box, who each came down on opposite sides, nearly got a divorce!

A Prosecuting Good Time

Of course, no matter how the modern jury votes, the play's ending is a foregone conclusion. Once the jurors return to the box, Anna Hauptmann screams and collapses after her husband is declared guilty. That part of the drama never changes, which, as Kazan admits, can please one section of the audience more than others. "Prosecutors," he said, "seem to like it particularly."

DID YOU KNOW?

When Meryl Streep placed her handprints in the sidewalk outside of Grauman's Chinese Theatre in Hollywood, someone asked her if, as a kid growing up in Summit, New Jersey, she thought that would ever happen. She quipped: "In New Jersey, we put other things in cement."

The AKA Quiz

Can you match these famous Jersey-born folks to their celebrated accomplishments? It's just a little tougher because we've used their original names. (Don't worry, their famous monikers are with the answers in case you get stuck.)

A. Susan Abigail Tomalin
B. Joseph (Jerome) Levitch
C. Jay Scott Greenspan
D. Concetta Maria Franconero
E. Dorothy Rothschild
F. Francis Castelluccio

1. Born in Newark in 1959, this actor entertained his classmates in Livingston with great comedy routines. He considers his bar mitzvah his "first paid gig." He's starred on Broadway, but the comic is best known for his role on *Seinfeld*. On that sitcom, he played chubby, neurotic George Costanza—a character who once approached a girl with the famous pickup line: "My name is George. I am unemployed and I live with my parents."

2. This Jerseyan is famous for her acting and commitment to social activism. Raised in Edison, she went to Catholic schools, where a nun notoriously noticed her "overabundance of original sin."

Undaunted, our heroine went on to be a Hollywood success story. She's most famous for her sensual roles—like the sex-therapist/baseball coach in *Bull Durham*. But ironically, she won an Oscar for her role as a saintly nun in *Dead Man Walking*.

3. She is a famous singer from Newark who grew up playing accordion. Her strict father wanted her to stick with it, but she sang her way to fame on *Arthur Godfrey's Talent Scouts* at the age of 9. She topped the charts with the 1958 recording of "Who's Sorry Now?" Her international singing fame brought her starring roles in movies like *Where the Boys Are* (1960). Sadly, in 1974, a rape in her hotel room after a performance traumatized her and kept her from performing for years. She made a comeback in 1981 for adoring fans—who never missed that accordion in the first place but sure missed her voice.

4. It's hard to tell if the voice of this Newark-born singer ever changed because he can hit the high notes. Born in 1937, this man and his singing group used their very distinctive sound and his high voice to put together a string of hits in the early sixties: "Sherry," "Let's Hang On," and "Walk Like a Man." The group named themselves after a bowling alley in Union City where they had their very first audition.

5. This Newark native had parents in vaudeville, who put him onstage in 1928 at age five. The little fellow accidentally tripped, fell down, broke a footlight, and got a huge laugh. He kept to that spastic, pratfall style through his many wacky routines and movies. At 15 he dropped out of high school to perform a comedy act, where he lip-synched to records. In 1946, while appearing in Atlantic City, he teamed up with singer and

fellow performer Dean Martin; the pair rocketed to Hollywood stardom. When they broke up 10 years later, our hero starred in films like *The Nutty Professor* and remained a king of comedy.

6. Born in 1863 in West End while her parents were at their summer home on the Jersey shore, she became one of America's wittiest writers. At 24 she took a job as theater critic for *Vanity Fair* magazine, allowing her to write quips like: "*The House Beautiful* is The Play Lousy." She went on to write poetry, fiction, and reviews for the *New Yorker* and to cofound the Algonquin Round Table, where the literary lights of the day met to lunch and knock back a few. Some of her witticisms, such as "Men seldom make passes at girls who wear glasses," have become part of common conversation.

Turn to page 321 for answers.

DID YOU KNOW?

Edgar Allen Poe's "The Mystery of Marie Roget" was inspired by a real-life murder mystery in New Jersey. Mary Cecilia Rogers had been missing from her mother's boarding house when her battered body was found in the Hudson River near Hoboken in 1841. Miss Rogers had a pretty face and a questionable reputation (she once worked in a cigar store), and the mystery surrounding her death became headline news. One of the newspaper accounts caught Poe's attention, and he based his detective story on it.

Jersey Speak

Communication is so difficult when you don't speak the language. Well, Uncle John has thought ahead and put together a short list of tricky terms to help build your Jersey vocabulary.

A.C.

This abbreviation stands for Atlantic City (which may be pronounced *'Lanic City*), not air conditioning.

Arthur Kill

It's not a command, it's a body of water. *Kill,* a Dutch word for strait or channel, is a holdover from the time the Netherlands colonized New York and New Jersey. The 15-mile Arthur Kill separates New Jersey from Staten Island, New York. At its northern end, it connects with the Kill van Kull and Newark Bay—at its southern, the Raritan Bay.

Benny

A term of obscure origin, benny refers to a day-tripping tourist at the Jersey Shore; usually seen on bumper stickers that say, "Bennies go home." See also "shoobie."

G'head

An abbreviated term for "Go ahead." Usually said when letting somebody go in front of you in line.

Great Adventure

Located in Jackson, New Jersey, this is an amusement park in the Six Flags family. Garden State natives never call the park Six Flags; it's referred to as Great Adventure.

Joisey

How out-of-staters pronounce Jersey. People from the Garden State never say it that way.

Jug Handle Turn

A genius civil engineering advance that allows motorists to make left turns from the right lane. Successful jug handle navigation is a sure sign that one is from New Jersey.

The Ledger

Nickname for the *Star Ledger,* the state's largest newspaper.

The Oranges

A collective term for the towns of Orange, East Orange, South Orange, and West Orange. Rarely used in reference to colors or to citrus fruit.

The Parkway

Nickname of the Garden State Parkway.

Pineys

When a Jerseyan mentions a Piney, they're not talking about trees. Pineys are people who live in the Pinelands.

Route

When giving directions, Jerseyans put the word route (pronounced like *root*) in front of the highway number. It's not "the 46," it's "Route 46."

Self-service Gas Stations

You'll never hear this term because these don't exist in New Jersey.

Shoobie

Another locals' derogatory term for tourists at the Jersey Shore. There are two stories behind its origins. The first: shoobies are people who wear their shoes at the beach. The other: these day-trippers brought their lunches to the beach in shoeboxes.

The Turnpike

Shortened form of the New Jersey Turnpike.

DID YOU KNOW?

It's hard to believe that at the turn of the 19th century, white-tailed deer almost disappeared from New Jersey—thanks to overhunting and habitat loss. But they've made a huge comeback. Today, there are more than 200,000 white-tailed deer in the state.

The Hindenburg Mystery

Lakehurst, New Jersey, was the site of one of the most famous disasters of the 20th century—the crash and explosion of the Hindenburg. *But what was the cause of this terrible accident?*

In the 1930s there wasn't much of a jet set, but the transatlantic travelers in the know did travel by air—airship that is. Airships, also called dirigibles, were metal-framed, cigar-shaped balloons filled with lighter-than-air gas; they were equipped with systems for steering and engines for propulsion. And they were the only way to fly—until airplanes carried passengers over the Atlantic in 1939. The greatest, most luxurious of all the airships was the *Hindenburg*.

With a top speed of 84 miles per hour and a cruising speed of 78 miles per hour, *Hindenburg* passengers could travel from Frankfurt, Germany, to Lakehurst, New Jersey, in 48 hours. The *Hindenburg's* luxury was on the level of that of most ocean liners. For a $400 one-way ticket, this "floating palace" provided passengers with comfortable state rooms, a smoking room (with a built-in lighter), the sounds of a grand piano, gourmet meals on fine china, and dedicated service from the crew. As *Time* magazine announced, "Certainly for trans-oceanic trips, the airship is the thing."

But on May 6, 1937, on a stormy evening at the Naval Air Station in Lakehurst, the *Hindenburg* crashed after a flame burst out near the tail of the ship. The disaster killed 35 out of 97 passengers and one crew member on the ground. Reports (carried via photographs, newspapers, newsreels, and radio) killed public trust in lighter-than-aircraft and marked the end of commercial airship travel. The fiery tragedy also made Lakehurst, New Jersey, the site of one of history's famous mysteries: What caused the demise of the *Hindenburg*?

Fly Me to Lakehurst

The German Count Ferdinand von Zeppelin was the world's great dirigible pioneer. His company so dominated dirigible invention and production that folks began calling airships "zeppelins." And Lakehurst, New Jersey, was an important destination in the Zeppelin Company's fleet itinerary.

Why Lakehurst? When it seemed that airships would dominate the future, the United States was determined to catch up with (and hopefully surpass) Germany in the creation of dirigibles. In 1919 Franklin D. Roosevelt, as secretary of the navy, founded the Lakehurst Naval Air Station for use as a dirigible field. It was eventually equipped with hangars for the airships and a large expanse of sand for landings. From 1924 on, transatlantic airships docked at Lakehurst. In 1937 Lakehurst was a U.S. focal point of zeppelin mania as camera crews, family, friends of the passengers, and spectators traveled to the naval air station to watch the magnificent *Hindenburg* come in for a landing.

The Late, Great Hindenburg

As the largest and grandest airship of the Zeppelin Company, the *Hindenburg* was 804 feet long. Sometimes called the Titanic of the Sky, it was only 78 feet shorter than that ill-fated ocean liner.

The steel frame was about as tall as a 10-story building (skyscraper height in those days). The *Hindenburg* reached 135 feet at its widest point, and it could lift 112 tons beyond its own weight. To this day the Hindenburg holds the record for the largest aircraft to ever fly.

Inside the craft, large bags of hydrogen gas (called hydrogen cells) were stowed to make the ship lighter than air and let it lift off the ground. Catwalks inside the craft gave the crew access to the hull, allowing them to service the ship. A gondola underneath the zeppelin carried the passengers and supplied their luxurious accommodations. Four diesel engines made the *Hindenburg* the fastest airship ever built.

All of the construction details came under scrutiny after the *Hindenburg* disaster. Everything from the ship's hydrogen cells to its fabric covering—painted a beautiful silver—to the black swastikas painted on the tail (a national symbol of Germany at the time) was considered a clue to her demise.

Eve of Destruction

But on May 6, 1937, there were no worries on the *Hindenburg*. The ship had already made 10 successful trips between Europe and the United States, and this one seemed routine. Storm conditions and high winds over Lakehurst delayed the landing; however the commanding officer of the ship, Captain Max Pruss, ordered a flight over New York City. This gave passengers spectacular views, including the Empire State Building, the Statue of Liberty, and Ebbets Field, where the Brooklyn Dodgers were battling the Pittsburgh Pirates. Then the aircraft circled the Jersey area until 6:12 p.m., when Commander Charles Rosendahl, the officer in charge of the air station, informed Pruss that conditions were suitable for landing.

On the ground 92 navy and 139 civilian ground crew personnel waited to help the airship land. They planned to use ropes from the *Hindenburg* to secure it by its nose to a mooring mast. At 7:25 the ship reversed its engines and stopped, hovering about 300 feet over the mooring mast. Onboard crew members dropped ropes to the ground crew so that they could tow the airship into position and winch it down to the ground.

What happened next was immortalized by a radio reporter, Herbert Morrison of station WLS in Chicago. He covered the airship's arrival and delivered one of the most famous live radio accounts ever. As the ship ignited, he fearfully described it, "It's burning, bursting into flames and is falling on the mooring mast, and all the folks agree that this is terrible. This is the worst of the worst catastrophes in the world! . . . There's smoke, and there's flames, now, and the frame is crashing to the ground. . . . Oh, the humanity, and all the passengers screaming . . ."

Half a minute after the first signs of flame were spotted near its tail section, the zeppelin lay on the ground burning. As the enormous metal skeleton fell, some passengers and crew were caught in the wreckage or thrown to the ground while others jumped from the windows or suffered burns in the fire. New Jersey's ground crew became a rescue crew as ambulances rushed to the scene.

What or Who Dunnit?

As the United States and Germany investigated the explosion, several theories emerged:

Crummy Weather. Did the storm over New Jersey take down the *Hindenburg*? That theory was put forward but discounted by scientists who pointed out that the ship had been battered by storms and struck by lightning before—and had survived.

Mechanical Failure. Some of the ground crew pointed out to investigators that the *Hindenburg* was coming in too fast. They speculated that when the airship was thrown into a full reverse to slow it down, a mechanical failure sparked a fire in the tail section. But little evidence was found to support that idea.

Sabotage. The *Hindenburg*, with large swastikas painted on its tail fins, was an important symbol for the Third Reich. It had flown over the 1936 Olympic Games in Berlin as a symbol of Germany's technological prowess under Hitler. The destruction of the *Hindenburg* would rob Hitler of a powerful propaganda tool. Some eyewitnesses reported seeing the glow of fire begin inside the rear of the ship. One of the passengers or crew members could have placed a time bomb on an interior rear catwalk, not knowing that the landing would be delayed for hours and that the bomb would explode while the *Hindenburg* was in the air. Though nothing was ever proved against them, two men are still discussed as suspects. Passenger Joseph Spah, who survived, brought a dog along in the cargo hold. Spah visited his dog several times, which could have given him the opportunity to plant an explosive device. Erich Spehl, a crewman who died in the fire, was also suspected because he was believed to have anti-Nazi beliefs.

An Act of God. After the investigation was over Hitler declared that no sabotage was involved and that the explosion was "an act of God." Not surprisingly he was accused of a cover-up—

the German crew had been ordered to say as little as possible. While much of the public, some passengers and crew, and some historians continued to believe that the zeppelin had been sabotaged, a more accepted theory eventually took hold.

A Flying Bomb? The *Hindenburg* carried hydrogen, a highly flammable gas. For many years the most accepted theory was that somehow (perhaps with a cut from a snapped wire) a leak had formed in one of the gas cells and a spark, whether from static electricity or lightning, had caused the hydrogen to explode. But that theory, considered the most credible for six decades, has recently come under fire.

A Bad Paint Job. Sixty years after the disaster, the cover story of the May 1997 issue of the Smithsonian Institution's *Air & Space Magazine* was authored by retired NASA engineer Addison Bain. Bain's research revealed that hydrogen wasn't the culprit in starting the fire because hydrogen only burns upward, and its flames are colorless. The *Hindenburg* fire burned in many directions and with bright orange and red flames. Bain fingered the likely culprit: the *Hindenburg's* beautiful silver outer skin, treated with an aluminum powder solution to stretch and waterproof the hull. "The *Hindenburg* was literally painted with rocket fuel," Bain reported. Original samples of the zeppelin's fabric still burned in laboratory tests. Bain (and, it turned out, some German engineers in 1937) concluded that the stormy weather allowed electrostatic charges to build up and ignite the highly combustible fabric covering the *Hindenburg*.

Lakehurst Today

Today the strip where the *Hindenburg* crash changed aviation history is part of the Lakehurst Naval Air Engineering Station. Visitors can take a tour that includes the *Hindenburg* memorial at the crash site and pay their respects to the victims of one of history's greatest disasters.

DID YOU KNOW?

New Jersey takes pride in native son World War II hero Sergeant John Basilone, who grew up in Raritan. In 1940 Basilone joined the U.S. Marines and fought on the Pacific front. During the Battle of Guadalcanal in 1942, Basilone bravely held his battalion together—calming soldiers, repairing equipment, replacing guns, and ensuring that his men had enough ammunition—even if it meant crossing enemy lines himself to get it to them. Because of his bravery and perseverance, Basilone won the Congressional Medal of Honor. After that, he could have taken a stateside post, but Basilone wanted to return to battle. "I'm a plain soldier. I want to stay one," he said.

On February 19, 1945, the first day of the Battle of Iwo Jima, Basilone was mortally wounded. He was posthumously awarded the Navy Cross and Purple Heart—thus becoming the only enlisted marine in World War II to win the Medal of Honor, the Navy Cross, and Purple Heart. Raritan still honors its native son with an annual John Basilone Day parade and a bronze statue of this brave, humble hero.

New Jersey by the Numbers

Interested in some quick New Jersey facts? Want to see them by the numbers? Well, here you go:

0

The number of big rigs you'll see on the Garden State Parkway. They're not allowed down that highway, good buddy.

3

New Jersey's place in the order of acceptance into the Union. It became the third state to ratify the Constitution, on December 18, 1787. It's also the number of states that New Jersey borders on: Delaware, New York, and Pennsylvania.

4

The number of major battles fought on Jersey soil during the American Revolution: two in Trenton, one in Princeton, and the last in Monmouth. General Washington and his army spent more time in this state than any other.

6

The current number of area codes: 201, 609, 732, 856, 908, and 973.

8

The current number of minor league baseball teams in the state.

Baseball fans can watch these teams play ball: the Atlantic City Surf, the Camden Riversharks, the Lakewood Blue Claws, the Newark Bears, the New Jersey Cardinals, the New Jersey Jackals, the Somerset Patriots, and the Trenton Thunder.

15

The number of active missile sites in New Jersey during the Cold War. Because of its strategic location, New Jersey housed these defensive sites from 1955 to 1974 to protect both New York City and Philadelphia from Soviet bombers.

21

Total number of counties. Hudson County (62.24 square miles) is the smallest, and Burlington County (819.27 square miles) is the biggest.

32

The number of New Jersey state parks. These parks occupy more than 90,000 acres and attract over 15 million people every year. Kittatinny Valley State Park has over 47 miles of abandoned railbeds for hiking and biking. Liberty State Park is right across the Hudson from Manhattan. Visitors there can take the ferry to Liberty Island and Ellis Island.

79

The number of New Jerseys that would fit into Alaska, the biggest state (over 591,000 square miles). New Jersey's square mileage (7,417) makes it the fourth smallest state, behind Delaware, Connecticut, and Rhode Island.

123

The number of butterfly species native to the Garden State. Most recognizable: the orange and black monarch.

130

If you traveled down the Atlantic Ocean coastline from Sandy Hook to Cape May, this is how many miles you went.

1,138

The number of malls. The biggest shopping center is also the oldest—Garden State Plaza in Paramus. It opened in 1957 and takes up over 2 million square feet.

1,186

The number of lakes in New Jersey. Some of the largest: Lake Hopatcong, Round Valley Reservoir, Dallenback Pond, and Mohawk Lake.

1,500

The average number of vendors at New Jersey's largest flea market, Englishtown Auction in Manalapan. Operating since 1929, this market is open every weekend, rain or shine, all year long.

3,155

With so many vehicles traveling through the state (see below), the number of gas stations almost doesn't seem to be enough, does it?

36,000

The number of roadside miles. New Jersey's roads are the most heavily used in the nation—over 18 million vehicle trips every day.

8,400,000

The approximate number of people in New Jersey. If you do the math (and we have), that's more than 1,000 people per square mile. Most of New Jersey's masses live in the northeastern section of the state with the westernmost and southernmost counties having lower populations.

Jon Stewart
Fake Newsman Extraordinaire

Funnyman and fake news anchor Jon Stewart has attracted a lot of attention in the past few years. He has the uncanny ability to take the most serious topics of the day and extract the humor, irony, and incongruity from them. The result: a brilliant career in political and media satire. So what's the story on this Jersey boy turned funny?

Personal History

- Born Jon Stuart Leibowitz on November 28, 1962, in Trenton

- His father was a physicist, his mother an educator who specialized in gifted education. His parents divorced when he was 10, and Jon went to live with his mother in Lawrence Township in Mercer County.

- He graduated from the College of William and Mary in Williamsburg, Virginia. ("I wanted to explore the rich tapestry of Judaica that is Southern Virginia.")

- In college Jon was a member of the men's soccer team. An award in his honor, the Leibo, is given out annually to the team member who makes his teammates laugh the most in a season.

Jack of All Trades

Before turning to stand-up, Stewart had an array of interesting jobs:

- Woolworth's stockboy in Quaker Bridge Mall. Destroyed $10,000 worth of tropical fish aquariums; fired by his older brother Larry, who also worked there.

- Contingency planner, New Jersey Department of Human Services

- Bartender

- Puppeteer. Performed shows in elementary schools

- Live mosquito sorter, New Jersey Department of Health

What Are You? A Comedian?

- In 1986 he decided to enter the comedy business and moved to New York City, home of many funny people.

- Around this time, he dropped his last name and became just Jon Stewart. (He claimed it was because no one could pronounce it right.)

- After years performing in comedy clubs, Stewart caught a break in 1993 when David Letterman helped him get *The Jon Stewart Show*, the first talk show on MTV.

Fake Newsman

- In January 1999 Stewart succeeded Craig Kilborn as host of *The Daily Show*, a late-night, made-up-news program that airs on Comedy Central. Since then the show's nightly ratings have more than tripled as the show has become smarter and funnier.

- In June 2004 a survey found that more than 20 percent of young voters get their news from *The Daily Show.*

- With Stewart at the helm, *The Daily Show* has won numerous prestigious awards—including five Emmys and a Peabody.

Other Careers

- **Actor:** Stewart has appeared in a number of movies, but has no illusions about his acting abilities. "I can be in 20 movies, but I'll never be an actor."

- **Author:** He is the author of two best-selling books: *Naked Pictures of Famous People* and *The Daily Show with Jon Stewart Presents America (The Book): A Citizen's Guide to Democracy Inaction. America (The Book)* was named the 2004 Book of the Year by *Publishers Weekly.*

DID YOU KNOW?

President James Garfield spent his final days in Elberon. After being shot by Charles Guiteau, Garfield lived for 80 more days. His physicians thought the Shore climate would help him recover, but they were wrong. After arriving at the Shore, he died two weeks later.

State Fruit
The Highbush Blueberry

"Enacted by the Senate and General Assembly of the State of New Jersey on January 12, 2004."

We know, we know. When people talk about blueberries, New Jersey isn't the first place that leaps to mind. But hold on one second there, because the Garden State has a pretty strong claim to the official blueberry legacy. According to the U.S. Department of Agriculture, New Jersey is second-largest producer of cultivated blueberries in the country (Michigan is the first)—not to mention the birthplace of the cultivated blueberry.

A Berry's Beginnings

It all started at Whitesbog, a cranberry plantation in New Lisbon, New Jersey, run by the White family since the 19th century. The Whites have long been expert cranberry growers (they literally "wrote the book" that set cranberry standards). Cranberries, however, did not intrigue the eldest White daughter, Elizabeth. She was a blueberry gal. In 1911, when Elizabeth heard that researcher Frederick Coville was studying blueberry propagation, she invited him to Whitesbog. Together they searched for the perfect blueberry.

By cross-fertilizing different plants, the team of White and Coville produced several new types of blueberries. It took them five years, but by 1916 the duo grew the first commercial blueberry crop at Whitesbog. They called their harvest Tru-Blu-Berries, and a brand-new agricultural industry began. Tru-Blues proved so popular that the cranberry farm eventually grew 20,000 barrels of them each season, in addition to their cranberries.

But White's innovations didn't stop there. She was the first to protect her berries by wrapping them in cellophane. She also helped organize the New Jersey Blueberry Cooperative Association in 1927. Nowadays the Garden State grows about 40 million pounds of blueberries each year on over 200 farms covering approximately 7,500 acres of New Jersey soil.

Blueberry Bill

It would take almost 90 years for New Jersey to recognize the official importance of the blueberry to the state—and it took some fourth graders to lead the way. Two fourth-grade classes at Veterans Memorial Elementary School in Brick were surprised to learn that Jersey had no state fruit. They put their heads together, researched the issue, and decided that the blueberry deserved the official honor. The students successfully lobbied state senators and assemblymen to introduce a blueberry bill and make it all official. In January 2004 Governor McGreevey signed on the dotted line, and Jersey got its own state fruit.

New Jersey Television
The Triple-Threat Quiz

There's more to Jersey TV than The Sopranos. *Think you know it all? We'll be the judge of that!*

All right, get on your thinking caps, because we've got a challenging triple-threat quiz for you here. We've selected five little-known television series with New Jersey locales for you to identify. They weren't all on the air for very long, so if you blinked, you may have missed them. See if you can . . .

Match this series title...

> 1. *Aqua Teen Hunger Force*
> 2. *Clerks*
> 3. *Come to Papa*
> 4. *Like Family*
> 5. *That's Life*

With this series description...

A. A newspaper reporter (Tom Papa) decides to bust out of Jersey by writing comedy. But in the meantime he has to deal with a dunderheaded boss (Steve Carell), a goofy pal (Robert Patrick

Benedict), and a hostile, 7-foot-tall mail carrier (former NBA star John Salley). Thank goodness he has a long-suffering wife (Jennifer Aspen) by his side!

B. Plucky Jersey bartender Lydia DeLucca (Heather Paige Kent) decides there has to be more to life. So at age 32 she breaks off her six-year engagement and enrolls in college. Will her friends and family understand her need for a better life? Will her former fiancé, Lou, want her back? And will she date that hunky 23-year-old in episode three?

C. Two slacker retail slaves (Brian O'Halloran and Jeff Anderson) work at a Leonardo convenience store and video rental. Despite this, they manage to have adventures and accrue nemeses, including Leonardo Leonardo (Alec Baldwin) and NBA star Charles Barkley (NBA star Charles Barkley—really).

D. When plucky single mother Maddie (Diane Farr) needs a little help from friends, her best pal, Tanya (Holly Robinson Peete), invites Maddie and her son to move in with her New Jersey family, which includes husband Ed (Kevin Michael Richardson) and their two kids. Need we say that hilarious high jinks ensue?

E. This animated New Jersey–based trio isn't your usual team of crimefighters: Master Shake is a giant, obnoxious milkshake, Meatwad is a shapeshifting ball of meat, and Frylock is a goateed order of french fries. They live next door to human neighbor Carl, who drives a Camaro. The team fights everything from two-dimensional aliens from the Moon to the creations of Dr. Weird, a mad scientist who lives at the Jersey Shore.

With how long this series lasted...

I. Four episodes in June 2004. You know, when your show debuts in June, that's a pretty good sign you won't be around for the next season.

II. Three seasons—55 shows—and still going strong as of this writing. It's the longest lasting of all the shows here.

III. Two seasons, from October 2000 through January 2002. Thirty-six episodes were filmed, but the last four went unaired.

IV. A mere two episodes, which aired in May and June 2002, although six episodes were created. Weirdly, the first episode aired was supposed to be the fourth episode; the supposed first episode was widely disliked by test audiences, so it was eventually scheduled to play fifth. But the series was canceled by then.

V. One season, beginning in 2003. Twenty-three episodes were filmed, but the final one—tantalizingly titled "We're Gonna Need More Peanut M&Ms"—never made it on the air.

Turn to page 322 for answers.

Hometowns
A Whole Lot of Nuts

The world has a lot of things to thank Nutley for: Valium and Martha Stewart, to name a couple.

The Town: Nutley
Location: Essex County
Founding: The slice of land that is now home to all things Nutley used to be part of Newark, Bloomfield, Belleville, and Franklinville. Nutley became its own little town in 1902.
Current Population: 27,362
Size: 3.43 square miles
What's in a Name? This town was named for the many nut trees found there, including beech, hazel, chestnut, hickory, and walnut.

Claims to Fame

- Although born in Jersey City, Martha Stewart grew up in Nutley, where she first honed her impressive domestic arts skills at 86 Elm Place. She was treasurer of the Nutley High School class of 1959.

- Nutley lost nearly 3,000 of its residents in World War II. Their names are listed on the town's World War II memorial.

- Robert Blake, star of the TV hit *Baretta* and of the *Our Gang* comedies, was born in Nutley.

- The Nutley Museum, a prime attraction, contains many relics of former Nutley resident Annie Oakley—including three of her guns: a Lady Derringer and two Colt revolvers.

- Meanwhile, down on the pharm, Nutley is home to pharmaceutical giant Hoffman-La Roche, New Jersey's first major vitamin manufacturer and the developer of Valium.

DID YOU KNOW?

Thomas Nast, the 19th-century political cartoonist, lived the last 30 years of his life in Morristown. In the 1870s, after attacking New York City politicians and officials with a series of harsh yet effective cartoons, Nast felt unsafe in New York. He and his family relocated to Morristown for their personal safety.

Got Wheels?

Driving along New Jersey roads during the summer, there is no escaping the ear-wrenching radio ads announcing the weekend lineup at "Oh ha-ha-ha-ho-ho-ho-ho . . . RRRRRRACEway PARK!" one of the premiere drag racing facilities in the United States.

If you've "got a need for speed" of the two- or four-wheel sort, Raceway Park is the place to go, either to participate or to watch the best racers in action. Nestled in a 320-acre tract of land in Old Bridge Township, Raceway Park offers enthusiasts the chance to match their skill against others, while onlookers can still get elbow-close to the best drivers and mechanics in the sport.

For spectators on race days the price of admission includes not only a reserved seat to watch the four-second dragsters blast down the track but also a pit-side/crew pass. Fans can tour the pit area, where the racers and their teams prepare and repair the cars. Bystanders will see, smell, hear, and experience racing up close—the fumes from the clog of cars and the sweat from the workers tuning the machines, the cloud of smoke rising from the tires when a car burns out, and the anxiety of reacting to the Christmas-tree timing light that counts down to the start.

From Farmland to Dreamland
This motor sports venue was painstakingly dug out of hard-

packed clay on abandoned farmland purchased by the Napoliello family (now known simply as the Napps), who have owned and operated the facility since 1965. The project was the dream of brothers Vincent Sr. and Louis, who sold shares in a construction company to build the drag strip from scratch for Vincent's car-loving sons, Richard and Vincent Jr. The business has withstood not only the deaths of the original partners, but also several legal battles over noise pollution and other environmental issues. Now run by third-generation family members, the racetrack is open 40 weeks a year, from March to November.

Initially devoted to just ¼-mile drag racing, Raceway Park has successfully expanded since its founding into three racing venues, including motocross and karting. A road course for cars and motorcycles is planned for the park in 2005. This multipurpose racetrack also contains extensive grandstands, a state-of-the-art timing tower, and numerous refreshment stands.

Shortly after opening its first racing surface—a ¼-mile track that's 60 feet wide—Raceway Park received official sanctioning from the National Hot Rod Association (NHRA). Within three years the park was hosting championship drag racing, including the NHRA Springnationals, which attracts crowds of more than 85,000 people to the racetrack each June. Among the notable drivers who have won at Raceway Park are "Big Daddy" Don Garlits (the "father" of Top Fuel racing) and Shirley Muldowney (the greatest female driver in Top Fuel racing history).

"Sunday! Sunday! Sunday!"

For those unfamiliar with the sport, let us explain: Drag racing is a form of auto racing that originated in the United States. It tests both driver skill and engine power. Two cars line up side by side, accelerate from a standstill down a short, straight course (usually ¼ of a mile), and try to finish in the least amount of time.

There are many classes of racing, beginning with street cars, moving on to the heavily modified "funny cars," and ending with the exotic-looking Top Fuel dragsters. The latter are fueled by nitromethane and can reach speeds of more than 330 mph in 4½ seconds over the ¼-mile distance. Because this type of racing can be extremely hazardous (one professional Top Fuel driver was killed in 2004 at an Ohio track), Raceway Park has installed state-of-the-art equipment along the tracks to prevent accidents and has full medical teams on hand to respond to emergencies.

Competition at the ¼-mile track is known as eliminator racing: the losing car from each race is eliminated from the contest, and the winner goes on to race again—until only one car remains. During formal competition, racing begins on Friday evening, when local cars usually take part. The professionals are added into the mix on Saturday, when qualifying whittles the field to the top 16 in each class. The finals take place on "Sunday! Sunday! Sunday!" afternoon.

More Than Just Drag Racing

In 1975 Raceway Park added a one-mile motocross track that soon received sanctioning by the American Motorcyclist Association (AMA), the national organization for professional motorcycle sport. The park hosts 11 races, including championship events sponsored by the Suzuki, Yamaha, and Kawasaki motorcycle companies.

Karting

Karting is another popular activity at Raceway Park, as the whole family can enjoy it. Karting is the most basic form of four-wheel automobile racing, utilizing lightweight, nimble karts (often called go-carts) powered by engines of various sizes and power. Virtually all top racing professionals began their careers in karting.

Races are known as sprints, usually 10 or 15 laps on a ½-mile road course or approximately 20 laps on a ⅕-mile track. While karting is technically a no-contact sport, drivers must wear safety equipment for their protection: a leather coat or karting suit, helmet, gloves, shoes that cover the ankle, long pants, and a neck collar.

DID YOU KNOW?

One expansion attempt didn't go as well as motocross and karting did for the Napps. In 1977 the Napps scheduled a Grateful Dead concert at the Raceway Park complex. When their fans showed up, they turned the track and surrounding neighborhoods into a New Jersey Woodstock. Throngs of concertgoers (more than 100,000 of them!) clogged the local streets, forcing the police to shut down all roads in the area. People abandoned their cars and tried to walk to the site instead. Wisely, no large concerts have been held at the track since then.

Roadside New Jersey

What to see on a New Jersey road trip? Lucy the Elephant in Margate? The Milk Jug Lady in Mizpah? The Fairy Tale Forest in Oak Ridge? Wherever you drive in the Garden State, there's something interesting and fun to check out. Solve this puzzle to find three more attractions.

ACROSS

1. Meter maid of song
5. Afternoon socials
9. Frisky swimmer
14. Oklahoma city
15. Taj Mahal site
16. Impoverished
17. In Rio Grande, NJ, you can see a . . .
20. Resident of the Leaning Tower city
21. Low bow
22. Real thing
24. Lyricist Harburg ("Over the Rainbow")
25. Biggest cyberportal
28. ____ Dinh Diem
29. Architect Saarinen
32. Hits the books
34. Monet or Picasso, e.g.
36. Catcall
37. In Plainsboro, NJ, see the grave of the beloved . . .
40. Speedy steed
42. Wiggle room
43. Stroller
46. Play the field
47. Good times
50. Essen exclamation
51. Sue Grafton's "____ for Alibi"

53. "Simpsons" bully
55. Teammate's help
58. Home of Busch Gardens
59. In Bayville, NJ, don't miss . .
63. Classic toothpaste
64. Roof ornament
65. Mosaic piece
66. Court cloaks
67. Squeezed (out)
68. Lost traction

DOWN

1. Look into again
2. Diamond period
3. Has ____ (is connected with)
4. Statesman Stevenson
5. Playground game
6. Meringue need
7. Neck of the woods
8. "I'm sorry to say . . . "
9. Like books for drivers
10. Bulls or Bears, e.g.
11. Asian holiday
12. School ending, in e-mail
13. Pocket filler of rhyme

Turn to page 322 for answers.

18 Goes into
19 Ship's canvas
23 Sasquatch's cousin
25 Get one's ducks in ___
26 Lennon's lady
27 W.W. II craft: abbr.
30 Cambodian cash
31 Big name in blenders
33 Mate's shout
34 "Dark Angel" star Jessica
35 Telly's character on "Kojak"
37 Every partner
38 "Trainspotting" actor McGregor
39 Totaled
40 Khan title

41 Bird of myth
44 Sporters of dreadlocks
45 "Addams Family" nickname
47 Label on a street-corner box
48 Vox ___
49 Caught, as in a trap
52 Blabbermouth
54 Holds up
55 Tip-top
56 Mont. neighbor
57 Pea picker-upper
59 Head honcho on a movie: Abbr.
60 Wall St. newbie
61 Collar
62 Beatty or Rorem

Rotten Tomatoes
The Final Chapter

The last of the truly bad digs at New Jersey.

It turns out that making fun of New Jersey has a long history. According to the *Encyclopedia of New Jersey*, the magazine *Picturesque America* reported in 1872 that New Jersey "has been the butt of sarcasm and wit of those who live outside her borders."

Ben Franklin, New Jersey Basher

"New Jersey is like a barrel tapped at both ends."

"[New Jersey] is a valley of humility between two mountains of conceit." (The mountains being New York City and Philadelphia.)

Tourism Turnoffs

Failed State Motto: "New Jersey: Landfill of Opportunity."

The Last Word

Out-of Stater: "Are people who live in New Jersey sensitive about Jersey jokes?"

Lifelong Jerseyan: "If we were that sensitive, we'd live somewhere else."

Answer Pages

Jersey Basics, page 6

1. B. Trenton
2. A. Newark. Its population is approximately 274,000.
3. D. 8.4 million. New Jersey is a densely populated state. It averages about 1,134 persons per square mile.
4. D. Two. The northern copperhead can be found in north Jersey, and the timber rattlesnake can be found in both the northern and Pinelands regions.
5. D. All of the above. Coyotes and eagles and bears! Oh my!
6. D. Verrazano Narrows Bridge. This bridge connects Staten Island to Brooklyn.
7. D. Great Egg. Great Egg is a Parkway toll plaza, not a rest stop.
8. B. High Point. Part of the Kittatinny Ridge, High Point is located in Sussex County in High Point State Park. A 221-foot-tall obelisk serves as a veterans memorial and marks High Point, too.
9. A. 65 mph. On certain highways, drivers can go up to 65 mph; however, if they go as little as 10 mph over that limit, they pay double fines.
10. E. None of the above. New Jersey has no official state song.

Down the Shore, page 44

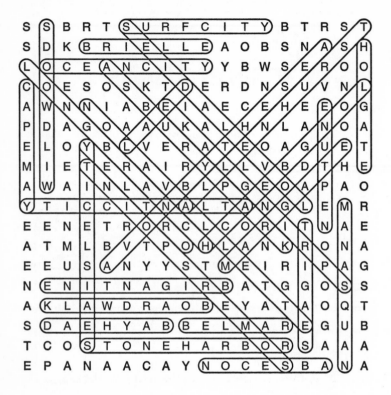

New Jersey Notables, page 56

1. Charles Addams, C
2. Donna Weinbrecht, O
3. William J. Brennan Jr., K
4. Grover Cleveland, M
5. Lauryn Hill, E
6. Dorothea Lange, B
7. Patricia McBride, H
8. Joe Theismann, N

9. Molly Pitcher, I
10. Queen Latifah, F
11. Antonin Scalia, L
12. H. Norman Schwarzkopf Jr., J
13. Ruth St. Denis, G
14. Alfred Stieglitz, A
15. Dionne Warwick, D
16. Franco Harris, P

Famous Turnpike Stops, page 106

Sons of Jersey, page 179

1. Edwin "Buzz" Aldrin, K
2. David Copperfield, A
3. Lou Costello, H
4. Savion Glover, N
5. William Halsey Jr., O
6. Ice-T, F
7. Alfred Kinsey, G
8. Ernie Kovacs, L
9. Ray Liotta, J
10. Zebulon Pike, M
11. Paul Robeson, B
12. Philip Roth, C
13. Amos Alonzo Stagg, E
14. Dave Thomas, D
15. Edmund Wilson, I

The E Street Band, page 192

1. Roy Bittan; G. Piano; V
2. Clarence Clemons; H. Saxophone; I
3. Danny Federici; F. Organ; VII
4. Nils Lofgren; E. Guitar (joined in 1984); II
5. Patti Scialfa; A. Backing Vocals; IV
6. Garry Tallent; B. Bass; VIII
7. Steven Van Zandt; D. Guitar (1975–1984. Rejoined in 1999); VI
8. Max Weinberg; C. Drums; III

The Wizard of Menlo Park, page 233

1. **False.** Thomas Edison was born in Milan, Ohio, in 1847. He didn't start working in New Jersey until 1870.

2. **True.** Samuel Edison took part in the 1837 Mackenzie Rebellion against the British crown. When the rebellion failed, Edison and his wife fled to Ohio.

3. **False.** His nickname was Al.

4. **False.** Edison only married twice. His first wife, Mary Stillwell, died in 1884. Mina Miller married Edison in 1886.

5. **D. Dash.** Thomas Alva Jr. was nicknamed Dash, and his sister Marion was called Dot. The nicknames were based the dots and dashes that make up Morse code.

6. **False.** Because Menlo Park had a train stop and a post office many believed it was a town, but it was just a neighborhood in what was then Raritan Township.

7. **False.** Ford wanted to recover buildings from the original Menlo Park site in New Jersey, but they had fallen into disrepair. Ford's staff used photographs and *some* original materials to reconstruct the buildings at the Henry Ford Museum.

8. **True.** In 1937 Raritan Township (called Edison Township since 1954) built the Memorial Tower and Museum where the Menlo Park Laboratory stood. The museum contains some of Edison's inventions and products from the Thomas A. Edison Company.

9. **True.** After the staff abandoned the building, Menlo Park was used as a theater, a dance hall, and a chicken farm.

10. **D. All of the above.** Among other things, Edison and his team worked on perfecting the telephone and inventing the electric fuse.

11. **True.** Edison put his name on 1,093 patents, to be exact. Four hundred were filed during his seven years at Menlo Park.

12. **True.** He applied for the patent on October 28, 1868, but the vote recorder was not a resounding success. The experience made him determined to devote his efforts to projects for which he believed there was a strong public demand.

13. **False.** Edison filed for his last patent just a short time before his death in 1931. The patent for the "Holder for Article to be Electroplated" was granted posthumously two years later.

14. **D. All of the above.** He also patented, among many other things, a vacuum pump, an electric chandelier, and a typewriter.

15. **False.** The first electric light is attributed to Humphry Davy, an English chemist, in 1809. In 1820, inventor Warren De la Rue made an incandescent lamp using a platinum coil, but the platinum was too costly. It wasn't until late 1879 that Edison developed the carbon filament bulb that was commercially practical.

16. **True.** Edison's first recording was about Mary's little lamb.

17. **False.** West Orange, New Jersey, was home to the first-ever motion picture studio.

18. **True.** The film *Edison Kinetoscopic Record of a Sneeze, January 7, 1894* is better known as *Fred Ott's Sneeze.*

19. **True.** In 1899, he formed the Edison Portland Cement Company. To create demand for the cement, Edison conceived an entire house (roof, sides, ornamental ceilings, fireplace mantles, and even bathtubs) that was poured from a single mold, but no builder was interested. Eleven prototypes were built in Union—10 of which are still standing!

20. **A. Hello.** Edison preferred "Hello" to Alexander Graham Bell's "Ahoy, ahoy."

Are You Game for Monopoly? page 264

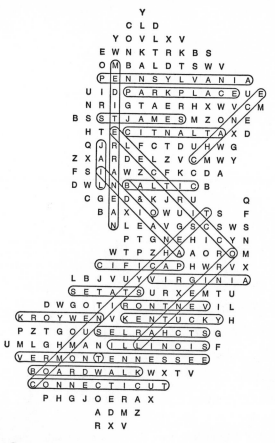

The AKA Quiz, page 282

1. C (Jason Alexander)
2. A (Susan Sarandon)
3. D (Connie Francis)
4. F (Frankie Valli)
5. B (Jerry Lewis)
6. E (Dorothy Parker)

New Jersey Television, page 303

1. *Aqua Teen Hunger Force,* E, II
2. *Clerks,* C, IV
3. *Come to Papa,* A, I
4. *Like Family,* D, V
5. *That's Life,* B, III

Roadside New Jersey, page 312

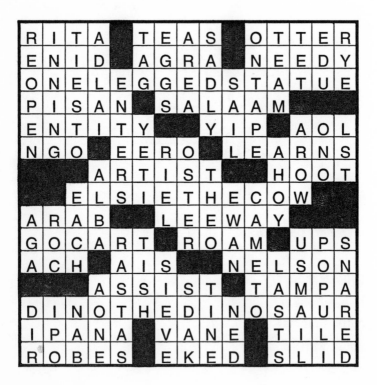